CONSCIENCE IN REVOLT

Sixty-Four Stories of
Resistance in Germany, 1933–45

ANNEDORE LEBER

WITH THE ASSISTANCE OF
WILLY BRANDT & KARL DIETRICH BRACHER

WITH CONTRIBUTIONS FROM
HILDE WALTER
WOLFGANG STEGLICH & HARALD POELCHAU

TRANSLATED FROM THE GERMAN BY
ROSEMARY O'NEILL

Westview Press
BOULDER • SAN FRANCISCO • OXFORD

Der Widerstand: Dissent and Resistance in the Third Reich

Copyright © 1994 by Westview Press, Inc.

Published in English in 1994 in the United States of America by Westview Press, Inc., 5500 Central Avenue, Boulder, Colorado 80301-2877, and in the United Kingdom by Westview Press, 36 Lonsdale Road, Summertown, Oxford OX2 7EW

First published in English in 1957 by Vallentine, Mitchell & Co. Ltd.

First published in German in 1954 by Mosaik-Verlag, Berlin.

Unless otherwise indicated, all photographs in this book were privately owned.

A CIP catalog record for this book is available from the Library of Congress
ISBN 0-8133-2185-9

Printed and bound in the United States of America

The paper used in this publication meets the requirements
of the American National Standard for Permanence of Paper
for Printed Library Materials Z39.48-1984.

10   9   8   7   6   5   4   3   2   1

CONTENTS

TRADITION

CHRISTIANITY

FREEDOM AND ORDER

FOREWORD

By K. D. Bracher (Bonn, February 1994)

THIS BOOK, edited by the widow of Julius Leber, leader of the Social Democratic resistance, was collected and written with the assistance of Willy Brandt, the young friend and political heir of Leber, and myself, a contemporary historian and the husband of a niece of Dietrich Bonhoeffer. When first published forty years ago, the story of the German resistance against National Socialism was still little known; at home the resistance was contested and defamed by old and neo-Nazis, and abroad it was only rarely taken seriously. Three years later a second volume of resistance portraits followed: *Das Gewissen Entscheidet.*

Today, as we debate again how democracy may be defended against its radical enemies in Germany and Europe, *Conscience in Revolt* reminds us of the continuing dangers of totalitarian ideologies and dictatorial rule. I welcome this new English edition and Andrew Chandler's thoughtful introduction.

RESISTANCE AND CONSCIENCE

An Introduction by Andrew Chandler (Birmingham, 1994)

I

The reality of the German resistance to Hitler has not always appeared clear to those outside the country. During the war against National Socialism it was difficult for many abroad to believe that Hitler was much opposed, if at all, by the Germans themselves. Those who argued that Germany was a society governed against its wishes were hard put to substantiate the case. A few scattered fragments of resistance might come to light, and people might talk vaguely of what they called the 'Confessional' Church, which they had seen as a statement of resistance to the Nazis before the war. They might then invoke the name of Bishop von Galen, whose sermons had been conveyed across Germany by couriers on motorcycles. But even these examples could appear vulnerable to criticism. It was soon known that the celebrated pastor Martin Niemöller, bundled off to a concentration camp by the secret police in 1938 for his stand against 'German Christianity', had earlier offered his services to the state that now put him in prison. In the Great War he had commanded a U-boat.

English opinion became bitter. The British public saw nothing to suggest that the German people desisted from the evil purposes wrought by their leaders. Instead, Poland was annihilated, Rotterdam was bombed, France fell, and soon the *Wehrmacht* confronted Britain itself across a bare twenty-one miles of water. When London was bombed it became even more difficult to maintain that any 'good' Germans existed. When in December 1942 the awful truth of the massacre of Jews was acknowledged by the British government in Parliament, those who spoke of good Germans were driven further into retreat.

If on the one hand the idea of a decent Germany appeared hard to justify, those who on the other hand declared that Hitler represented the beliefs of the German people sensed that they stood boldly on ground that was hard to contest. In Britain the hatred of Germans found its prophet in a retired diplomat, Lord Vansittart, whose robust little polemic, *Black Record*, stated the case pungently. It was Vansittart's argument that Nazism was no accident, looming suddenly out of the fog of history, but rather a natural expression of the German character as history itself had revealed it; indeed, the logical outcome of German history itself. After all, what kind of a people were the Germans? Ardent columnists in newspapers would say that they were a people given to discipline and conformity; when attached to a sinister purpose they became a menace to the world. Where, asked Lord Vansittart, as Nazi crimes accumulated, was there evidence of protest? 'Hardly a German soul bothers—not even the women'. Meanwhile, the British government doubted reports of a resistance movement inside Germany; the government required proof of the movement's existence and found none.

II

Nothing could be worse than that a civilized nation, without any show of opposition, be 'governed' by an irresponsible clique given over completely to their own lusts for power. Is it not so that today every honest German is ashamed of his government? And who amongst us has any idea of the extent of the outrages which we and our children must one day bear witness to when finally the shades are lifted from our eyes and we will behold in broad daylight all the hideous and monstrous crimes?

These words were written in Germany itself—in the heart of Bavaria, in Munich, near the concentration camp of Dachau. They were the work of two young students, Hans Scholl and Alexander Schmorell, who had acquired a typewriter and a mimeograph machine with which to publish seditious literature. Their first, 'Leaflet of the White Rose', was printed one hundred times and then circulated in the city. It raised again the question that preoccupied so many abroad and that continues to make work for historians today: How could a tolerant, democratic society pass into the hands of the violent racialist totalitarianism of National Socialism?

Adolf Hitler became chancellor of Germany on 30 January 1933. He came to power through a combination of popular approval in the first place and political mismanagement in the second. Hoisted into the heights of influence by a sizeable minority of the electorate, he was ushered surreptitiously through the doors of the Reichschancellory by an assortment of conservative politicians who sought to pursue their own ends. It was a resistable rise. His immense, but not overwhelming, popularity notwithstanding, Hitler was fortunate to succeed.

When the pastor and theologian Dietrich Bonhoeffer pondered the significance of the 1933 event from his prison cell at Tegel ten years later, he wrote, 'The great masquerade of evil has wrought havoc with all our ethical preconceptions. This appearance of evil in the guise of light, beneficence and historical necessity is utterly bewildering to anyone nurtured in our traditional ethical systems. But for the Christian it simply confirms the radical evilness of evil'. Today most might find it difficult to understand what Bonhoeffer meant. But for many Germans in 1933, depressed by political confusions and economic misfortunes and fearful of a loss of social coherence, National Socialism appeared to offer much. It seemed to them the best of all worlds; explicitly nationalist *and* socialist, revolutionary and yet, it was claimed, legal. The enthusiasts were exhilarated by the sense of vitality and vision that the party announced while the traditionally minded were reassured by its claims of respectability.

It was Hitler's achievement to voice, equally, the wishes of the radical and the conservative, the extremes and the middle ground of popular belief. Even the neutral, who suspected political opinions to be only the expressions of divisive partisanship, could embrace the new movement because it claimed not to represent the Left or the Right but to encompass them all. Hitler had seized the essential vulnerability of political neutrality. He declared that he offered to the Germans their sense of identity, community, and purpose. The muddle of political pluralism would be swept away. The confusions of aimless youth would be superseded, brilliantly, by splendid parades and benevolent social schemes. Submission was ennobled as self-sacrifice, and individualism, which had failed and which democracy had institutionalized, was repudiated and submerged beneath the wish to serve. Self-denial was exalted. Many though that Hitler represented an appeal to idealism, to all that was good and distinctive in German life. To millions that was compelling.

Within this confident ethic of unity, Hitler exploited the grievances that rumbled below the surface of a fundamentally unhappy, divided society by voicing his anti-Semitism for the anti- Semites; promoting revision abroad for those who despised Versailles; promising safety from Bolshevism for those who feared it, security too for the beleaguered middle classes, and moral cleanliness for those who talked anxiously of dubious nightclubs and blatant brothels in Berlin. Hitler's genius lay, in part, in his ability to embrace the various aspirations of a diverse public while simultaneously affirming a clear identity and a powerful sense of purpose. He stood as the inheritor and the prophet of recognizable German values, taking them to new heights and fashioning them with a new heroic grandeur. To vote for him was, for many, a respectable and responsible political act. And millions of humane, thoughtful, and devout men and women went into the voting booth and did so.

The subsequent establishment of the Nazi state was testimony to the continued failure of western societies to mark their fundamental political values and protect them. On the other side of the imposing images of the state were the persecuted Jews, the political victims, the Socialists, Communists, and pacifists. Most Germans disliked the intimidation and violence of National Socialism but did not find it hard to believe that every great popular movement had its unfortunate elements, its fanatics and thugs, busy on the fringes, and that these were momentary and secondary phenomena. They might ask how many other revolutions had been accomplished with so little bloodshed. Instead, Hitler, the visionary who had saved his country from Bolshevism, and the eager youths whose ardent idealism marched in ranks through the streets of Germany, represented the essence of National Socialism.

Opinion abroad was also divided. As the history of the Third Reich unfolded, liberal observers could lament the incarceration of men like Carl von Ossietzky, whom Annedore Leber eloquently commemorates, and claim them as examples of the truth that Nazi Germany was fundamentally rotten. But others would still observe that the great truth of National Socialism lay not in matters that concerned mere individuals but in the confidence of the new society—its dynamism and its efficiency. To them, Ossietzky and others like him were merely incidental, personal dramas, lying on the periphery of a splendidly impressive whole. It was remarked, often enough, that all grand endeavours, lauded by contemporaries and commemorated fondly by histories, involved these personal tragedies. In fact, throughout European life there existed a division of opinion over what fundamentally mattered and by what lights the basic integrity of a society should be soundly judged.

Throughout her political life Annedore Leber had no doubts. Robert Birley, who wrote the introduction to the first English edition of *Conscience in Revolt,* later encountered her at a political meeting in West Berlin in December 1948: 'I remember that I said that in all elections it became clear long before what were the dominant issues and I asked her which they were in this one. "There is only one issue," she replied, "and it is the old question: Are you, or are you not, against the concentration camp?"' But in Germany, as elsewhere in Europe in 1933, much of society was not so sure.

The English academic Amy Buller knew Germany well and visited the country regularly between 1933 and 1939. On one occasion she was a guest of a conservative family in East Pomerania. Her host, an advisor to the Ministry of Agriculture, viewed the National Socialist regime with distaste. His nephew, an officer in the Luftwaffe, perceived its benefits. It was the younger of the men who met her at the railway station when she arrived and offered to take her to their home:

'I would like to take you a rather longer way round as it is a lovely drive and it will give us some opportunity to talk, because I think of things rather differently from my uncle and I would like to tell you that perhaps he is a little extreme in his views about the National Socialists'.

'Yes, do tell me. But surely you are not a Nazi?'

'No', he replied, 'not exactly. There is much that they do and say that I hate, so much is vulgar and false, but then the leaders are not educated men. But I cannot forget two things. First of all I and most of my friends did not know what we could do because there was no opportunity in the army or in the air force, and now Hitler has made it possible for us to have a future and I cannot forget that. Secondly Hitler has given some of us an idea that there must be more fair play for all classes and that whatever class people belong to they are Germans and that in the days of Germany's disasters all Germans must hold together'.

'Yes, my dear Ernst, that is all very well, but what about concentration camps for those who do not agree, and what about the Church and the Press and the universities, all of which have lost their freedom?'

'I know, and at times I have felt very troubled about these things, but is it not true that you always get excesses in times of revolution? I am sure that when things are more settled in Germany and there is no fear of a counter-revolution there will be more freedom again. In war-time we all give up freedom and I think Hitler is right and that the state of Germany in 1933 was much worse than war and that we all must give up much to get things right'.

Before January 1933 Hitler had sought to undermine authority, disturb social order, and lay siege to the law. Now he represented these institutions. The National Socialist movement became, alarmingly quickly, the National Socialist state. On 28 February, following the Reichstag fire, a decree suspended the liberties of the individual, the freedoms of speech and assembly, and the rights of the Press. On 24 March a majority in the Reichstag passed an Enabling Act that granted Hitler arbitrary power for the next four years. Hitler had conciliated the centre, thrown out the Communists, and defeated the Social Democrats who withstood the fearful violence that hung over them and voted against the act. On 7 April a new law purged the civil service of political opponents, Jews, and 'Non-Aryans'. In April the Gestapo was created. On 2 May the trades unions were banned and on 14 July so were all other political parties. Every citizen who had held a critical view of the Nazis had now to reconsider. One might criticize a political party, but to oppose the will of the state was a profoundly different matter.

Moreover, it was another powerful mark of Hitler's success that he persuasively equated the German people with the Nazi movement and the Nazi movement with the German nation. Could dissent come from a law-abiding citizen, or from a patriot, or from a devout Christian who read Romans XIII? Evidence of Hitler's success could be found in Protestant churches across the country, where congregations hung swastika flags in their churches. Perplexed English visitors were assured that this was entirely consistent with the historic practice of suspending national flags from the vaulted ceilings, to be found in the cathedrals of England itself. The National Socialist state presented itself as a compelling moral gesture. Its claims of public legitimacy were affirmed by the vivid demonstrations of assent and enthusiasm that it generated, orchestrated, and sustained throughout its twelve-year life. The emotional power of a Nuremberg rally was the result of an extraordinary fabrication of social assent and communal unity. There the individual counted for nothing, and the crowd for everything. This, on a national scale, was what the dissenting conscience confronted.

Perhaps the most disturbing truth of the National Socialist state lay in its destruction of the personal relationships that sustain a civil society and its utter exploitation of the European idea of citizenship. The morality of the individual was trapped inside the institutional morality of corporate life. Hitler did not create a totalitarian society by ruthlessly suppressing what he inherited. He did not need to. Instead, he only purged or abolished what clearly appeared irreconcilable—the political parties, the trades unions, and the Jews. The facade of a civilized, orderly, humane society remained reassuringly intact. The institutions were maintained, if refashioned and often unsettled, and by their very existence the past endorsed the present, perpetuated the new powers, and served their ambitions. The ongoing activities, however unhappy, of the civil service or the judiciary were valuable evidence of civilization and tradition.

Hitler cancelled the potential threat of pluralism and institutional independence by merely reinforcing and extending the values that already existed in the institutions themselves. The duties of the private citizen were sharply defined—they were not 'political'. To judge the morality of government lay beyond the professional duties and cultural rights of the individual. The duty of a civil servant was to shuffle papers, not to write them. As a consequence, decent, tolerant people proceeded after 1935 to administer the Nuremberg Laws. Army officers must obey their oath and not question their orders. Accordingly, they invaded Poland, France, and the Soviet Union. The responsibility of the church was to administer the sacraments and pastor the congregation. It therefore avoided politics where the politicians left its own province undisturbed. The Confessing Church of the Barmen Bynod sought to affirm the integrity of the church and to contest the influence of the political world in the life of the church. Accordingly it rebelled at the imposition of an 'Aryan Clause' inside the church; it did nothing, however, to condemn the 'Aryan clauses' that existed in the civil service, in the judiciary, and elsewhere.

In short, where the Hitler regime could not induce the citizen to adopt its own vision, it sought to relieve individuals of the burden of a contrary conscience. That this regime eventually devastated the continent and virtually destroyed the Jewish community of central Europe was as much a testimony to man's cultural amorality as to his capacity for evil. The essential paradox of the National Socialist state lay in the fact that its thorough political mobilization of the public coexisted beside—and was even made possible by—a cultivation of apolitical and amoral institutional values.

Amy Buller's conversation with the young officer illustrates how profoundly the moral ground had shifted in Germany in 1933. In supporting a powerful peoples' community and a totalitarian state, her young host had become the moderate in the family. His uncle, who disapproved of the state, had become the 'extremist'. The decision to resist an authority that in the eyes of the public was legally constituted, accepted, and upheld by national institutions and was supported by the broad public was the act of an extremist. Such resistance was perilous both in principle and in reality. No common sense recommended it. It was the choice of the individualist in a society where individualism had become anachronistic; the treasonable, where the wicked governed; the eccentric, where prevailing definitions of responsibility were sharply defined and prohibited political opposition; the perverse, when the new state rapidly accumulated, at home and abroad, a sense of success and vindication; the archaic, where it represented a dynamic modernity; the irresponsible, when one must care for one's family. The moral imperative had not merely become confused—it appeared to have been converted altogether.

And yet, in the face of these inestimable pressures, there existed from 1933 to 1945 fragments of dissent, opposition, and fundamental resistance. Observers abroad recognized evidence of it, although they found it difficult to assess. In 1933 the World Committee for the Victims of Fascism, whose president was Albert Einstein, estimated that as many as 35,000 to 40,000 prisoners were held in some forty-five concentration camps. Now it is believed that between 1933 and 1945, 3 million were confined for political crimes; 800,000 were sentenced for active resistance; and 32,600 were executed—of these, 12,000 had been convicted of high treason.

In a society in which institutional values had failed, resistance was the act of the individual. This was the fundamental argument of Annedore Leber's book: 'For there is one fact that we should never forget: it is the very foundation of our spiritual and intellectual life that the individual, whenever the need arises, should be ready to come forward and to answer for the rights, the lives and the souls, of his fellow human beings'. That Hitler was resisted at all testified to the continuing vitality, in the face of constant intimidation and persecution, of humane convictions and to the fragile endurance, despite all the discouragements and prohibitions, of moral precepts established by generations of Christian faith. Fabian von Schlabrendorff claimed, 'The truth is that our—the resistance movement's—battle against Hitler and National Socialism was based not upon consideration of material or military success or failure, and not even primarily on political ideas, but upon the moral and ethical concepts taught by the Christian faith'. Caesar von Hofacker, who on 22 December 1944 was executed for his links with the 20 July 1944 conspiracy, once wrote to his children, 'The fact is that in all history up to this time there has appeared no spiritual force that has been able, as Christianity has, to bring man to a realisation of his own limits, to make him desire the good and resist evil'. Resistance was, for some, an act of national atonement. When Dietrich Bonhoeffer met his friend Bishop George Bell in Stockholm in May 1942, Bonhoeffer stated firmly that the political conspiracy with which he was associated must be seen as 'an act of repentance'. This was crucial. Principle lay at the root of resistance and transcended its overpowering adversities. Ernst von Harnack, a government official and the son of the great German theologican Adolf von Harnack, was heard to say before his execution, 'The decisive thing is not attaining the goal, but rather holding to the right road'.

The fundamental crisis of resistance lay in the relationship between individuals and institutions. What some have seen as the moral inconsistencies, or even the lateness, of collective resistance may be largely explicable in these terms: No institution represented opposition, so that resistance had to be created on a foundation of personal convictions, private relationships, and shared interests. And the very prerequisites of effective resistance appeared to some to involve a degree of moral compromise. Should one resign from positions of public service and escape or go abroad, to live without the taint of compromise or corruption but also without hope of influence? Or should one more truly pursue the moral course by continuing to live in the heart of a corrupt society, sharing the degradation of its values but working against its designs?

By 1939, 40,000 had gone into exile. But many stayed. Rudiger Schleicher was a civil servant in the Reich Aviation Ministry who was soon haunted by the prospect of joining the Nazi Party in order to retain his post. After the war his son, Hans Walter, wrote: 'I still remember how on the evening of the last possible day before the deadline for registration in the party in May 1933, my father paced back and forth with me in front of the door of the party office until the office closed and he had to knock in order to be able to declare his entry into the party'. Schleicher was later sentenced to death and executed for his participation in the revolt of 20 July 1944. The story of Ludwig Beck illustrates how many individuals struggled to align personal principles, institutional interests, and national values. From 1933 to 1938 General Beck was chief of the General Staff of the German army and substantially the author of Germany's rearmament programmes during those years. He then became a critic of military policy. In five years—and it is hardly a long time in which to move from legal and military obedience to active conspiracy— he was planning the destruction of the regime. By then Beck perceived that fundamental resistance was an ethical responsibility. He renounced the oath of loyalty that he had sworn to Hitler, repudiated the apoliticism of many of his fellow officers, and shunned the pragmatism of those who argued that it was the soldier's duty to win the war and, perhaps, to deal with Hitler once it was over. Beck became the catalyst for consistent, committed resistance. After its failure he shot himself on 20 July 1944.

Not always was the character of resistance determined by institutional and denominational forces. In the heart of a society riven by rigid and unyielding social distinctions, Ewald von Kleist-Schmenzin, a Prussian monarchist and ultraconservative, became a close friend of Ernst Niekisch, a socialist who worked with the German Communist Party. They met whenever they could in Berlin, where Niekisch had an apartment. During the purge of 30 June 1934 Kleist, threatened by death, hid in Niekisch's apartment. Afterwards, the same apartment became the venue for a number of secret political meetings. Those on the Left would consort in one room while Kleist talked with fellow conservatives in another. By the summer of 1944, the German resistance gathered around Beck, which included the conservative Carl Goerdeler as well as Annedore Leber's husband, the Social Democrat Julius Leber, had become an enormously complex spectacle embracing a variety of political persuasions. In that summer the resistance group reached out to the Communists, too. Its leading lights sought to frame an inclusive political programme that could transcend partisan politics, articulate Christian morality, and unite the worthiest values of the German people. Annedore Leber had known well the very heart of the resistance movement whose final and disastrous statement was the 20 July 1944 revolt. In part the purpose of her book was to commemorate that heart.

But *Conscience in Revolt* did not only portray those who sought to overthrow the Hitler state. Many of the thousands interned in concentration camps for 'political' offences were the victims of a system that politicized and punished discontent, black humour, demoralization, and private criticism. Many of those who were sentenced to imprisonment in concentration camps as enemies of the state were not engaged in fundamental resistance, conscious opposition, or even sporadic dissent. They were innocent men and women like Heinz Bello, Erich Knauf, and Gertrud Seele, who were guilty only of exasperated words, hostile opinions, or stray gestures. Meanwhile, the suicides of Joachim and Meta

Gottschalk were a clear act of dissent in a society in which a racialist state had made their lives together impossible. With their inclusion the argument of the book was significantly expanded.

At her trial in February 1943 Sophie Scholl declared, 'What we have written and said is in the minds of you all, but you lack the courage to say it aloud'. The remark must have struck a chord. By then the continent of Europe had been devastated by war, and Germany itself had been shaken deeply. No doubt, millions of Germans loathed these bitter realities, but most also sensed how utterly they were trapped by it all. Consciences did not always revolt, but they often stirred miserably. Occasionally evidence of it came to light. In June 1944 a Swedish newspaper reported the discovery of a number of little leaflets in the railway carriage of a German train passing through Helsingborg. The leaflets, which resembled the mortuary cards distributed in Catholic districts of Germany, bore the Greek characters for the name of Christ. Below, in Gothic script, were the words:

O God forgive me my sins
Forgive me my share of guilt in Hitler's war
O Jesus I life for Thee
O Jesus I die for Thee
O Jesus I am Thine in life and in death.

III

The appearance of an English edition of *Conscience in Revolt,* translated by Rosemary O'Neill and published in London by Vallentine, Mitchell & Co., was significant. With the conclusion of the war against Hitler, the barely veiled suspicions of old allies had broken out into the Cold War. Germany remained divided, its geopolitical character unresolved. It was already apparent that the German resistance to Hitler had acquired a symbolic importance for a number of postwar interests. In the two Germanys, the resistance was pressed into the service of a new age that sought firm ground on which to stand. The politicians of both the Federal and the Democratic republics looked into the chaotic history of the resistance against Hitler for antecedents. If the National Socialist era had been a cataclysmic test of political values, it was important to show that the continuing political and religious traditions of European life had passed that test and were still credible. Outside Germany, the services of the Germans were required in the continuing struggle between Communism and capitalism. The fact that Hitler had been resisted in Germany itself did something to legitimize new military relaitonships—an obvious comment on the political utility of history. To some extent the publication of *Conscience in Revolt* in Britain illlustrated this climate. It was an argument against totalitarianism in any guise and demonstrated that the Germans too had participated in that argument. English opinion became more sympathetic.

The historiography of National Socialism was in its infancy in the immediate postwar period, and few accounts of the resistance against Hitler existed outside Germany. In October 1945 George Bell had published an essay, 'The Background of the Hitler Plot', in the *Contemporary Review*. Fabian von Schlabrendorff's memoir, *Revolt Against Hitler,* had been published in London in 1948. A slim volume of the last letters of Helmuth James von Moltke, *A German of the Resistance,* was printed in Oxford in the same year. Each of these stressed the religious and ethical inspiration of resistance. Since then much has happened. Historians have written less of moral values and more of political intentions. Arguably, the construction of general theories has become more important than portraits of individual personalities. The very language of resistance scholarship has been disputed intricately. But none of this serves to diminish the value of Leber's achievement. *Conscience in Revolt* remains a profound and significant work of history. In a recent article for the journal *Kirchliche Zeitgeschichte,* the distinguished historian John Conway observed 'the almost total disregard by secular historians of the affairs of the churches'. He continued: 'Such historians, by overemphasizing the political, military or diplomatic factors in their accounts, have largely ignored the religious lives of the people, or failed to see the relevance of moral and spiritual dimensions in the political and social arenas'. It is undoubtedly true. This new edition of *Conscience in Revolt* is a timely reaffirmation of the fundamental importance of these dimensions in National Socialist Germany, not merely for a small number of unusual individuals but for men and women throughout society.

INTRODUCTION

By Robert Birley *Headmaster of Eton College*

THE appearance in an English translation of this book on sixty-four Germans, the representatives of thousands, who died opposing the Nazis, is timely.

The acceptance of Western Germany as a member of the West European and Atlantic system of nations has been a decision of very great difficulty, and has caused political tensions in several countries, including our own. As long as Germany was entirely subjugated, the country might be the field of a diplomatic struggle between East and West, but the German people themselves seemed hardly to be part of the problem. However, when Western Germany became a possible partner in an alliance, the character and traditions of the people could no longer be ignored. It is not surprising, therefore, that several books, widely publicised and widely read, should have appeared, reminding Englishmen of the atrocities of the Nazi régime. This book is in no sense an answer to them. But it is an essential part of the evidence, and one largely neglected in this country, which must be considered if the problem of the German people, now, once more, one of vital urgency, is studied.

There is no answer to the accounts of the Nazi terror. Some may, perhaps, be inaccurate in points of detail and may at times rely too confidently on hearsay evidence, but the main facts about it are quite incontrovertible. This book will not appear, at first, in any way to lull the fears of those who are alarmed at the prospect of the rearming of Germany. Rather, the true picture of the horrors of the time is incomplete without it. But when Englishmen ask themselves the questions, which they certainly ought to ask: 'Can we trust a nation responsible for such deeds? Can we be morally justified in so close an association with it? Does such an association amount to a condonation of the Nazi period in its history?' They will find this book indispensable, if they are to find the true answer.

In order to understand this book, it is necessary to know something of the historical background of the Germany which saw the rise to power of the Nazis and their twelve years' rule. Not that a study of history will easily explain this phenomenon: Never before in European history has there been anything so astounding as the Nazi revolution. The rest of Europe was quite unprepared for such a cataclysmic return to barbarism. The first world war was a terrible catastrophe, but ten years later what seemed most obvious was the resilience of Europe, its ability to recover from the disaster. In 1928 an eminent English judge, Lord Maugham, wrote in a study of the case of Jean Calas, 'Things have changed very greatly in the west of Europe since the year 1761, and we can be assured that the tragic history of Jean Calas can never be repeated. The essential change is in the direction of greater humanity. A complete toleration of the religious views of others, a hatred of cruelty to man or beast, a more generous sympathy with others and a public opinion whose power is scarcely yet fully realised—these are the things which in a complex, unsatisfactory and often disquieting civilisation, may reasonably give us hope for the future of the world.' Five years later Europe saw established in one of its greatest countries a government which quite openly used as one of its chief weapons the ruthless infliction of physical pain. A few days saw the establishment, as part of the normal order of things, of the Concentration Camp: there had never been anything so horrible before in European history. A study of historical events, one might think, should be able to explain the violence which usually accompanies revolutions, excesses such as those which marked the Wars of Religion or the 'Terror' under the Committee of Public Safety in 1793 and 1794, but not this deliberate and organised system of cruelty.

Europe saw a return to the world of the Apocalypse. How pointless, how incongruous the absurd figures from that book have come to appear, the 'great red dragon, having seven heads and ten horns', the beast which had 'a mouth speaking great things and blasphemies', the other beast which 'exerciseth all the power of the first beast before him'. One day, not long after the end of the war, I visited the Spielberg, the great fortress standing above the town of Brno, in Czechoslovakia. It had been the headquarters of the Gestapo in that country, the scene of unimaginable cruelties. The chapel of the castle had been turned into a place of worship for the new Nazi pagan religion, and after the war the Czechs had left it untouched. In place of the altar was a huge block of stone, with an Iron Cross carved on the front, and on it was placed, lit with electric lights, the Gospel of the new religion, Hitler's *Mein Kampf*. Above, where before had hung a picture of the crucified Christ, was fixed an immense eagle, carved in stone, its talons reaching downwards. Never since then have the figures of the Book of Revelations seemed to me absurd or unreal.

We feel, indeed, that we are beyond the sphere of History. Yet these things actually happened, and we must examine, of necessity very shortly, the history of the period.

Germany at the end of the First World War established a parliamentary republican government. Mr J. W. Wheeler-Bennett, in his book, *The Nemesis of Power: the German Army in Politics, 1918-1945*, has seen in an incident on the very first day of its establishment, 9 November 1918, the fatal decision which ultimately condemned it to futility. A Socialist government was formed in Berlin under Fritz Ebert, which was at its birth menaced by a Communist revolution. That night over the telephone he came to an agreement with the Army. If the Government would restore order and co-operate with the Officer Corps in suppressing Bolshevism and in the maintenance of discipline in the Army, the High Command would bring the Army peacefully home and the safety of the Government would be assured. 'Thus, in half a dozen sentences over the telephone line, a pact was concluded between a defeated Army and a tottering semi-revolutionary régime; a pact destined to save both parties from the extreme elements of revolution, but, as a result of which, the Weimar Republic was doomed at birth.' With the support of the Army, even after it had been reduced by the Treaty of Versailles to 100,000 men, the Government was able to suppress attempts to overthrow it from the Left and the Right. Credit must be allowed, however—and it is often denied—to the German civilian statesmen of the first years of the Weimar Republic. They saw it through the crisis when the allied peace terms were almost rejected; the militarist *coup d'état* known as the Kapp Putsch, in March 1920, when indeed the Army all but abandoned it; the crisis in 1923, when Germany failed to pay reparations and the French occupied the Ruhr; and the great Inflation of 1924. After this the Republic sailed into calmer waters. The attempt to exact reparations from Germany was tacitly abandoned, the allied troops were withdrawn from the Rhineland, and the Locarno Treaty of 1925 paved the way for the admission of Germany to the League of Nations. With the election of Hindenburg as President in April 1925, the conservative parties seemed to have accepted the Republic, which up till then had had little real support, except from the socialist and the more liberal elements of the middle classes.

The Republic, however, was very far from safe. The Free Corps, illegal bands of unemployed and disappointed soldiers, called into being during the months of anarchy after the war, were dissolved in 1920, but many continued to exist as secret societies. The Communists, defeated in their initial attempt to seize power, were able to poll nearly two million votes for their candidate in the Presidential Election of 1925. Revolutionary groups proliferated; among them, with its leader an obscure ex-corporal, Adolf Hitler, the National Socialist German Workers' Party. This had attempted a *coup d'état* in Munich in 1923, which had failed ignominiously, but it somehow kept in being for the next few years. And the comparative economic prosperity of this period was an illusion.

The Republic was not nearly strong enough to resist the impact of the great industrial depression, which began in 1929. No one who was in Germany during this great disaster could fail to recognise its effects, the sense of frustration and despair which overwhelmed, in particular, the youth of the nation. It is more difficult to blame the German Government for failing to deal with this crisis than for its policy during the more prosperous period before it. The Chancellor, Heinrich Brüning, was the most honest and certainly one of the ablest statesmen of the Weimar regime. But he was never in a position to control the situation. The *Reichstag* gave him little support and he was forced to try to uphold a parliamentary régime by the use of decrees which received no parliamentary authority.

Englishmen should realise the difference between the situation in their own country and that in Germany during these critical years. Here the economic policy of the National Government may have been faulty, but the Government received solid backing at elections and in parliament. In Germany the Government could never rely on a parliamentary majority. Here the economic foundations of the country proved strong enough to stand the shock; in Germany they had never really recovered from the anarchy after the war and the inflation of 1924. Here the Communists were far too weak to make much capital out of a situation which was apparently so favourable to them; in Germany they were a large and well-organised party, skilled in the use of political violence and always ready to resort to it. And in Germany there was a party and a leader ready to exploit the situation.

The Nazis did not come to power as a result of an electoral victory. In July 1932, they became the largest party in the

Reichstag with 230 seats, more than double their previous number, but in a house of 630 members this was some way from a majority. The Social Democrats and the two Catholic parties had together exactly the same number. In November of the same year at another election their number declined to 196. Local elections in December showed that the loss of ground was continuing. And yet, on 30 January 1933, Hitler became Chancellor, being placed in this position as the result of intrigues by the Army and Nationalist leaders. Six weeks later, with the Communists eliminated by force, all the political parties, except the Social Democrats, united to place full powers in his hands. A few months later they all accepted dissolution without a murmur. In this way, without any long drawn out civil war, the revolution took place. It was the most appalling catastrophe in European history.

If one tries to discover in German history the reasons for this disaster, one finds oneself reciting a kind of parody of the House that Jack built. The Nazis came into power because of the failure of the Weimar régime. The difficulties of this régime were quite genuine. What else could Ebert have done on the night of 9 November 1918? Without the support of the Army for the Government, a Communist dictatorship seemed certain. Why were the Germans unable to form a strong government without relying on the Army? Because under the Empire they had never gained any true experience of parliamentary rule or any sense of democratic responsibility. Why was this? Because under Bismarck Germany had gained her legitimate goal of political unity through military victory. Why had she been compelled to accomplish it in this way? Because her attempt to do so by parliamentary means in 1848 had failed, so that Bismarck could say with truth 'What Germany wants in Prussia is not her liberalism, but her strength.' Why was the revolution of 1848 such a failure? Because the German principalities had been able to prevent the growth of liberal nationalism during the years of the French Revolution. Why were these principalities in a position to do this? Why was German unity so long delayed? Because Germany had failed during the later Middle Ages and the sixteenth century to develop, as France had done, into a National State. And so it goes on, until one may find oneself wondering whether the ultimate cause was not that Germany never became part of the Roman Empire. Was the reason in the end largely geographical, that Germany in the first century B.C. was a land of forests and swamps, which made any political cohesion impossible, compared with Gaul, which was

already a country with roads down which armies might march and enough unity at least to make it conquerable?

The whole process can be made to appear quite inevitable—until one remembers that other nations do not seem to have been so completely at the mercy of events. If they were able to attain a happier state of affairs, it was as a result of political decisions, taken by resolute men, *ready* to sacrifice themselves to secure them. They were acts of will. What seems to be missing in German history is the determination to control events, except in certain individuals, such as Bismarck and Hitler, who were ready to exploit this failing in the German character.

The Nazis, then, obtained power as the result of a surrender, a surrender especially by the more conservative elements in Germany. Even after the election of Hindenburg as President, they had steadily refused to accept responsibility for the government of the country. This goes far to explain the difficulties of those who opposed Hitler once he had gained power. There was no tradition on which a movement of resistance could be built, except among the Social Democrats, who were always a minority, and among the Communists, who were anxious to set up one kind of totalitarian régime in place of another. We must recognise also how the nature of the modern state, more powerful than any state has ever been before, plays into the hands of a totalitarian government. Opposition to any régime now needs a tradition that the government should itself make opposition possible.

Once the Nazi government came into existence, the great majority of Germans simply accepted it as inevitable. After all, most people in any country do not concern themselves much with politics, they merely ask to be allowed to live their own lives and do their own work. But it is futile for the Germans to excuse themselves by saying that they did not know what was happening. Most, no doubt, were not aware of the full horror of the Concentration Camps. But no party has ever been more open in avowing its aims and methods than were the Nazis. One had only to see them walking down the street to realise perfectly well what kind of people they were.

A far more serious charge lies against those, especially the well-educated, who in various ways actively supported the Nazi government, although they did not accept its principles. Not long after the Nazi revolution, a professor at one of the Rhineland universities, a genuine opponent, who had later to flee the country, had cause to visit the Ministry of Education in Berlin.

There he was astonished to meet among the officials one of his former colleagues, whom he knew to be no supporter of the Nazis. This man felt it necessary to excuse himself: 'Do not misjudge me,' he said, 'I am not a Nazi. Very few of us here are. They have put in a few members of the Party, of course, but they are quite useless. They have no idea what administration means. It is the rest of us who keep the Ministry going. No, we are not Nazis. We call ourselves the "Spezis" (*Spezialisten*: specialists).' This was worse than a conscious abandonment of responsibility; it was a complete failure to realise that they had any responsibility at all. Even then, one must recognise the dilemma in which many were placed who did not approve of Nazi rule or were even disgusted by it. Opposition would mean not only disaster, and quite possibly torture and death for themselves, but also utter ruin for their families. It is difficult for Englishmen to blame them. We have never been faced with such a dilemma. Nor need one wholly discount the plea, so often advanced, that they knew that, if they abandoned office, they would only be replaced by men who would carry out the intentions of the Nazis more vigorously.

In a sense, there was no Resistance Movement in Germany against the Nazis. In a modern totalitarian state such a movement is only possible if there is widespread popular feeling against the tyranny, as when a country is militarily occupied, and even then it depends on the hope of help from outside. Most men will only resist if they feel that an alternative government is at least possible. For the first five years of Nazi rule there could be little more than isolated acts of resistance and these could hardly take the form of more than outspoken criticism. For some time, however, there existed many groups of active opponents in the factories, who kept the spirit of resistance alive by secret meetings and the distribution of illegal pamphlets and who were in touch with German political exiles abroad. Among their leaders were Alwin Brandes and Else Nieviera. Brandes, a former Chairman of the Metal Workers' Union, was at the head of a whole network of such groups, which was broken up by the Gestapo at the beginning of 1936. Else Nieviera, also a prominent Trade Unionist, had done remarkable work among the women textile workers. The group, of which she was the leader, tried to keep in close touch with Trade Unions abroad but was broken up in the spring of 1939; she was herself sentenced to two and a half years' imprisonment and was killed in an air-raid in 1944. Altogether, thousands of workers suffered in concentration camps during this early period. Their history is almost unknown in this country. There were writers also who were not prepared to be subservient to the government, like Carl von Ossietzky who figures in this book, and, above all, Rudolf Pechel, the editor of the *Deutsche Rundschau*, the most resolute of all literary opponents of the Nazis, who survived imprisonment in concentration camps and is one of the leading political writers in Germany today. Some of the figures in this book belong to these early years of the tyranny and their lonely heroism is in some ways the finest of all.

In the meantime Hitler had crushed the dissidents in his own party and had murdered many of his old political opponents in the appalling massacres of 30 June 1934. A month later, on 1 August, Hindenburg died and Hitler succeeded him as Leader and Chancellor. Next day the whole Army took the Oath of Allegiance to him. It was, perhaps, his greatest victory. For the Army was the only power in Germany which could possibly resist the Nazis successfully. It was not until the great crisis of February 1938, when Hitler outmanœuvred the generals and himself became War Minister, that a movement grew up in the Army itself which was ready to overthrow the régime. It was to lead eventually to the great conspiracy of 20 July 1944. Because it is so much better documented, there is some danger that its development, along with that of various civilian groups closely connected with it, may come to be regarded as the only manifestation of resistance in Germany during the war. This book is enough to show that there were others.

Let Sophie Scholl, some of whose letters are printed here, stand for those whose resistance was a more desperate and lonely act of defiance. She belonged, with her brother, Hans, to a secret society of students at Munich University, known as the *White Rose*, who were assisted by one of their professors, Kurt Huber, of whom also an account will be found here. The group, which had been distributing anti-Nazi pamphlets, came into the open in February 1943, when the Nazi *Gauleiter* of Bavaria addressed the students on their patriotic duty. Characteristically, he called on the girls to bear a child each year of their studentship as their contribution to the nation. The students spontaneously demonstrated against him and three days later Hans and Sophie Scholl and other members of the *White Rose* scattered pamphlets, which Huber had written, from a balcony in the University. They were arrested, tortured and brought before the People's Court, which had been constituted by Hitler to deal with any manifestations against the government, under its President, Roland Freisler. His is a name which will often be met with in this book. In the whole long roll in history of judges who have used their position to show their venom and cruelty, his is without a peer. The brother and sister, with another student, were condemned to death on 18 April, and hanged. Huber and three other students were executed a few days later. Sophie's bearing at her trial was magnificent. Reading of it is like reading the trial of Joan of Arc. The rôles seem to be reversed: it is the prisoner who prosecutes.

Archbishop Temple said in 1943 that 'the one effective centre of resistance to Nazi oppression in Germany has been the Christian Church'. That may have gone too far. In the Protestant Churches in Germany there was a strong tradition against any intrusion into the political sphere; the Vatican concluded a Concordat with the Nazi government within six months of its establishment. It was not until some years later that the Churches can be regarded as in any way officially opposing the Nazis. But all the time there were individuals who protested and refused to accept the persecution of the Jews. Few finer statements were made against the Nazis than one by von Galen, the Roman Catholic Bishop of Münster, always an opponent of the régime. In a sermon in his Cathedral after a devastating air-raid on the city, he asked his congregation whether, when they had fled from their burning homes, they had remembered how the Jews had had to do the same on the night of the great pogrom of November 1938. Hundreds of Protestant Pastors, who joined the movement of the Confessional Church against the Nazi attempt to gain control of the Evangelical Church, suffered in concentration camps; many were executed. The resistance of Pastor Niemöller was the one act of opposition to the Nazis which was well known at the time to people in this country.

At least half of the persons of whom we read in this book, however, were members of the movement which reached its end on 20 July 1944. It may help the English reader if some account is given of it, with a description of the main groups of which it was composed, and also if some of the characters in the book are specially referred to.

The leading figure in the Army opposing Hitler was Ludwig Beck, Chief of the General Staff from 1935 to 1938. A remarkable number of the German generals were, at one time or another, fully aware of the plots against Hitler, even though most of them did no more than wait to see which way the cat would jump.

Among those who were wholly in support of the movement, however, were General (later Field-Marshal) von Witzleben; General von Tresckow, who had first supported the Nazis, but was to become one of the main figures in the conspiracy during the war; and General Olbricht, in 1944 Chief of the General Army Office and deputy to the Commander-in-Chief of the Reserve Army. One important group was to be found, incongruously enough, in the *Abwehr*, or Military Intelligence Service, whose head, Admiral Canaris, gave shelter in his organisation to many of the opponents of the régime, the most active of whom was General Oster.

We may consider next some highly placed civilians, of whom the most important was Karl Goerdeler, Mayor of Leipzig from 1923 to 1937, who had resigned from the post of Price Commissioner under the Nazi government when he saw that Hitler's economic policy was directed to a war, and from his Mayoralty in protest at the persecution of the Jews. With General Beck, he was the leader of the resistance to the Nazis; if the conspiracy had been successful Beck would have become *Reichsverweser*, or Head of the State, and Goerdeler Chancellor. Professor Popitz, who was Prussian Minister of Finance, represented the most conservative element in the conspiracy. Ulrich von Hassell, one of the leading German diplomats, had been Ambassador in Rome until 1937. His *Diaries*, which were preserved, tell us much of its history.

A very important part was played by a group of younger men, some of the leading members of which were closely related to one another: Dietrich Bonhoeffer, who had been Pastor of the Lutheran Church in London, was one of the chief figures in the Confessional Church, which led the resistance of the German Protestants to the Nazis; his brother, Klaus Bonhoeffer; their two brothers-in-law, Hans von Dohnanyi, the ablest organiser in the group until his early arrest, who was from the first in touch with Beck and Oster, and Professor Rüdiger Schleicher. One member of the group, who miraculously survived, was Fabian von Schlabrendorff, and his book, *Offiziere gegen Hitler*, gives an account of the conspiracy which perhaps brings us nearer to an understanding of the difficulties of the enterprise and of the courage of those who resisted Hitler, than any other.

Helmut Graf von Moltke was the leader of a group, known as the Kreisau Circle, from his home in Silesia, where they often met. It should not be thought of as in any way an organised society, but among its members were most of those who, one feels, had realised that opposition to Hitler made necessary a new and dynamic political philosophy, and that a return to the Germany of pre-Nazi days was no longer practicable. It started at the beginning of the war as a group of personal friends, in particular von Moltke and his cousin, Peter Yorck von Wartenburg. Among them was Adam von Trott zu Solz, a former Rhodes Scholar of Balliol College, and Hans-Bernd von Haeften, who were young members of the Foreign Office; representatives of the Churches, such as Father Alfred Delp and the Protestant Dr Eugen Gerstenmaier, one of the three men at the very centre of the conspiracy on 20 July who escaped, and now President of the *Bundestag*. In friendly relations with it were some leading members of the Social Democrat Party, Julius Leber, whose widow has written this book—he would have been Minister of the Interior, if the plot had succeeded: what would he not have given to Germany and to Europe if he had survived—Carlo Mierendorff, who was killed in an air-raid, Theodor Haubach and Adolf Reichwein. Of all four we may read in this book. The Kreisau Circle was to be deeply divided over the question of Hitler's assassination, which von Moltke could never accept as justifiable, but more than any other group they looked forward to the future and the death of nearly all of them was an irreparable loss to Germany after the war.

In May 1938, Hitler announced to his generals his decision to crush Czechoslovakia by the early autumn. They protested at what seemed to them to be a militarily indefensible policy. Hitler rejected their protest and Beck, then Chief of the General Staff, resigned. During the summer the first steps were taken in bringing together the various groups opposing Hitler and the association began between Beck and Goerdeler, which was to last until the final disaster six years later. A plan was evolved, largely under the direction of Oster, to seize Hitler as soon as he had ordered a war with Czechoslovakia and bring him to trial. It was supported by General Halder, who had succeeded Beck as Chief of the General Staff; von Witzleben, then in command of the troops near Berlin; the Police-President of Berlin; his second-in-command, Graf Fritz-Dietlof von der Schulenburg, and others. Whether the complete collapse of the plot, which was never attempted at all, was due to the decision of the British and French governments to abandon Czechoslovakia is one of the still unsolved problems of History. In any case, the intentions of many of those involved, like Halder, who now fades out of the picture, was not so much to eliminate Hitler as to prevent him from starting a war which in their view would be disastrous for Germany. The whole episode, however, made the task of those genuinely opposed to the Nazis far more difficult in the future, since Hitler's position in Germany was immeasurably stronger after the allied surrender at Munich.

For the next four years, though numerous plans were evolved, the chances of a successful coup against Hitler were small, owing to his extraordinary series of successes. But during these years the various strands in the Resistance were slowly wound together. Already among those who had been involved in the planning of the utterly abortive plot before Munich were several in the group to which the Bonhoeffers belonged. They now served in posts which brought them into closer touch with the military leaders. Von Dohnanyi and Otto Kiep, another member, joined the Intelligence at the beginning of the war and served under Oster, and Yorck von Wartenburg was on the staff of von Witzleben. Nothing could be done, however, without the Army. There was a moment, after Hitler had announced his intention, on the successful conclusion of the Polish campaign, at once to attack in the West, when the Generals, led again by Halder, came near to forestalling what they expected to be a disastrous campaign, in the same way as they had planned the year before. But the Generals fumbled and Hitler changed his mind.

It is impossible to say when the opponents of Nazism came to the conclusion that the only solution was to assassinate Hitler. Beck and Goerdeler only came slowly to accept it; many of the Kreisau Circle, and von Moltke in particular, were never able to do so. In August 1941, however, a definite plan to kill Hitler, when he visited the Headquarters of General Bock in Russia, was formed by General von Tresckow, who was on Bock's staff, and von Schlabrendorff, his A.D.C. But Hitler was far too well guarded for it to be carried out. This was only the first of his escapes from assassination, each one more astonishing than the last.

The Kreisau Circle, as has been shown, combined persons of very diverse political views. The association of this group with those which had already accepted the leadership of Beck and Goerdeler made something much more like a Resistance Movement. January 1943, with the end of the battle of Stalingrad, marked the turn of the tide in the war. On 22 January von Hassell wrote in his Diary: 'If the Generals had it in mind to withhold their intervention until it was absolutely clear that the corporal is leading us into disaster, they have had their dream fulfilled.' But most of the generals were only ready to act when Hitler was actually dead, and all the plots to assassinate him were abortive. The members of the movement have sometimes been charged as incompetent amateurs for their run of ill-success. That they were amateurs is indeed true. Men like von Schlabrendorff, who once succeeded in introducing two delayed action bombs, in a case of brandy, on to Hitler's aeroplane—they failed to explode—were not professional assassins, but honourable men forced to undertake assassination after deep searchings of heart. The professionals were on the other side.

It cannot be said that all those in the conspiracy were even reasonably careful. Goerdeler, in particular, talked a great deal too much. It is, in fact, surprising that the Gestapo did not find out more than it did. In course of time, however, a certain amount inevitably was discovered. In April 1943, Dietrich Bonhoeffer and von Dohnanyi were arrested and Canaris was forced to dismiss Oster from active employment. In January 1944, the Gestapo seized von Moltke and Otto Kiep. The latter had belonged to a group sometimes known as the Solf Circle. Under the inspiration of Frau Solf, the widow of one of the greatest diplomats of the Weimar Republic and a firm opponent of the Nazis, this group of people had done much to assist those sought by the Gestapo to escape from the country. Among its members was Elizabeth von Thadden, the headmistress of a well-known school for girls, another of the victims of the Nazis who are to be found in this book. A Gestapo spy attended a meeting at her house. Later, all those who had been present were arrested, and also von Moltke, who had been a friend of Otto Kiep. Elizabeth von Thadden had actually nothing to do with the great conspiracy; she was, in fact, quite unaware of it.

At this stage the most remarkable figure in the whole movement, Claus Schenck Graf von Stauffenberg, took over the initiative in organising the conspiracy. The fact that he actually carried out himself the final attempt on Hitler's life may give a false impression of his rôle and of his personality. It was indeed typical of him to undertake himself the most dangerous task of all. But he was also a very fine organiser and, what is more, a young man with the makings of a great statesman. Very severely wounded in North Africa in 1942, he was later appointed to be Chief of Staff to General Olbricht, who was by now a leading member of the conspiracy. The cousin of Yorck von Wartenburg, he became interested in the Kreisau Circle. Under his inspiration Beck agreed to the inclusion of the socialist leaders, Leber and Leuschner, in the future government of Germany. Later, Adolf Reichwein arranged a meeting at which Leber met some of the Communist leaders. The activities of the Communists against the Nazis cannot be ignored. Their actions have been quite unconnected with those of whom we have been speaking and they were, as was to be expected, directly in the service of Russia. Leber considered it important to find out how they would react if Hitler were assassinated. It was a tragedy that on this occasion one of those present was a spy, and that, as a result, both Leber and Reichwein were arrested.

After all these arrests it was decided that the plot must go forward, whether Hitler was successfully assassinated or not. The first move in the plan was to use those army officers who were in sympathy with the movement to set in motion troops who would seize Berlin and contain the Nazi SS there. As the Army was half expecting a rising of the SS against itself, it was thought that the troops would be ready to move without too great suspicion. As soon as possible more troops would be brought in from more distant commands to finish off the SS in Berlin. It was hoped that, once Hitler had been assassinated, the leaders of the Army would support the coup and accept the authority of Beck as head of the State and of von Witzleben as Commander-in-Chief. Von Stauffenberg, who had recently been appointed Chief of Staff to General Fromm, the Commander of the Home Army, was due to represent him at a conference at Hitler's Headquarters in East Prussia, the so-called *Wolfschanze* or Wolf's Lair, and was to carry out the assassination. Much was seen to depend on Fromm himself, who was well aware of much that was going on under his nose but had not committed himself. If, on hearing that Hitler was dead, he refused to join in the coup, he would be supplanted by General Hoepner.

Von Stauffenberg flew to the *Wolfschanze* on the morning of 20 July with Werner, brother of Hans-Bernd von Haeften. He entered the Conference Room, a large wooden hut, where General Heusinger, Deputy Chief of the General Staff, was explaining to Hitler the situation on the Eastern front. Then he placed under the table, on which were spread the maps needed for the meeting, his brief-case, in which was a bomb timed to go off in a few minutes, and left the room, ostensibly to make a telephone call.

He waited outside the hut until he saw the devastating results of the explosion, which took place at ten minutes to one o'clock. Then, fully satisfied with the result, von Stauffenberg and Werner von Haeften entered a waiting car, drove to the airport and returned at once to Berlin, which they reached about two and a half hours later.

But Hitler had not been killed or even seriously injured. He had been saved by the massive table under which the bomb had been placed. What is more, the general in charge of the communications at Headquarters, who was himself in the plot, failed to disrupt the telephone exchange and to inform those in Berlin of what had happened.

In Berlin, the members of the conspiracy met at the War Ministry and waited for news from Hitler's Headquarters. There was nothing but an ominous silence. Soon after half past three, however, Werner von Haeften rang up from the airport of Berlin and told them that the attempt had been successful. Von Stauffenberg and he went straight to join the others at the War Ministry; orders were despatched at once by telephone to the troops near Berlin and the initial moves of the coup were carried out. General Fromm, however, insisted on telephoning to the *Wolfschanze*, from which he was told that Hitler had only been slightly injured. The conspirators then seized him and those other officers at the Ministry who refused to accept the authority of von Witzleben as Commander-in-Chief. But already the plot was going awry. From the *Wolfschanze*, Field Marshal Keitel, the Chief of the Supreme Command, was ordering German armies spread all over Europe to disregard all orders unless they came from Himmler or himself. An astonishing battle of telephone calls was waged, von Stauffenberg from the War Ministry insisting in his turn that the Army Commanders were only to obey orders from von Witzleben or Hoepner. In Paris, the SS were actually seized and disarmed. At six in the evening an announcement over the wireless informed the German people that Hitler was alive.

The coup could now hardly succeed. The end came when Major Remer, an officer commanding one of the regiments which had been ordered to Berlin as part of the plot, saw Goebbels, who arranged for him to speak to Hitler direct. He was ordered to seize the War Ministry. Before he did so, however, Fromm and the other officers there, who had been arrested, succeeded in escaping and turned the tables on their captors. Beck was allowed to commit suicide. Four of the conspirators, among them Claus

Schenck von Stauffenberg and Werner von Haeften, were shot at once in the courtyard of the Ministry, for Fromm wished to silence all those who could tell of his own hesitations and his doubtful loyalty to Hitler. But before he could organise the execution of the rest, Gestapo officials arrived and arrested them. Among those of whom we read in this book were Yorck von Wartenburg, Fritz-Dietlof von Schulenburg, Hans Bernd von Haeften, Berthold von Stauffenberg and Ulrich Wilhelm Schwerin von Schwanenfeld. At midnight Hitler spoke to the German people and all was over, except the hunting down of the members of the Resistance, the interrogations, the torturings, the trials before the People's Court under the Presidency of Freisler and the executions of some thousands implicated in the conspiracy.

After the end of the war I worked for two and a half years in Germany and I was left with one very strong impression, that thousands of men and women in that country during the period of Nazi rule had found themselves faced with what seemed to be an impossible dilemma. They did not approve of the régime; many felt utterly ashamed of it. But what were they to do? Resistance seemed quite futile, and what would happen to their wives or husbands, their parents or children, if they made their protest? Most men and women are not strong enough to solve such a dilemma, and certainly someone who has not had to live in a totalitarian country has no right to condemn them. In Germany I had at one time to work with four *Land* Ministers of Education: three of them had been in concentration camps (two were Socialists and one had been a Deputy of the Catholic Centre Party); the fourth, who had been a Headmaster, was dismissed from his post the moment the Nazis gained power. We used to meet regularly to discuss our common problems, and I never met them without wondering whether I could have shown the courage they had shown. It is a sign of the decadence of a civilisation when ordinary men and women must expect to face an impossible dilemma. But those whose deaths are recorded in this book—and the photographs of each one of them bring them very near to us— were most of them not very remarkable people—and *they* solved the dilemma.

In this lies their importance for the future, and not only the future of Germany. We should not forget that all those in Germany today who believe in freedom, the claims of conscience and the sacredness of truth, carry with them always the burden of a terrible memory; the memory of a complete defeat when the Nazis gained power. This is the most serious of all the weaknesses in Germany today. Something, I believe, can be done if they can be convinced that there are those in other countries who are ready to help them. But the only thing that can really lighten the burden is the memory that there were those who were not defeated.

It is not enough for us to say that all this happened in another country and could not happen here. We may indeed believe that it could not, but that is irrelevant. For, if there is no condonation of the Germans in suggesting that they did not really know what was happening, there is none for us either. The Nazis, when they cynically avowed their ends and their means, spoke across the frontiers. We knew quite well what was meant by the murders of 30 June 1934. We read at the time of the persecution of the Jews and quite enough about the concentration camps to know what they stood for. And yet, until war began, how pitifully little we did to let those who resisted the Nazis in Germany feel that they had even sympathisers in this country.

Not long after the end of the war the Protestant Church in Germany said in a famous declaration that the guilt for the crimes of the Nazis lay with the whole German people. It was a courageous statement and I know that it found an echo in the minds of many in Germany. But the concept of national guilt is one to which it is difficult to give any meaning. Guilt can only be purged by sacrifice, and, by the mercy of God, provided that men's hearts are touched, by vicarious sacrifice. That is the historic rôle of martyrs. It was the rôle of the sixty-four men and women—representatives, let it not be forgotten, of thousands of others—whose stand for conscience is related in this book. Dietrich Bonhoeffer had said that the resistance to the Nazis must be 'an act of repentance'.

I remember meeting the author one evening in December 1948, in Berlin, during the blockade. Frau Leber had been addressing an election meeting in what must have been one of the strangest elections that ever took place. They were held, of course, only in West Berlin. Which party won did not seem very important. What mattered was that free elections were being carried out in a beleaguered city in the middle of the Soviet Zone of Germany. I remember that I said that in all elections it became clear long before what were the dominant issues and I asked her which they were in this one. 'There is only one issue,' she replied, 'and

it is the old question: Are you, or are you not, against the concentration camp?' We should not forget that in Eastern and
Central Europe there are thousands today who face the same
dilemma as did the men and women in this book, and that there
are those who are making the same answer. For these men and
women, who raised the Revolt for Conscience against the Nazis,
are not yet merely figures in a page of history. They fell in the
struggle against the totalitarian state which still continues, and it
will be long before the cause for which they died will have been
won.

Preface to the Original German Edition

I FIRST thought of writing this book many years ago when I saw some photographs taken in the People's Court, apparently by order of the highest Gestapo authorities, during the trials which followed the attempt on Hitler's life on 20 July 1944. At the time, neither the general public nor the families of those concerned knew of their existence, but after the final collapse of Germany in 1945 they were made available to me.

Even at first glance I felt that these photographs explained more powerfully than any words the realities of life under a modern totalitarian dictatorship. Here is the individual going out to meet his fate: he emerges from the countless mass of Nazi victims, known and unknown, to give his own personal testimony. We are confronted by his courage, his suffering and his spiritual strength. He commands our attention and asks whether we understand, or whether we want to evade the real issue.

Since then I have given much thought to the question of finding the right framework for these documents of recent German history. I wanted to present them in a manner which would make more generally understood the individual need to protest against tyranny, and I felt that the strength of the spirit that withstood all the grisly methods of the totalitarian state should stand out as the connecting link in the story of resistance and endurance.

There were men and women, young and old, of all classes and from all parts of the country, who could not and would not come to terms with injustice, and sooner or later they resisted. Resentment and rebellion brought together people of every kind and drove them to action, and in the end their outraged consciences found a common outlet on 20 July 1944. This book, published ten years later, is dedicated to their memory.

After much thought I decided to present a more general picture and for this purpose to collect other stories. But difficulties soon arose. Circumstances made it hard to get hold of material from the Eastern Zone of Germany; relatives and friends had either died or were difficult to contact; photographs and documents had been lost in the confusion of the immediate post-war years. As a result many personal stories have never come to light. For all that, the most difficult task was to make a selection from the wealth of material which was available without implying that the selected cases were of greater significance than the rest. This book does not claim to tell the complete story, but simply to convey in the stories of the life and death of sixty-four people the motives and manner of resistance. The task of finding the right framework for further studies to fill in the gaps which a book of this kind must inevitably leave, will be well worth while.

But an ambitious task is absorbing, and one is almost sad when even a part of it is finished. That this book appears at all is due to the help and encouragement of the relations and friends of the men and women whose stories it tells, whom we in Germany have lost and whom we miss so much today, and it therefore incorporates many of the thoughts and views of the people who were closest to them.

Human beings, seeking, hoping, straying, struggling, suffering— that is what they were. In them, as in each of us all, conflicting forces wrestled with one another. They stood the test, for their conscience was strong enough in the hour of decision. By some unexpected stroke of fate any one of us might find himself in a similar position, and we hardly dare to say how we should conduct ourselves; and all the less so in face of the complicated political and social situation of today, which might so easily present us with desperately difficult decisions.

Perhaps we might react the right way, perhaps not. But the essential is that we should continually remind ourselves of what is right and therefore of what our own decision ought to be. For there is one fact we should never forget: it is the very foundation of our spiritual and intellectual life that the individual, whenever the need arises, should be ready to come forward and to answer for the rights, the lives and the souls of his fellow human beings.

ANNEDORE LEBER

I YOUTH

GERMAN YOUTH, the men and women who grew up after the 1914-1918 war, provided much of the enthusiasm and support which brought Hitler to power. Many of them first became politically conscious in the days of the Weimar Republic. This was a period when good intentions and great efforts at reconstruction, often unappreciated, failed to bring about economic stability and failed also to give young people a purpose in life or a loyalty to democratic society. Strong parties of both Right and Left attacked the foundations of the state. During the economic crisis of 1929-30 subversive activities increased alarmingly and inflation was let loose, working men brought home their wages in suitcases and university students queued up for the dole with millions of unemployed. The ground was well prepared for unscrupulous adventurers; and when the adventurers came, under the banner of a corrupted nationalism, it was above all the young who followed them into the darkest period of German history.

These same men and women, and others who grew up later, also had to bear a very heavy share of the misery meted out by National Socialism. They had to kill for it and die for it and at the end even children, boys of 15 or 16, were put into uniform and sent out to stand between the *Führer* and his henchmen and the encircling armies, to delay by a few weeks or days or hours the inevitable retribution. But the young had to suffer far more than this: they grew up in an atmosphere of authority, fear, distortion, propaganda and hysteria; they were fed with false history and false ideology, and confused by callous invocation of freedom, patriotism and social justice; they were taught to despise individuality and to glory in the corporate bleating of the totalitarian state. Many of them saw through the façade, some sooner and some very much later; but whenever it was that disillusionment came, the whole edifice of habit and loyalty crashed; they were left with no faith, no background, no purpose, no confidence and very little knowledge of the outside world, other than a slow realisation that it looked with disfavour on all that had been done in their name. Those of them who survived the war had to start again among the ruins, to live down twelve years of Nazi tyranny, and some sought to keep alive the memory of those of their contemporaries who died in the struggle against it.

For many of them had resisted and many had been prepared to die. In 1933 there was still an organised opposition, and the young people in the Labour Movement, in the—greatly reduced—ranks of the liberal groups, in the *Reichsbanner* (the militant socialist organisation), and in many denominational and other youth and sports organisations, all played their part in the genuine, if inadequate, efforts to ward off disaster. But the Nazis made it clear that they would not tolerate independent youth movements. Sons followed their fathers into prison, even young girls were not spared the brutalities of the SA and the tortures of the Gestapo: the aim was to line up the young in one state-controlled youth organisation—the Hitler Youth—and to use it as an instrument of power. A bitter fight was waged against the few remaining independent organisations until they were finally brought to heel. But even the Nazis, though they might destroy the organisations themselves, could not altogether obliterate the spirit of opposition among the young, and the spirit of opposition grew.

As in every sphere, the motives and the manner of resistance varied widely. Some opposed from the beginning, others began as enthusiastic Nazis. Many were indifferent, and were more concerned with their next examination or with plans for their summer holiday than with the demerits of a political régime which, for the moment, enjoyed obvious success; and were stung to awareness by some particular event or personal experience—a relation who fell foul of the authorities, a Jewish friend who was in trouble, or a soldier with long hours of boredom during a bitter winter on the eastern front in which to think. Many came up against the compulsory measures imposed upon them, and took refuge in home life. Tradition often proved stronger than the Nazis would have wished, and many parents were able to foster in their children a basically critical attitude, supported sometimes by religious faith or by humanitarian feeling. The liberal ideas of the earlier youth movements were kept alive, and as time went on and those who deviated from the Nazi pattern were branded as 'liberalistic' or 'individualistic', the struggle against standardisation acquired a new significance.

2

Experiences at the front led many young men to reflect, or to seek refuge in basic impulses of love, loyalty, comradeship and mutual trust. *Letters from German Students Killed in Action, 1939-1945*[1] gives many examples. The young men no longer knew what they were fighting for; liberty had become a legendary concept; some simply believed they must defend their country, others that the essential task was to be rid of the National Socialists; but they were not traitors, and certainly not cowards, merely young and bewildered and disillusioned, and trying to follow their consciences.

The world took notice when a year before the attempt of 20 July 1944 against Hitler's life the Munich students, the Scholls and their friends, came out in open defiance of the Nazis, knowing quite well that they would pay with their lives and that they had no prospect of tangible success. A friend wrote of Willy Graf, who was arrested just after the Scholls and had to wait seven months in the death cell before his execution: 'At the age of sixteen he first met members of the *Jungenschaft* and belonged to this group up to his death. After the ban on all youth organisations (save those sponsored by the Nazis), the *Jungenschaft* continued in being and rejected all enticements from the National Socialists. Most of his friends shared his fate, they were killed either in action or in the struggle against Hitler.'

Hope was never quite abandoned; as late as January 1945 a young member of an illegal group in Berlin still found it possible to be optimistic, and wrote in a most moving memorandum: 'Let's make a new start. Really. Let's plough up the earth once more so that we are ready to sow good new seed. And it will happen, oh, it will!'

---

[1] *Kriegsbriefe gefallener deutscher Studenten 1939-1945*. Rainer Wunderlich Verlag, Tübingen and Stuttgart.

ANTON SCHMAUS

19 April 1910—January 1934

ANTON SCHMAUS was one of five children and the second son of Johannes Schmaus, a trade-union official and a member of the *Reichsbanner* in Berlin-Köpenick. He served his apprenticeship as a carpenter and attended evening classes at a technical school for builders. He also joined the Socialist Workers' Youth Organisation and later the German Socialist Party, and in 1931 became a member of the *Reichsbanner* Youth Organisation. There he was much respected but was unable, for lack of time, to play any very active part.

The following story was told by Willy Urban and Paul Hasche, friends and neighbours of the Schmaus family:

'In February 1933 the district of Köpenick was thrown into a state of extreme alarm: SA[1] gangs, in laundry vans, would pull up at the houses of people known to oppose the Nazis and cart them off to the various SA headquarters, and no-one knew if he would return safe and sound from these ordeals.

'On 21 June the terror reached a climax, when the Köpenick SA seized more than 200 people during the day. On his return in the evening Anton Schmaus was warned at the station that the SA had been to his home looking for his father and himself. The Schmaus family were widely respected for their independence of outlook and Anton firmly refused to take flight, saying he was "fed up with all this lawlessness" and did not intend to spend his time permanently in hiding.

'Anton was already upstairs in bed when the SA forced their way into the house late that evening. They kicked his mother, who barred their way, and knocked her down. Anton was woken by her cries for help and found himself at the top of the stairs confronted by the SA. He told them to get out of the house, otherwise he would shoot. They took no notice, and closed in on him; and so as a last resort he pulled out a pistol. According to the police report of 5 July 1933, File No. IAdVI, three storm troopers were badly wounded and later

[1] *Sturmabteilungen*—Hitler's Brownshirts.

4

died in hospital and a fourth was fatally wounded by a shot
from one of his companions.

'Anton Schmaus jumped out of the window and then gave
himself up to the police. The SA began to search for him and
demanded of the police that he be handed over to them. The
police refused, but for his own safety they sent him to Police

5

Headquarters in Berlin, guarded by two constables. Suddenly the policemen found themselves surrounded by thirty or forty storm troopers who clearly intended to seize their prisoner. According to the same police report, a shot was fired at him out of the crowd. Anton Schmaus was paralysed through an injury to the spinal cord, and died in a police hospital in January 1934. The day of his death is unknown.

'On 22 June 1933, the day after the SA raid, the Brownshirts hanged Anton's father, Johannes Schmaus, in his own house. There were many other fearful acts of revenge. A few days later a number of sacks containing corpses were washed up by the river Dahme, near the Grunau ferry. Among those which were identified were Johannes Stelling, a former Prime Minister of Mecklenburg-Schwerin, Paul von Essen, the leader of the *Reichsbanner* and Pokern, a prominent communist.'

HELMUTH HÜBENER

8 J 1271 42 g
2 H 141/42

Secret!

In the Name of
The German People

In the criminal proceedings against:

1. Helmuth Günther Hübener, born 8 January 1925, in Hamburg, civil servant in the Hamburg Welfare Department, lately resident in Hamburg.

2. Rudolf Gustav Wobbe, born 11 February 1926, in Hamburg, locksmith's apprentice, lately resident in Hamburg.

3. Karl Heinz Schnibbe, born 5 January 1924, in Hamburg, house-painter, lately resident in Hamburg.

4. Gerhard Heinrich Jacob Jonni Düwer, born 1 November 1924, in Altona, civil servant in the Hamburg Welfare Department, lately resident at Hamburg-Altona, all at present held in custody

for plotting high treason

the Second Chamber of the People's Court, in its proceedings on 11 August 1942, in which there took part:

Presiding Judge: Judge Engert, Vice-President of the People's Court;
Judge Fikeis;
Brigadeführer Heinsius, of the National Socialist Motor Corps;
Herr Bodinus, Magistrate;
Herr Hartmann, Chairman of the District Court, as representative of the Chief Prosecutor of the Reich;
Dr Drullmann, State Prosecutor, as an official of the court;
Herr Wöhlke, Clerk of the Court;
has decreed and passed sentence as follows:

7

Hübener, for listening to foreign broadcasts and for spreading the news so heard; and simultaneously for plotting high treason and treacherously supporting the enemy, is sentenced to *Death* and to the loss of civil rights for the rest of his life;

Wobbe, for listening to foreign broadcasts and for spreading news so heard, and simultaneously for plotting high treason is sentenced to *10 years' imprisonment;*

Schnibbe, for listening to foreign broadcasts and for spreading news so heard, is sentenced to *5 years' imprisonment;*

and *Düwer,* for spreading news from foreign broadcasts is sentenced to *4 years' imprisonment.*

EXTRACTS FROM THE COURT CASE BOOK

'The defendant Hübener is now 17 years of age. His father is at present employed in the Security Service, his mother is at home.

'He attended an elementary school and moved on to a secondary school in 1938. His school leaving report was excellent. In April 1941 he joined the civil service, executive grade. In 1938 he joined the junior section of the Hitler Youth Organisation, and later became a member of the Hitler Youth proper and was a member until the time of his arrest. Since early childhood he has been a member of the "Church of Jesus Christ of the Latter-Day Saints".

'Since the summer of 1941, Hübener has spread the contents of British news bulletins in leaflets and handbills. . . . All in all twenty different propaganda leaflets of this kind, either drafts or mimeographed copies, have been confiscated. In addition to the British bulletins on the war situation, the handbills contained insults and insinuations against the *Führer* and his lieutenants and inflammatory attacks on the measures and institutions of the National Socialist government; they also demanded that the war be ended by the overthrow of the *Führer.* . . .

'All the defendants have admitted that they were aware of the ban on listening to foreign stations and on the spreading of foreign news detrimental to the Reich. They have also made the following statements:

'*Hübener:* Unlike the German news bulletins, British bulletins to which he had listened had reported events in a manner

favourable to England and detrimental to the Reich. But since they went into far more detail than the German reports, he believed that on most points they were true; and had considered it his duty to let other people know about them, so that they would also hear the truth and be better informed. . . .

'Hübener, whom the witness Mons has called an excellent and reliable colleague, has shown in his work at the Central Administration an intelligence far exceeding that of the average

9

boy of his age . . . an impression that is borne out by the fact that he reached an educational standard beyond that of the Elementary School. Moreover, in his final school examination, he submitted a political essay entitled *War of the Plutocrats*. Although this was in the main a compilation, it was hard to believe that the author was only 15 or 16 years old; both in content and maturity of style this essay appears to be the work of someone far older. The same applies to the leaflets which Hübener drafted on the basis of the news broadcasts; no one could imagine that their author was only 16 or 17, even if he knew that they were composed with the help of notes. Thus the defendant had to be punished as an adult person.

'The death sentence was carried out on 27 October, 1942.'

HILDA MONTE

31 July 1914—18 April 1945

WHEN HILDA MONTE was 15 years old, she was writing for *Der Funke* (The Spark), the Berlin organ of the Socialist

11

International. Three years later, when the Nazis seized power in Germany, she was in England. Although as a Jewess she had reason enough to worry about her own future, she devoted all her strength and her short life to the organisation of an international resistance movement against the Nazi régime and to the liberation of the German people. Through the Socialist International she got in touch with political friends in many countries and also, with great skill, in Germany. In speeches and in writing she advocated the decisive blow against Nazism—the removal of Hitler. Under the pseudonym of Hilda Monte (her real name was Hilde Meisel), she kept her friends in Germany well informed, warning them when danger threatened and helping them to escape.

During the war she published in English a short story entitled *Where Freedom Perished,* in which she tried to make it clear to other nations that Germans, too, were being oppressed by Nazi dictatorship; and about the same time she published a book, *The Unity of Europe*, which reveals her understanding of political and economic affairs.

Even during the war she tried to reach Germany; in 1939 she got as far as Lisbon, but had to return to England. In 1944 she managed to make her way to Switzerland, hoping to go on to Austria and Germany. In the spring of 1945 she was shot dead by an SS patrol when attempting to cross the frontier, illegally, on her return to Switzerland.

Nora Platiel, one of her closest friends, has written of her:

> 'Hilda Monte, physically delicate, mentally lively and pre-cocious, turned to political journalism at an age when other young people are still working for their examinations. Her clear mind quickly grasped the salient features of our social structure. Though she never completed her formal education, her many theses on social economy and political affairs testify to her ability.
>
> 'She has left behind her a number of poems. They have no great literary merit, and yet are strangely moving. Is it her deep community with nature, with the arts, with the world of beauty which appeals to us so directly? Or is it the deep sincerity, the passion for justice? Perhaps we come closest to Hilda Monte's character and to the meaning and value of her poems when we take them as expressions of a passionate and restless heart, which never yielded to cowardice or inertia.'

12

Do Not Speak of Courage

Do not speak of courage,
O do not speak of heroes,
Heroism too;
I know there are some heroes
To whom all praise is due
But my case was quite different:
To praise me is absurd.
Life is sometimes so oppressive,
So unbearably hard,
One must be brave to live at all;
Far braver, than to hear the call
Of some great cause, to give
One's life, and be done with it all.
So, one learns that death may be
Despised: it's good to learn that truth.
But they who get as far as this
Can best give proof
Of courage, by retreat: by living on
For years—and decades—long
Vistas of living. Do not make a hero
Of her for whom life was too strong.

(From Poems by Hans Lehnert, Hilde Meisel. Europäische Verlagsanstalt, Hamburg.)

JONATHAN STARK

8 July 1926—October 1944

His parents were Jehovah's Witnesses and gave Jonathan a strict religious upbringing. On leaving the elementary school he learned lithography at an art school in Ulm, where he was regarded as one of the best pupils. On 1 October 1943, when he was 17, he was ordered to report to the National Socialist Labour Service, which he did with a heavy heart because he knew that even boys of 16 were being taught to use arms. True to his faith, he refused to swear the Oath of Allegiance to Hitler, and after three days at a labour camp he was arrested by the Gestapo.

Soon after this his father was likewise arrested, remaining in prison until after the end of the war. Jonathan Stark himself was taken to the concentration camp of Sachsenhausen, and there, at the end of October 1944, was hanged.

Herman Scheffel, who was in the same concentration camp and who, as a Jehovah's Witness, was later sentenced to a long term of penal servitude in the Soviet-occupied zone, told the following story:

'In the autumn of 1944 I heard that the young brother Jonathan Stark had arrived at the camp. He was put in the punishment cells in Block 14 and immediately given a special uniform. We all knew what these uniforms meant: they were death uniforms. When I heard this I tried to get in touch with him, which was of course strictly forbidden. But I succeeded, and talked to him for over an hour. His companions were impressed by his exceptional behaviour, and he was much beloved. He was quite calm on that first evening that I was with him, though he had no illusions about his fate. He remained serene and in control of himself to the end, so much so that his behaviour won the admiration even of the SS. He was the sensation of the camp and everybody talked about him.

'One Tuesday afternoon his last hour was at hand. We saw him once more, from a distance, but were unable to get near him. He was standing by the gate, upright and quiet. A professional criminal had been ordered to hang him in the presence of the camp commandant. His neck was put in the noose. The hangman hesitated and the commandant forgot to give the

order. Suddenly the boy asked: "Why do you hesitate? Bear witness for Jehovah and for Gideon!" These were his last words.'

At the time, Jonathan Stark was one of 6,034 Jehovah's Witnesses in Germany. Of these, 5,911 were arrested between 1933 and 1945. Over 2,000 of them were either executed, or died of ill-treatment, hunger, disease or overstrain in the course of forced labour.

SOPHIE SCHOLL

9 May 1921—22 February 1943

SOPHIE SCHOLL was born in the small town of Forchtenberg (Württemberg). She was the daughter of the local mayor, and grew up with four brothers and sisters. In 1940 she left the secondary school at Ulm and spent two years training as a kindergarten teacher. She was then called up by the Labour Service and later by the Auxiliary Military Service. In May 1942 she began to study biology and philosophy at Munich University. She belonged to the resistance group known as the 'White Rose', composed of students, artists and scientists who called for a clear rejection of Hitler and his régime in order—as one of their leaflets put it—'to strive for the renewal of the mortally wounded German spirit'.

On 18 February 1943, Sophie Scholl and her brother Hans were arrested at the university; they were sentenced to death by the People's Court, with Freisler as the presiding judge,

on 22 February 1943, together with Christoph Probst, a friend of Hans. The sentences were carried out a few hours later. The nucleus of the group consisted of Professor Kurt Huber, Willi Graf and Alexander Schmorell. They too were executed.

'My heart soon gets lost in petty anxieties and forgets that death is near. It is quite unprepared, quickly distracted by frivolous incidentals, it could easily be taken by surprise when

17

the hour comes and miss the one great joy for the sake of little pleasures.

'I realise this but not so my heart. It continues to dream, refuses to listen to reason, is lulled into safety by the consoling words of irritating warders and fluctuates between joy and sorrow. Sorrow is all that is left, paralysis, utter helplessness, and a faint hope.

'My heart clings to these treasures, to the promise of a sweet life; tear me away against my will, because I am too weak to do it myself. Let me wait till I am miserable and in pain before I dream away salvation.

SOPHIE.'

*   *   *

From Sophie Scholl's letters and entries in her diary:

9 November 1939.

'. . . After all, one should have the courage to believe in what is good. I do not mean that one should believe in illusions, but I mean that one should do only what is true and good and take it for granted that other people will do the same, in a way one can never do with the intellect alone. (That is to say—never calculate).'

16 May 1940.

'. . . I hope very much that you will survive this war and this era without becoming its *slave*. We each have our own standards of values, but we don't use them enough. Perhaps because they are the most exacting standards.'

13 January 1941.

'. . . In the train I longed so much to see a face which would remind me of my brothers and sisters and friends. Does that make sense? Not exactly home-sickness, but awareness of being different. Even the young people, and there were lots in the train, weren't young any more, they seemed to think the only purpose of youth is pleasure. But my family and friends—even if they were sometimes clumsy or ignorant, were at least full of goodwill—full of the will to do what is good.'

July 1942.

'I want to shout for joy at being so alone, with the wild rough wind pouring all over me. I'd like to stand all by myself on a raft, upright above the grey river which rushes along so fast that the wind cannot touch it. I'd like to shout out that I am so gloriously alone.

'The wind tears open the blue sky, out comes the sun and kisses me tenderly. I'd like to kiss him back, but my wish is forgotten in a moment as the wind grasps me. I feel the wonderful firmness of my body, I laugh aloud for the sheer joy of finding I can resist the wind. I can feel all my own strength.'

10 February 1943.

'I shall probably be called up for labour service next summer. I am not entirely unhappy about it, because I still want to suffer, to share the suffering of these days (that is putting it too strongly; I mean that I want to be affected more directly). You will understand, sympathy is often difficult and soon becomes hollow if one feels no pain oneself.'

HEINZ BELLO

5 September 1920—29 June 1944

'How helpless we human beings are in the face of death. What would life be without faith? We should have to despair if we expected merely to revert to dust and ashes'.

Heinz Bello, a 24-year-old Sergeant in the Medical Corps, said those words just before his execution by a firing squad and his family were told of them by an army chaplain, Herr Kreuzberg. This chaplain, who accompanied many young soldiers to execution, gives the following account of the events of that day:

'It was 6 a.m. when Heinz Bello was told at the office of the Military Remand Prison in Berlin that his petition for mercy had been rejected and that the death sentence "would be carried out at 8 o'clock this morning by a firing squad". Heinz accepted the sentence gravely and calmly. I then went back with him to his cell. When we had sat down he said something like this: "I suppose it is God's will. Yesterday I was transferred to this place from Spandau. Last night I didn't sleep as well as usual. The thought struck me that if I should have to die today it would be on the day commemorating the death of the martyrs Peter and Paul. I will die for a Christian Germany. I want to die for the re-unification of the Churches in Germany so that all people can live in peace again. My last words shall be: *Omnia ad majorem Dei gloriam!* All for the greater glory of God. . . ."

'In a closed car, I drove with him and the Protestant chaplain and another young soldier to the place of execution. We arrived at 7.55 a.m. The other soldier went first with the chaplain. When the volley was fired, Heinz said: "Lord, give him eternal peace!" We prayed. Then our time was up. I went with him all the way. The sentence was read over again. He was asked whether he had any final wish, and said he wanted to die as a free man, without a bandage over his eyes and without handcuffs. His wish was granted. He stood upright, ready for the end. I gave him the blessing once more, and shook hands with him. Then he prayed, his lips moving gently, his eyes lifted to heaven.'

Heinz Bello was born in Breslau on 5 September, 1920, and was the son of a tax collector. He passed his matriculation in

Wesel in March 1939, then completed his compulsory period with the Labour Service. After the outbreak of war he was called up for the Armed Forces. He was later exempted from military service to study medicine, and began his studies in January 1940 at Münster University, but in October he was called up again. He took part in the advance on Moscow, as a corporal, and was awarded the Iron Cross (2nd Class) and the East Medal. He was later transferred from the front to a students' company at home which enabled him to resume his medical studies. For his courageous rescue work after an air raid on Münster on 10 October 1943, when he received a head injury from a bomb splinter, he was awarded the Badge for Wounded Soldiers.

On 18 March 1944, Heinz Bello stood before the Central Military Court in Berlin-Charlottenburg. Two so-called friends had informed on him. On 20 July, 1943, the day before he was due to take his preliminary medical examination, he had been detailed for fire-watching at the barracks where the students' company was housed. Annoyed by this inconsiderate order, he gave vent to his feelings with some hard words against militarism, National Socialism and party informers. He also pointed to a cross which happened to have been left in the building now serving as barracks and said: 'So long as there is a God in Heaven, there is a limit to what can happen on earth.'

From the time when proceedings against him began, up to the time of his trial, Heinz Bello was not actually under lock and key. During this interval he turned down offers from friends to help him to go to Switzerland, because he did not want his family to suffer the consequences; and on the date set for the trial, he and his father went to Berlin. The hearing began at 1 p.m. but was very soon interrupted by an air-raid warning. During the alert, which lasted two hours, his solicitor made it quite clear to him that, judging by proceedings so far, things looked extremely serious, and urged him to seize his chance and escape from the unguarded air-raid shelter. He again refused to take advantage of such a situation.

At 4 p.m. the trial was resumed and in less than an hour the court pronounced sentence as follows: 'For undermining morale, Heinz Bello, a Sergeant of the Reserve and Officer-Cadet (civilian occupation: medical student) is sentenced to death, to dishonour and to loss of civil rights for life.'

After the sentence had been pronounced, Heinz Bello was taken to the military prison in the Lehrter Strasse. It was impossible to appeal, so the defence took the only course open to them and, on 19 April 1944, filed a petition for mercy with the court at the *Wehrmacht* Headquarters in Berlin-Charlottenburg. But on 10 June 1944, on the strength of opinions submitted by the leader of the students' movement and by the *Führer's* Chancellory, the sentence was confirmed. Heinz Bello was shot on 29 June 1944, on the machine-gun ranges in Berlin-Tegel.

FRIEDRICH KARL KLAUSING

24 May 1920—8 August 1944

FRIEDRICH KARL KLAUSING, being a member of the
Christian Boy Scouts, was automatically transferred to the
Hitler Youth in 1933. In 1938 he passed his matriculation in
classics, and after serving six months with the Labour Service
joined up with the 9th Infantry Regiment, as an officer-cadet,
in the autumn of 1938. He took part in the Polish and French
campaigns, was awarded the Iron Cross (1st Class) and
received his commission. He was seriously wounded at the
battle of Stalingrad, when he was promoted to 1st Lieutenant;
and when he was again badly wounded in Russia in 1943, he
was transferred to G.H.Q. for home service.

This young officer is a true representative of a whole
generation who grew up under the influence, and indeed in
the spirit of National Socialism; but each of whom, sooner or
later, was brought by his own thinking or experience to the
point where he was forced to listen to the voice of conscience,
and to find his own answer. For Klausing, the conflict began
at the front, when he began to ask himself what sense there
was in the war; it deepened when he was sent on home
service, after being wounded. Then he met a friend from his
regiment, an older man, Fritz von der Schulenburg, who
opened his eyes and won him over to the cause of the resistance group. Klausing then cast aside the tarnished ideals of
his youth, betrayed as they were by criminal leaders, and
became Adjutant to Stauffenberg, whom he admired with all
the enthusiasm of youth but also as time went on with a more
mature political outlook.

There now began a life of self-denial and conspiracy which
led by way of many setbacks and long waiting to 20 July.
Although ill himself, Klausing was in the War Office in the
Bendlerstrasse at mid-day, ready to carry out his appointed
task, which was to keep other key members of the plot, in
Potsdam, in touch with events. He witnessed the arrest and
execution by a firing squad of the officers nearest to Stauffenberg, but himself escaped late at night. He took refuge in the
Zehlendorf house of Vera Gaupp, a doctor, as he had often

24

done in the past weeks. He spent the next few hours with
Wolfgang Gaupp, one of the conspirators, trying to decide
what was the right thing to do. Finally he chose neither
suicide nor flight, but gave himself up to the authorities the
next morning. He was sentenced to death by the People's
Court, and died with some of his friends on 8 August, 1944.

Vera Gaupp has written the following account, based on
her brother's story of Klausing during the last few hours
before his arrest.

'He came to my house at midnight, white and distraught.

My brother was there too. Klausing laid his pistol on the table. He said that he would now have to shoot himself, since all was lost and he must share the fate of his friends. The discussion lasted half the night, and ranged over the alternatives of flight, suicide or a common death with his friends. He soon gave up the idea of suicide, because he didn't want to endanger the rest of us; also, on reflection, he decided it would be no real solution, but merely an evasion. Flight he regarded as cowardly, and thought this too might lead to trouble for those who would wish to help him. And so in the end there seemed to be only one thing to do: openly to declare himself for Stauffenberg and his venture, and return to the Bendlerstrasse. Wolfgang was unable to convince him of the senselessness of this sacrifice, which could no longer serve the cause. The deciding factor in Klausing's decision was his loyalty to his friends, for which his life seemed to him to be the appropriate price. When he set off at eight o'clock the next morning to give himself up he was calm, sure and fearless. He knew what he was doing.'

MICHAEL KITZELMANN

29 January 1916—12 June 1942

MICHAEL KITZELMANN was the son of a farmer in the Allgäu; he went to the elementary school and to a boys' school in Dillingen. He served his term with the Labour Service, and then studied for three terms at St. Stephan's Theological School, in Augsburg; after that he joined the 20th Infantry Regiment in Lindau to complete his compulsory military service. He had no love of soldiering and as early as 9 January 1938, he wrote to a friend: 'So for two years I must submit to this horrible yoke of ridiculous and dreary military drill, which I find quite soul-destroying after only a few weeks.' Before his two years were up, the war began. Michael took part in the Polish campaign as a private soldier and wrote to a friend who lived near him at home: 'Never will I tell anybody what I have seen and experienced here.' He later went on a course for non-commissioned officers in Döberitz, got his commission during the French campaign in 1940, and was awarded the Iron Cross (2nd Class).

During the Russian campaign, Michael Kitzelmann was a company commander in the 199th Infantry Regiment. On 3 April 1942, he was sentenced to death by a Court Martial for what was called 'undermining the German Army'. The sentence was carried out by a firing squad in Orel on 11 June 1942. Details of the Court Martial proceedings are not known. But there was no concealing Michael Kitzelmann's bitter criticism of the government, which found expression in, for instance, such remarks as: 'If these criminals should win, then I would have no wish to live any longer.'

The following are extracts from the diary which he wrote while he was in prison:

'On 11 April 1942, I walked into the military prison of the fortress of Orel. The fortress, a huge squat building, distempered pink, with massive round turrets at each corner, lies to the north of the town on the steep banks of the river Oka. There is a dark stone passage on the upper floor where the air is dank and chill; and here I was handed over to the prison guards.

'My cell is in the north-east turret and is about 14 feet wide

27

and the same height. It has a wooden floor and a vaulted brick ceiling. To the west an arched window pierces the wall, which is over three feet thick, and across the window there are strong iron bars, let into the wall. In the evening and then only, a few golden sunrays briefly penetrate to my dreary solitude. A massive oak door, reinforced by heavy iron-work, shuts out the world.'

'Darkness and terror paralyse my being. The stillness is unbearable. Helpless and abandoned I am left to myself, alone, sentenced to death. . .!

'Now I know the full fury of these Military Laws. Overnight I was branded as a criminal just for making a few derogatory remarks about the government. And for that apparently I must lose my life, my honour, my friends and my place in human society. How could all this happen? I had a good enough reputation up to now, and so far as I know I was regarded as a decent man with a normal sense of duty. What are right and justice in this world? Haven't I served my country honourably for four years? I was at the front for two years, took part in three campaigns and proved my loyalty often enough. Is this the thanks I get from my country?

'Apart from all that I am beginning to be afraid for my family at home. Letters have been taken from my trunk, and others from the post, and confiscated by the Court, letters from my father and mother and from friends. What will happen to them? Will the law get on to them too? That would be terrible. But I suppose there is nothing to be done and . . . events must take their course. I am so much afraid: my fears follow me day and night like horrifying ghosts, and all the time this awful loneliness, this claustrophobia, this oppressive silence. For hours on end I pace up and down my cell, just to hear my own footsteps. I light a fire in the stove just to hear it's crackling. I pray aloud to hear my own voice; and I call upon Heaven, asking God to help me in my agony. . . ."

'Home-sickness grips my heart, and that is the worst of all my troubles. My beloved, beautiful home seems so far away. I suppose I shall never see it again: my parents' house with its garden in front, the fruit trees, the green meadows and the rustling woods, the waterfall, the quiet little church in the Argental valley, the hills on the other side. A paradise in this world of woe. . . .

'But what fearful suffering has my clumsiness brought on my beloved mother and father, on my brothers and sisters, my relations and friends? To have to hurt love itself: it is then, surely, that the human heart suffers its greatest pain.

28

Photo by Atelier Sauter

'Who would blame me for these earthly ties, this agony, this burning home-sickness? Was not Christ Himself, the Son of God, overcome on the Mount of Olives at the prospect of His sacrifice for mankind? Even He suffered when saying farewell to those He loved. He let them wait at the gate leading into the garden, He asked His friends to pray for Him, three times He interrupted His prayers to go back to them, for He did not want to be alone. He longed for the sympathy of His friends.

'I pray to Jesus the Crucified, who has led the way through the most bitter pain. And He answers me: "If you will be My disciple, take up your cross and follow me!"

'But I appeal to Him: "Lord, I am still so young, too young for such a heavy cross; I have not lived my life, all my hopes, plans and aims are unfulfilled." And he says: "Behold, I too was young, I had yet to live my life, and as a young man I carried the cross and sacrificed my young life."

'Again my soul complains: "Behold my bitter home-sickness, the sufferings of my family. Let me return to life and let me not hurt their love."

'But Jesus replies: "If you cannot leave your belongings and all your earthly love, you cannot be my disciple. Follow me!"

'Again my soul rebels: "O Lord, the burden is too heavy; relieve me of this terrible yoke; shorten my sufferings and dry my tears!"

'Lovingly He speaks: "My son, be brave and do not despair! I have suffered so greatly for humanity, and for you too; I have opened Heaven for you. And I shall remain with you until the end."

'I answer my Saviour: "Thank you a thousand times for your endless love, my Redeemer! I shall be your disciple and I will carry your cross after you. So take me by the hand and lead me to my blessed end in all eternity."

'The morning is the worst. Every time I wake up, I am almost crushed by the horror of my fate. Fear of death fills my heart; how many more times shall I be able to lie down in my cell and rest? Shall I still be alive tomorrow? I feel like a drowning man. Desperately I look for some support. I cling to the Cross of the Saviour and implore Him to give me comfort and strength. I start my prayers in the morning and go on praying until my heart is calm again.'

'24 May, Whitsunday. Whitsuntide in prison and in the shadow of death! The storms in my soul are calmer. The Whitsuntide sun, the Holy Spirit, the Comforter and Saviour, lightens even my desperate solitude. And while I rejoice in the return of the Holy Ghost, in my solitary cell, I am reminded of the splendour of my own countryside at this time of the year. It is as if I were standing at home with the choir in the church, and I sing once more the old, immortal hymn *Veni Creator Spiritus*. I know that I am near to God. Human misery retreats, even death loses its horror. . . .'

'Now I live the life of a hermit. My day's work consists of praying, reading the Bible, occasionally scribbling something in my diary or writing letters. It is very painful, this separation from life, from the past, from all fond hopes and plans and particularly from my nearest and dearest. It is terribly hard to submit wholly to God's will in such agonising circumstances: but the only attainable comfort is to hold out to the end despite all suffering. . . .'

'On 11 June 1942, at 5 p.m., I was told that my petition for mercy had been rejected and that the sentence would be carried out on 12 June 1942 at 8 a.m. Lord, Thy will be done. In the evening I knew great joy. Dear, good Pastor Schmitter has come back and wants to stay with me during my last hours on earth. He was here till after midnight. I told him my final wishes, asked him to give my love to my people at home and talked over with him what would happen at the end. He has promised to return punctually at 6 a.m. Then I will confess once more, for my whole life. We shall celebrate Mass and take Communion together. . . .

'God has granted me great joy, for the hour of my death is a merciful one.'

2 LEARNING

THE National Socialists were not content with political mastery. They demanded also that their doctrines and ideologies should be accepted by each and every individual and that the state should order the *Weltanschauung*—the whole attitude—of all the people; to this end they embarked on a ruthless course of suppression and annihilation.

Many of their methods are well-known: the police state, the censorship, the control of education and the propaganda machine. When Goebbels' Ministry of Propaganda and a central Ministry of Education (education was normally the concern of each *Land*) were set up, the intention was all too clear. Among the earliest measures taken by the new government were the 'cleansing' of the universities and schools, the banning of dissident newspapers and periodicals, the suppression of writers whose opinions did not conform and the barbaric public burning of books. The inquisition of the mind reached a climax on 10 May 1933, ten weeks after the Reichstag fire and while the atmosphere of political terror still reigned, when huge bonfires raged in the Gendarmmarkt in Berlin and in many other public squares. Many famous books by living authors who had added to Germany's fame as a literary and scientific nation, and practically all European literature since Voltaire which might possibly stimulate the German reader to reflect on the spirit of the new régime, belonged to the *Schmutz-und-Schundliteratur* which was sent up in flames by order of Goebbels.

Hundreds of writers and scientists had to leave the country of their birth. Many lost their lives. Others were frustrated by the ban on speech and publication, or driven to other and unaccustomed occupations; if, that is, they were spared the concentration camp, or death. Emigration, actual or spiritual, became the only alternative to subservience. The National Socialist state had in its hands all the weapons it needed to enforce compliance.

Anti-Semitism was one of them; it was in fact a corner stone of Nazi policy. Economic, social and racial prejudices were systematically fostered, built up into a philosophy of envy and hate. The amateurish racial theories of Hans F. K.

Günther and Alfred Rosenberg purported to give to the despotism a pseudo-scientific basis and to provide in the primitive cult of the 'master race' an intellectual justification for its policy: the policy whose practical results were the gas chambers of Auschwitz.

The propaganda for the 'master race' theory was carried into the smallest villages; the notice 'The Jews are our misfortune' appeared everywhere in shop windows; *Der Stürmer* carried endless perverted scandal stories. The Nazis were at some pains to give a legal veneer to their annihilation campaign, and one inhuman law succeeded another. First came the dismissal of all Jewish officials, then their exclusion from all professions; followed by deprivation of citizenship, imposition of higher taxes, compulsory labour and finally discrimination in private as well as public life: they were branded with yellow stars, not allowed to have pets, cars, telephones or wireless; to buy books or newspapers, nor even to use automatic ticket machines or public telephones. On the notorious *Kristallnacht*, in November 1938, a mob, organised by the authorities, demolished their shops and burned down their Synagogues, without opposition from the police, in every German town.

Those people who retained their independence in face of such doctrines came up against the full power of the machine, and found that they too incurred, first, defamation, then persecution and finally death. But there were scientists, teachers, journalists and men of learning who stood up to the Nazi disciples of 'Culture' and 'Race' against the bogus racial theories, the abuse of medicine to allow euthanasia, forced sterilisation, experimental murders and finally against legal mockery and the national policy of war. They were ready to give up their lives in defence of the freedom of the mind, and by doing so they challenged the arrogant belief of the tyrants in power that the mind is something that can be bought, conditioned, degraded and enslaved.

CARL von OSSIETZKY

3 October 1889—3 May 1938

CARL VON OSSIETZKY came from a lower-middle class Catholic family in Hamburg. He won an international reputation as a journalist and died on 3 May 1938, as a prisoner of the Gestapo in Berlin.

He was one of the first victims to be arrested on the morning after the *Reichstag* fire, and his martyrdom in concentration camps lasted for more than three years. But when the Berlin Propaganda Ministry learned that he was being seriously considered in Oslo for the award of the Nobel Peace Prize, the Gestapo were obviously much embarrassed and ordered that he should be taken to a prison hospital in Berlin.

Four months later, a few days before the final decision of the Norwegian Nobel Prize Committee, Hermann Göring had the powerless 'deadly enemy' brought into his office, so that he could talk to him; and there, now with threats and now with flattery, he tried to extract from Ossietzky a promise to the effect that, should the Nobel Prize decision fall in his favour, he would reject it with some sort of personal declaration as to his unworthiness; if he would do this he would be allowed to go free and to enjoy material security, and be left in peace. Ossietzky said 'No', and went back to his prison.

A week after this discussion, while German newspapers and broadcasting stations were spreading the provoking news—and describing it as 'an impudent challenge to the "Third Reich"'—the prize-winner had been moved, on Göring's orders to a municipal hospital, where he lay under strict arrest and special supervision. In Oslo however, the President of the Nobel Prize Committee received the following telegram: 'Grateful for the unexpected honour—Carl von Ossietzky.' The sender had to pay for it by life-imprisonment, but no one had dared hold up his message. This courageous decision, in spite of all the pressure which was put upon him was in fact the measure of Ossietzky's character, for such decisions determined the part he played in public life in Germany.

In his youth, in Hamburg, Ossietzky's fight—a journalistic fight—was directed against the influence of the army in the home and foreign affairs of the Reich. When he was thirty he came back from the western front, where he had fought as a private soldier, deeply shaken and embittered by the war experiences of his generation, and brought back with him the firm resolve to devote his energy and talents to opposing all and any forces which might bring about another war; and to work no less energetically to build and to protect a free, democratic Republic, ruled by citizens who were glad and proud of their responsibilities.

Photo from Tagesspiegel files

Carl von Ossietzky in Papenburg-Esterwegen concentration camp, where he received the following information:

THE NOBEL COMMITTEE of the NORWEGIAN STORTHING has in accordance with the provisions laid down by
ALFRED NOBEL
in his Will of November 27 1895 awarded the
NOBEL PEACE PRIZE for 1935 to
CARL VON OSSIETZKY
Oslo, December 10, 1936.

To those ends, he first went to Berlin as Secretary of the German Peace Society, then became editor of liberal newspapers and periodicals and found, in 1927, as editor of the *Weltbühne*, a platform which satisfied his insistence on complete freedom of speech and which was well suited to an intellectual guerrilla who lacked only the sharp elbows of the successful politician.

Ossietzky wrote in a brilliant, versatile, aggressive and often bitingly witty style. As German politics degenerated into a latent civil war between the left-wing radicals and the right-wing and conservative groups, Ossietzky emerged as a bulwark against the National Socialist threat; and as a critic of the parties of the right which were friendly disposed towards Hitler and of the military and legal forces which were prepared to compromise with Nazism.

Ossietzky brought to light in his periodical the work of many pro-Soviet writers, but he himself complained that 'the word "freedom" is given no place in the vocabulary of Red Russia', and that Moscow wanted to pack the European affiliations of the Communist Party with their 'weak-willed satellites and half-witted slaves'; meanwhile the men charged with the protection of the Republic and of freedom in Germany were clearly told where they had gone wrong, by commission or by default as the case might be: so it was not surprising that he had to meet attacks, as he himself put it, 'from the Right, accusing me of betrayal of national interests, and from the Left, charging me with irresponsible carping aestheticism'.

The first great test came with the famous Leipzig trial before the Reich Court, which took place in secret in 1931. Ossietzky was sentenced to 18 months' imprisonment on a charge of 'treason and betrayal of military secrets'; the result of violent attacks in the *Weltbühne* in which he had stated that camouflaged funds, withdrawn from parliamentary control, had been put at the disposal of certain military departments, and that they were being used on Soviet territory, with the co-operation of the Soviet government, for the secret but intensive production of air armaments for Germany. Ossietzky could easily have avoided his prison sentence by going abroad, for the guilt-ridden authorities would have been in no position to interfere. But he maintained that the *Weltbühne* could remain true to its reputa-

36

tion only if its editor identified himself with its policy and if, when things became difficult, he chose 'not the convenient solution, but the necessary one'. Ossietzky remained in Germany and went to prison.

Seven months later, after he had been released under the Christmas Amnesty of the Chancellor, von Schleicher, he again refused, in February 1933, to choose a 'convenient' solution. After Hitler had become Chancellor, his friends implored him to save himself in time by going abroad. 'After my final election article,' he replied. He did not want to leave until he had made this last attempt to avert evil. On the same night that Ossietzky's last warning cry was printed, the *Reichstag* was set on fire, and at 5 o'clock in the morning they came to fetch him.

In the concentration camp, whenever Ossietzky bled from the blows of his tormentors or collapsed with a heart attack during hard labour, they would allow him a few days rest on his wooden bunk, and then a high Nazi official would appear and suggest that he should sign a release petition saying that he had 'revised' his opinions. To this compromise with dictatorship Ossietzky said 'No', and for his 'No' he was silenced by slow, murderous 'special treatment' until, ill beyond hope, his life quietly slipped away in the darkness of isolation.

FRITZ SOLMITZ

22 October 1893—19 September 1933

FRITZ SOLMITZ was born in Berlin, the only son of well-to-do parents. He studied national economy at Freiburg University for one term and in August 1914 volunteered for military service, but owing to an accident his call-up was postponed until 1915.

Fritz Solmitz's experience of war on the western front made him a pacifist. On his return in November 1918 he took part briefly in the fight against the Sparticists in Berlin, but was soon demobilised, took his degree in political economy and became an official in the public welfare service in Berlin. In 1924 he entered the field of political journalism, and for the last nine years of his life he was political editor on the staff of the *Lübecker Volksbote,* where he worked closely with Julius Leber. Until 1933 he was also a member of the Lübeck City Council.

He seems to have made up his mind quite early to devote his life to the cause of justice; and the two main driving forces which combined to shape his personality were his Jewish faith and his insight into the injustice of the social and economic conditions of his time. 'For me, politics have never been anything but a means to justice,' he wrote in a passage taken from his posthumously published work. He lived up to his beliefs, and was unassuming so far as he was himself concerned but always ready to help anyone who was in need. He served the cause through his allegiance to the Social Democratic Party, and in the work he did for associations with social, educational and pacifist aims. He followed his course passionately and, with an uncompromising love of truth, he wrote while in prison in Lübeck: 'I believe that absolute honesty with oneself is the most important axiom of religion. Lies are the beginning of all that is ungodly."

His mind and his words were clear-cut, and so was their warning. His insight and his almost prophetic anticipation of the political developments in Germany enabled him to foresee the consequences of Nazi tyranny in their true horror,

and as time went on he made it clear, in many grave and profound discussions, that he was quite aware of the insecurity of his own life. In all his political and journalistic activities and in particular in his work with the young, he tried above all to arouse people to their responsibilities as citizens of a democratic republic. On 24 May 1925, he wrote on the occasion of a meeting of the *Reichsbanner*: 'But we want to create a fatherland which is a real home to each of us. We want a Germany that we can love freely and without shame, love not only the country and the people but also the state, which is the synthesis of the two. But we can love only a state which builds its greatness not on blood and iron, but on prosperity and shining armour, a state which is based on work and justice, a state which we, as free working men and women, can fashion according to the image we each have in our own minds.'

On 19 February 1933, three weeks after Hitler's assumption of power, Lübeck witnessed a mass parade of workers and liberals such as it had not seen since 1918. Speaking at the demonstration, Fritz Solmitz said: 'Are you merely a motley crowd which will fall apart as soon as the first shot is fired? I am convinced of the opposite. Threats and terrorism will only unite us more closely.' And the next day he wrote in the *Volksbote*: 'We will not gain our end without sacrifices. The soldiers of the Republic know why these sacrifices must be made.'

On 11 March 1933, Fritz Solmitz was arrested in Lübeck. Friends had advised him to take flight, but he wanted to share the hardships of the Lübeck workers. For a short time he was kept in custody at the Burgtor prison, and then in May 1933 he was sent to Fuhlsbüttel concentration camp near Hamburg. At the beginning of September Karoline Solmitz succeeded in persuading the National Socialist Senate in Lübeck to order her husband's release; but the release never in fact came about.

On 13 September, after the Chief of the Lübeck Gestapo had just visited Fuhlsbüttel camp, Solmitz was placed in solitary confinement and so brutally treated that death came as a relief during the night of 18-19 September. Dying, and in great agony, he wrote a few words of farewell to his wife, on cigarette paper which she found later in his watch case. They ended with the last verse of Hebbel's poem: '*Dem Schmerz sein Recht*'.

Many people went the same way as Fritz Solmitz, silently, with dignity, and simply because it was not in them to be different, and others made heroic protest. But all these had one thing in common which distinguished them from the rest: they had recognised evil and could not, and would not, take it upon themselves to live together with it.

While he was in prison Fritz Solmitz seems to have been

much aware of the limits imposed on individual destiny, and its relation to the future; he wrote to his children:

'I feel all too clearly that anything I have been able to give has been crude and poor, but I have always believed that it is best in these disordered days to live out one's life in the service of God and otherwise to keep quiet. For it is not my job to tell what is going on in the minds of the multitude, and today I am speaking only to you, and quite softly; may God grant you true innocence and true kindness, that gladden the heart.'

KURT HUBER

24 October 1893—13 July 1943

KURT HUBER was born at Chur, in Switzerland, where his father taught at the Canton school. In 1897 the family moved to Württemberg and Kurt passed his matriculation in Stuttgart. He studied the theory of music and philosophy in Munich, took his degree in 1917, and in 1920 was formally admitted to the Faculty of Philosophy and Psychology; he became a regular lecturer in 1925 and an Extraordinary Professor in 1926. In 1937, at the request of the Prussian Ministry for Religion, Education and Culture, he established the folk-song department of the archives for German music research, but he soon came into conflict with the leaders of the students' and Hitler Youth organisations, and as a result went back to his old post in Munich. Huber was an intellectual, he was deeply religious and he was a man of complete integrity, whose refusal ever to compromise inevitably brought him up against his superiors in the state hierarchy, and set him at loggerheads with the measures of state compulsion. No less inevitable were his ties with student resistance groups, and he was particularly close to the group round the Scholl family. At the turn of the year 1942-43 there was endless discussion in these circles, on means of resisting the growing terror, on the futility of prolonging the war and on the way to a spiritual and moral regeneration of Germany.

On 8 and 9 February 1943, Kurt Huber himself drafted the leaflet which the Scholls, ten days later, scattered in the Munich university courtyard.

'. . . In the name of German youth we demand of Adolf Hitler that he return to us the personal freedom which is the most valuable possession of every German, and of which he has cheated us in the basest possible manner. We have grown up in a State where freedom of speech is brutally muzzled. During the most formative years of our lives, the Hitler Youth, the SS and the SA have tried to standardise us, to coerce us and to drug us. "Indoctrination" is the despicable method by which all independent thinking and values have been choked with platitudes. . . . We are concerned for true knowledge

and for genuine freedom of the spirit. No threat can intimidate us, not even the closing of our universities. . . . The name of Germany will be sullied for ever unless German youth now at last rises to crush its tormentors and to restore the spirit of Europe. Each and all of us must fight for the future, for liberty and for our own honour in another kind of state, one which is confident and united. . . .'

On 27 February 1943, the Gestapo carried off Kurt Huber from his flat. On 19 April he was sentenced to death together with Willi Graf and Alexander Schmorell, two of his students. On 13 July he was beheaded. These are some of the notes he made for his final pleading before the Court:

'As a German citizen, as a German university teacher, and as a man who is politically alive, I regard it not only as my right but also as my moral duty to help to decide the fate of Germany, to expose obvious defects and to combat them. . . . I have set out to arouse the students, not by the establishment of some sort of organisation, but by simple words; not by any act of terrorism, but by helping them to gain an insight into the serious deficiencies of our political life. A return to clear moral principles, to the constitutional state and to mutual trust of man to man—all that, far from being illegal, is simply the restoration of law. Following Kant's Categorical Imperative, I have asked myself what would happen if this, my individual maxim, were to become general law. There can be but one answer; in that case order, security and trust would return to our country and to our political life. Every morally responsible person would raise his voice with us against the menacing ascendancy of might over right, of dictatorship over the will of the morally good. The demand for self-determination, even on a purely local level, has been stifled all over Europe, no less than the demand that traditional and racial customs be protected. The pre-requisite of a true national life has been destroyed by the systematic undermining of trust between man and man. There can be no more deadly condemnation of a national community than the confession we all have to make; that no-one can trust his neighbour, that a father no longer feels sure of his sons.

'There is a point at which the law becomes immoral and unethical; that point is reached when it becomes a cloak for the cowardice that dares not stand up against blatant violations of justice. A state which suppresses all free speech and which, by imposing the most terrible punishment, treats each and every attempt at criticism, however morally justified, and every suggestion for improvement as "plotting high treason", is breaking an unwritten law. . . .

'I beg and entreat you on this occasion to judge these young defendants opposite in a truly constructive manner, to seek and to hear not lip-service to power, but the clear voice of conscience; and so to consider the motives which prompted the deed. These motives were in fact the most selfless and the most idealistic that one can imagine. They were striving for absolute justice, integrity and truthfulness in public life.

'For myself, I claim that my warning to reflect on the lasting principles essential to the existence of a constitutional state is the supreme need of our time; and that to ignore it would mean the destruction of the German spirit and eventually of the German nation. I have achieved one object, in that I have made this statement and given this warning before the highest court in Germany and not before some insignificant private debating club. I stake my life in its support and in support of this my most solemn entreaty to turn back. . . .

'History will vindicate what I now say and do; of that I am quite sure. Before God I hope that the spiritual strength which is the justification for my own actions may also and before it is too late take hold of my compatriots. I have done what I had to do, what my own conscience required. I take the consequences upon myself. . . .'

ELISABETH von THADDEN

29 July 1890—8 September 1944

THE following account was found among the papers which Ricarda Huch left behind at her death:

'I met Elisabeth von Thadden at the home of a mutual friend in Heidelberg. I had been rather dubious about meeting her, for when I tried to imagine the Pomeranian headmistress of a Protestant boarding school which recruited its pupils from army circles, I was left with a picture of some kind of bespectacled female sergeant major, perhaps not unpleasant, but rather strange. But I had not been with her for a quarter of an hour before I took a great liking to her. In her presence one forgot, for the moment, her origin, standing and profession and was aware only of her human qualities, although she was in fact a typical representative of her homeland and of her calling. She was tall, strong and stately, and the utter confidence of her bearing reminded one of a matriarch who ran a large estate and held sway—just and kindly—over a big family and an army of servants.

'She was no blue-stocking, neither pedantic nor dogmatic, and her sense of humour and cheerfulness were most to the fore. Her friends knew that she was deeply religious and her Protestant faith was so much a part of her nature that there was no need for her to emphasise it. I doubt if one would have got anywhere with her by discussing theology or philosophy. She probably never went through a period of doubting or had any difficulty in accepting the conventional dogma. Faith was for her a matter of course, like her love of her country and her own people, something with which she lived and died and which could never be taken away from her. Above all there was something peculiarly childlike about her, which in contrast to her portly bearing was particularly attractive. She tackled every task with the confidence, curiosity and candidness of a child.'

Elisabeth von Thadden was born on 29 July 1890, at Mohrungen, in East Prussia, where her father was chairman of the local council. In 1905, the family moved to Trieglaff, a country estate in Pomerania. After her mother's death Elisabeth, then twenty, took charge of the household and of her younger brothers and sisters. In 1920 her father married

again, and she took up teaching and passed her examination in youth leadership at the Anna von Gierke training school in Berlin. After a teaching job at the youth camp of Heuberg, in the Swabian mountains, and another at the school in Salem castle, she founded, in the spring of 1927, a Protestant boarding school at Schloss Wieblingen, near Heidelberg. Her school flourished, but in the summer of 1941 she was forced by various new state regulations to resign from the management. She then began to work for the Red Cross, where, according to her sister Ehrengard, she was much distressed

47

to find that some of the letters from prisoners of war in Russia were destroyed, because Hitler considered they might be bad for the morale of the troops at the front.

From 1943 onwards Elisabeth von Thadden worked at various soldiers' recreation centres in France. On 10 September 1943, while she was on leave, she invited a young man to tea because an old friend in Switzerland had asked her to introduce him into Christian and conservative circles in Berlin, saying he had had terrible experiences with the Nazis.

This young man reported to the Gestapo all that was said at the tea party and as a result the guests who had attended the party were arrested in the course of the next few months. On 1 July 1944, the People's Court sentenced Elisabeth von Thadden to death, together with Otto Kiep, a Minister in the diplomatic service, on the grounds that the conversation in question were detrimental to fighting morale, and tantamount to high treason.

During the weeks that followed her sentence, Elisabeth von Thadden was kept in handcuffs, but she was able to dictate to Pastor Ohm, the prison chaplain, and thus to communicate with her family:

'I was arrested at Meaux, in France, at 8 a.m. on a January morning in 1944. I was brought by car from M. to Paris where I was interrogated from 9 a.m. to 6 p.m. and then, after one hour for supper, the cross-examination continued throughout the night. The next day a warrant of arrest was issued. I had several opportunities to escape but I did not make use of them because I did not want to incriminate my brother. I was then taken to Berlin and again cross-examined all night. The inquisition was quite terrible. I was asked about the Confessional Church and the *Una Sancta*. I said nothing that might incriminate others. Ravensbrück concentration camp was awful. I have had nothing to do with the 20 July uprising, I know none of the people involved. We ourselves wanted to help in the field of social service whenever the need should arise. It was clear that the time would come. We wanted to be good Samaritans.'

Pastor Ohm, who on 8 September 1944 accompanied Elisabeth von Thadden to the door of the execution chamber, said that her steps were sure and her bearing steady. Her last words were those of a verse from the hymn by Paul Gerhardt: 'Put an end, O Lord, to all our sufferings.'

NIKOLAUS GROSS

30 September 1898—23 January 1945

N I K O L A U S G R O S S came from the river Ruhr, the son of
a labourer. After he left the elementary school he went into
the mines and also attended evening classes and a school for
public speaking, and at the age of twenty he founded the
first youth groups of the Christian Miners' Movement. He
himself became secretary of one youth group and later Trade
Union Secretary in Niederschlesien, Zwickau and the Ruhr.
In 1930 he became editor of the *Westdeutsche Arbeiterzeitung.* In everything he said or wrote, he consistently
opposed Nazism and all its works, and continually asserted
his fundamental precept, that 'Christian family life is the
basis of society'.

When the *Ketteler Wacht,* the successor to the *Westdeutsche Arbeiterzeitung,* was finally banned, he continued
to air his convictions by any possible means, in talks to small
groups and in private conversation. He also worked in close

co-operation with Bernhard Letterhaus in building a network among trade unions and Catholic working-men's associations in preparation for the attempt of 20 July 1944, and for this he was arrested on 12 August, sentenced to death on 15 January 1945, and executed on the 23rd.

* * *

The following extracts from one of Nikolaus Gross's earlier works, *Sieben um einen Tisch* (Seven round a Table) give some indication of his attitudes and ideas:

'Childish dreams pale and a guiding purpose for living takes their place: it is our task to arouse this purpose in children.'

'What kind of a picture should we set before them? I believe it should be a picture of a man of character and maturity; of a man who develops his individuality in freedom, but without losing his way; of an independent man to whom ability is both a goal and a serious responsibility, who masters unruly dreams and longings by the strength of his mind and discipline of his will; of a man whose wealth lies within him, who seeks simplicity and integrity, is true to himself.'

'Sometimes my heart is heavy and the task seems insoluble when I measure my own imperfections and my own inadequacy against my obligations and responsibilities. When I look at my children at meal times, and listen to their gay chatter, when I reflect on the many roads which must cross, converge and part in the course of their lives, when I look into this life and seek an answer to its problems, then I find only one. Every human being is the keeper of his own destiny. He cannot evade or mitigate it in any way without being untrue to himself.'

In a farewell letter to his wife and seven young children he wrote:

'. . . Do not fear that I feel any great dismay in the face of death. I have prayed every day that God will give us both strength to accept with patience and humility whatever He decides or permits. And in prayer I find peace and calm.

'I think of you with love and deep gratitude. How good God is, and how rich He has made my life. He gave me love and mercy and a loving wife and good children, and I shall be grateful for that for the rest of my life. I thank you my dear ones for everything you have done for me; forgive me if I have ever hurt you, or failed in my duty towards you . . .

'Sometimes in the long months of my captivity I have wondered what will become of you when I am gone. I realised long ago that your fate does not depend on me. If it is God's will that I should no longer be with you, then He has help ready for you which is independent of me. . . .'

ERICH KNAUF

21 February 1895—2 May 1944

ERICH KNAUF came from a working class family in Saxony.
At fourteen he began his apprenticeship as a compositor; and
in the spring of 1914 he spent a few weeks wandering through
Italy, Greece and Turkey. From 1915-18 he was on active
service, and in 1920 took part in the suppression of the Kapp
Putsch in Gera.

After teaching for a year at a college in Tinz, Knauf
turned to political and literary journalism and from 1922 to
1928 was editor of the Plauen *Volkszeitung*. His articles on
painting and pictures and his theatre reviews were widely
admired, but also involved him in a series of law suits and
fines. For several years after this he worked with the Gutenberg Book Guild and at the same time wrote a novel about
the Kapp Putsch, a biography of Daumier and a book of
profiles of twenty-two artists from Daumier to Kollwitz.
When the Nazis took over the Book Guilds in 1933 Knauf
resigned and a year later, as the result of a review in the
8-*Uhr-Abendblatt*, he was expelled from the Reich Press
Association and had to spend ten weeks in the concentration
camps of Oranienburg and Lichtenburg.

After his release he turned to advertising for industry and
for films, and continued this work until, on 28 March 1944, he
and Erich Ohser, who had become famous, under the name
of E. O. Plauen, for his human and loveable drawings in the
Father and Son series, were arrested.

The following extracts from the documents in the case
against Erich Knauf and Erich Ohser speak for themselves:

From Captain Schultz   *Berlin*
To F., for the attention of the   *22 February 1944*
Head of the Department.
WPr F/H

Since the destruction of my flat at Trabenerstrasse 49, my
wife and I have been living in Berlin-Kaulsdorf, Am-
Feldberg 3. The Publicity Officer of the Terra Film Company,
Erich Knauf, and Erich Ohser, a cartoonist, live in the same

house . . . The following are remarks made by one or other of them on various occasions, and are rendered word for word whenever possible:

Knauf, discussing an article by Dr Goebbels which appeared in *Das Reich*, said *inter alia*: 'This little rat is paid 1,500 marks for each article, even though he is the Propaganda Minister and ought to write them for nothing. . . .'

Ohser agreed, saying that he, as a regular contributor to *Das Reich*, knew all about it, and that Dr Goebbels, as so-called Minister, had so strangled and enraged all German artists that German art, as any blind man could see, had gone to the dogs. . . .

Ohser: 'Himmler only keeps his job by ordering between 80 and 100 executions a day . . . I know that from the way my own circle of friends is dwindling. . . .''

Knauf: 'All the worst shirkers are in the SS. . . .'

Knauf and *Ohser*: 'A German victory would be the greatest misfortune, for only then can Hitler, so he himself says, become a real National Socialist. . . .'

I have held up this information until now in order to be quite sure that I had interpreted Knauf and Ohser's views correctly.

(*signed*) SCHULTZ

From The Under-Secretary   **Berlin**
To The Minister   **29 March 1944**

The first reports on the interrogation of the accused in the state-loyalty affair are to hand. . . .

The Gestapo official in charge, Lietzenburg, hopes to extract a confession from the accused in the course of further interrogation. If however no results are forthcoming, the accused will be confronted with Captain Schultz.

I will keep you informed.

Heil Hitler!

(*signed*) GUTTERER

Office of the Under-Secretary   **Berlin**
Memorandum on the discussion with   **1 April 1944**
the Under Secretary

Subject: *Ohser and Knauf*

. . . The Minister now wants Freisler to handle the main proceedings himself, if possible before Easter. The Minister also requests, as the matter concerns him personally, that Freisler should consult him by telephone before sentence is passed, as he may wish to reduce it. R. is not convinced that this is the best way to handle the matter and suggested that Freisler might, when he had given some thought to the matter, get in touch with the Minister by telephone.

The Under-Secretary thereupon telephoned Freisler and fixed the proceedings for next Tuesday or Wednesday, before the People's Court. It has proved impossible to obtain the services of independent judges at such short notice, so Freisler will have to select judges from the ranks of the Berlin Party Leaders, in so far as they have been appointed judges of the People's Court by the *Führer*. Freisler must get in touch with the Minister again *before* the proceedings begin.

Action: Consult Dr Metten, Public Prosecutor's Department.

(*signed*) DR PRAUSE

From The Under-Secretary   **Berlin**
To The Minister   **1 April 1944**

. . . Captain and Mrs Schultz have agreed to give evidence on oath against the accused. They give the impression of being reliable. The matter is now being passed on to the Chief Public Prosecutor at the People's Court. Care will be taken to expedite affairs.

I will keep you informed.

Heil Hitler!

(*signed*) GUTTERER

Berlin
R. 1403/3.4.44/372-1,4   3 April 1944
From Dr Schmidt-Leonhardt,
Ministerial Director,
To The Minister

Subject: Case against Ohser and Knauf

According to my instructions I called on President Freisler
and discussed the matter with him in detail, and afterwards,
at his request, with Lautz, the Chief Public Prosecutor. Ohser
has now retracted his partial confession, so that new witnesses
will have to be called to ensure his conviction. These are now
being questioned. For this reason the documents cannot as yet
be sent to the Chief Public Prosecutor, much less to the Court,
in fact the transfer certainly cannot take place before tomorrow
morning. In spite of these difficulties, matters will be expedited
so that the main trial can take place on Wednesday at 9 a.m.
President Freisler, who will be the Presiding Judge, is giving
the matter his personal attention . . . he says he never, on
principle, predicts the outcome of a trial, but implies that two
death sentences are probable; an opinion which, in view of the
severity of the charges, I am inclined to share. . . .

                                        Heil Hitler!

                                                  pp. S

R.M.f.V.u.P   **Berlin**
R. 1403/3.4.44/372-1,4   4 April 1944

Subject: Material from Dr Metten, Public Prosecutor

To Dr Freisler
President of the People's Court   U R G E N T
Berlin W9, Bellevuestrasse   *By Special Messenger*

Dear Mr President,
    At your request I am sending you the following documents
concerning the trial of Ohser and Knauf:
    1. A facsimile and 10 photostat copies of the caricatures
signed **Plauen**.
    2. Two newspaper cuttings of speeches by the *Führer* and
by the Minister of Propaganda, Dr Goebbels, which are concerned with German artists.
    3. A letter from the Personnel Office, dated 4 April 1944.
    So far as (1) is concerned, the photostat copies of the cari-
catures might be included in the material for the proceedings.
But I must ask you to return the other items to me as soon as

possible, as they are the only copies we have and are in frequent use.

The selection under (2) is very meagre, as the press-cutting section cannot for the moment find quotations to meet your requirements. I have given instructions for further searches and if anything turns up I will let you have it at once. May I have these two cuttings back?

The information from the local Personnel Office is also very meagre, for although it contains useful personal particulars, especially about the events of the day the two of them were bombed out, there is really nothing of any political significance. The Personnel Office say they cannot get hold of any such information until this afternoon at the earliest, as they must consult the Party Offices in the districts where the accused formerly lived, as the Office in the district where they now live has nothing. There is no other relevant information about either of them, either political or criminal, but if anything else comes in you shall have it as quickly as possible.

Heil Hitler!

Yours sincerely,

pp.

(*signed*) Dr M.

R.1403/4.4.44/372-1,4   *Berlin*
Official in Charge: Dr Metten,   *4 April 1944*
        Chief Public Prosecutor
To The Minister

Subject: Case against Ohser and Knauf

A new problem has arisen: Thierack, the Minister of Justice, who is responsible to the *Führer* for all cases concerned with the undermining of morale, has asked for an interview and, so I am told, demanded that he shall be fully informed of the facts of the case tomorrow morning. The proceedings scheduled for tomorrow morning cannot therefore take place. Herr Thierack will however see to it that they are held on Thursday, if this is at all possible. He has been informed of your interest and of your desire for speed. I will hear his views tomorrow morning, and will then know whether the proceedings have in fact been fixed for Thursday. I will then report to you immediately.

The Minister of Justice's request to be informed in advance of the facts cannot be refused.

Heil Hitler!

(*signed*) Schmidt-Leonhardt

R.1403/4.4.44/372-1,4　　　　　　　　　　5 April 1944
Official in Charge: Dr Metten　　　　　　Berlin
To The Minister

Subject: Case against Ohser and Knauf

President Freisler informs us that the proceedings are
definitely fixed for tomorrow, 6 April, at 9 a.m. Dr Metten of my
department will be present, and a report will be sent to you
immediately afterwards. President Freisler also hopes to be
able to send you details of the sentence early tomorrow afternoon.

Heil Hitler!

(signed) SCHMIDT-LEONHARDT

From Dr Metten,　　　　　　　　　　　Berlin
Chief Public Prosecutor,　　　　　　6 April 1944
To The Minister

Subject: Case against Ohser and Knauf

The session was postponed until 10 a.m. owing to the
announcement at 9 a.m. that Ohser had committed suicide. The
proceedings were conducted by President Freisler in his
capacity as Chairman of the Criminal Committee of the
People's Court; with him was another professional judge and
also, in an honorary capacity, Ahnels, Chairman of the District
Council, Winter, a local Party Leader and von Mangold, a
Labour official.

As soon as the charge (continual undermining of morale and
aiding the enemy) had been read out on behalf of the Chief
Public Prosecutor the accused, Knauf, was given a hearing.
Interrogation revealed that he was married, had no children,
had fought in the war, had been awarded the Iron Cross
(Second Class) and a medal for wounds received in action, and
that he was the author among other things of the songs *The
Stars of my Homeland* and *Bells from Home*. With regard to
his political activities it was established that he, like his father,
was a former member of the Social Democratic Party and that
he had worked on *Tribune*, a Social Democratic newspaper
appearing in Plauen, and with the Gutenberg Book Guild.
Knauf denied every charge.

57

The chief witness for the prosecution, Captain Schultz, then gave evidence. He repeated his accusations against Knauf. His wife, who was then called to the witness box confirmed and amplified all he said. Both witnesses were quite convincing. Captain Schultz's evidence was reinforced by the fact that he had made detailed notes of the relevant remarks made by Ohser and Knauf.

The death sentence, which the accused heard with composure, is absolute on pronouncement, since there is no legal appeal against sentences of the People's Court. After the report of the Judge's summing-up has been completed, the documents go to the Minister of Justice. He, by virtue of the special powers invested in him by the *Führer*, may order the execution on his own responsibility; or, should he decide that a pardon might be granted, or should any further evidence be laid before him, he may put the matter before the *Führer* for decision.

Heil Hitler!

(*signed*) DR METTEN

President of the People's Court
Berlin W9, Bellevuestrasse 15

11 April 1944

Extracts from the Summing-Up:

'. . . It is easy enough to understand how the accused came to make his demoralising and defeatist remarks, when one considers his observation that our victory would be the greatest possible misfortune, because only then could the Führer become a real National Socialist. It is in fact hate of National Socialism, and of our uncompromising achievement in carrying out the programme which is the synthesis of our way of life, that has driven him to it. He has dug his own grave, his political development has gone full circle . . . He, a man who had an important position in the cultural life of our country, a man whose honour should have kept him to the straight and narrow way, has come to this!

'We would not be true National Socialists if we were to match such deeds—the deeds of a man who has lost his honour for ever—with anything less than the death penalty.

'Knauf, since he has been found guilty, must also pay the costs.

(*signed*) FREISLER (signature illegible)

Offices of the Minister of Justice　　　　*Berlin W. 8*
IV g 10b 668b/44　　　　　　　　　　*Wilhelmstrasse 65*
From Dr. Franke,　　　　　　　　　　　*21 April 1944*
Office of the Public Prosecutor,　　　　　URGENT
To The Chief Public Prosecutor,
People's Court, Berlin
Personal (or official representative)
Enclosures: Order of 20 April 1944 (original)

1 copy of the Order

With reference to the trial before the People's Court on
9 April 1944, in which Erich Knauf was condemned to death,
I am sending you the original order of 20 April 1944, together
with a certified copy, with the request that the necessary further
steps may be taken with all possible speed.

Please do not make this information public, either through
the press or by proclamation.

pp.....

(*signed*) WOLLMER

Office of the Public Prosecutor
People's Court
Ref. 4 J 777/44

Account
for the case against Erich Knauf

Fee for the Death Penalty (see Articles 49/52 of the Penal Code)	300.
Postage (see Article 72(1) of the Penal Code) ...	1.84
Fee for the Counsel for the Defence, Ahlsdorff, Barrister, Berlin-Lichterfelde-Ost, Gärtnerstrasse 10a (Article 72(6) of the Penal Code)	81.60
Charge for Prison Maintenance, 6 April-2 May 1944	44. 0
Costs for carrying out the sentence	158.18
Postage for sending Account	.12

TOTAL R.M. 585.74

59

Responsible for Payment: The Heirs of Erich Knauf. For the personal attention of Mrs Erna Knauf, Berlin-Tempelhof, Manfred-von-Richthoven-Strasse 13, bei Fa. Gilbert, Mach.

The President *of the People's Court*	*Berlin W 9* *6 April 1944* *Bellevuestrasse 15* *Tel. 22 18 23*

Business Ref.....

    (Please quote in reply)

To The Minister for Popular Enlightenment
and Propaganda, Dr Goebbels
Berlin W. 9
1 Enclosure

Dear Minister,

    I have the honour to send you the Sentence, passed today in the People's Court, on Knauf.

Heil Hitler!

Yours sincerely,

(FREISLER)

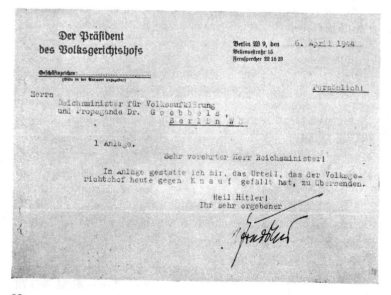

The President
of the People's Court

Berlin W 9
11 April 1944
Bellevuestrasse 15
Tel. 22 18 23

Business Ref. . . . .
    (*Please quote in reply*)
Enclosures

Dear Ministerial Director and Party Member
        Schmidt-Leonhardt,
    Now that the case against Knauf is complete, I do not want the moment to pass without thanking you once more for the material you put at my disposal, which was most useful during the proceedings and in the preparation of the case.

Heil Hitler!

Yours sincerely,

(FREISLER)

Der Präfident
des Volksgerichtshofs

Berlin W 9, den 11. April 1944
Bellevuestraße 16
Fernsprecher 22 18 23

Geschäftszeichen:
    (Bitte in der Antwort anzugeben)

Anlage.

Sehr verehrter Herr Ministerialdirigent!
Lieber Parteigenosse Schmidt-Leonhardt!

    Nach Beendigung der Hauptverhandlung gegen K n a u f möchte ich nicht verfehlen, Ihnen nochmal für die Übersendung des für die Verhandlung und ihre Vorbereitung sehr wertvollen Materials herzlich zu danken.
    In Anlage gestatte ich mir, zu meiner Entlastung das Material Ihnen wieder zu übersenden.

Heil Hitler!
Ihr sehr ergebener

ADOLF REICHWEIN

8 October 1898—20 October 1944

ADOLF REICHWEIN grew up in Oberosbach and as a boy ran wild in the Taunus hills. He matriculated in 1916 and was immediately conscripted. In 1917 he was seriously wounded. After the war he studied philosophy, history and political economy and became a Doctor of Philosophy as early as 1920. His thesis appeared as a book under the title *China und Europa: geistige und künstleriche Beziehungen* (China and Europe: Intellectual and Artistic Ties).

While still quite young he entered the Prussian Ministry for Religion, Education and Cultural Affairs, but soon turned to practical teaching, first in a college for adult education and later as a university professor. He published four books, *Die Rohstoffe der Erde* (The Raw Materials of the Earth), *Mexiko erwacht* (Mexico Awakes), *Erlebnisse mit Mensch und Tier* (Experiences with Man and Beast), and *Schaffendez Schulvolk* (Creative Work in School).

Susanne Suhr, who was in touch with him from the time he was in Jena up to the resistance days, says of Adolf Reichwein:

'He was an unusual man, with unusual intellectual and human qualities—everyone said so. This must have been the secret of his fascination, for he had no trace of self-satisfaction. It was as though the charm of youthfulness, of early promise, surrounded him like a tragic aura: for he never really reached maturity. Reichwein was the child of the youth movement, but tried always to live it down; and fate seems to have lent a hand while he was still young. At the age of twenty-two as a young Doctor of Philosophy in the Ministry he was able to try out his theories and ideals on adult education, and soon afterwards as director of the College of Thuringia, to put them into practice. In this work, with students and workers of the Zeiss factory in Jena, he came in touch with all manner of men and remained in touch for the rest of his life. He longed for the day when new intellectual and ethical bonds would break down the time-honoured acceptance of a class-ridden society. He also realised that enthusiastic idealism must sooner or later give way to

Photograph taken in the People's Court

political activity, but it was a long time before he moved in that direction.

'A romantic love of adventure went side by side with a capacity for sober and disciplined work. He tramped through America, went to Japan as a seaman, smuggled weapons for the Kuomintang, fought against the rebels in Mexico, and thereby but quite incidentally collected a wealth of material for his books and lectures.

'In the Prussian Ministry, as Personal Adviser to the Minister

(Becker), Reichwein played a decisive part in the founding of teachers' training colleges, and himself went to the Teachers' College in Halle in 1930 as Professor of History and Social Studies. He rated example high, as an essential to all facets of teaching (perhaps even to the teaching of physical discipline for he himself flew a small sports aeroplane!). Up to this time he had always avoided connection with any political party, or any active political work: but as Hitler stood menacingly at the door and many people began fearfully to disown their former opinions, Reichwein avowed his allegiance to the Social Democratic Party; just as after 1933, when every aeroplane had to be marked with a swastika, he gave up his first machine because he could no longer fly as a "free man".

'The National Socialists soon removed him from his professorship. He retired into the isolated existence of a village schoolmaster, although many glittering offers came his way.

'He enjoyed his work, but developments under the Hitler régime troubled him deeply and he began to take an increasingly active part in resistance. Known only to a few trusted friends, he became a sworn member of the group planning the attempt on Hitler's life, and thanks to his unusually wide circle of friends he was able to tie up many of the loose ends; he was for instance the main link between the Kreisau and other resistance groups, particularly with those among industrial workers. He worked closely with many old friends and many new ones, all at one in their intent and purpose; and his office in the Prinzessinnen Schlösschen, Unter den Linden—he was then working at the Folklore Museum in Berlin—was a cover for many secret meetings and discussions. The way from ethics and awareness to political action had not been easy for him; but his courage, his loyalty to his friends and his sense of the moral obligation to do what was necessary, whatever the consequences, led him without faltering on the path he had chosen.

While the secret preparations were in full swing, Reichwein was betrayed by a police spy, arrested and imprisoned. During the trial before the People's Court, under the presidency of the raging Freisler, he, who was as gentle as he was indomitable, must have suffered greatly. On 20 October, he was executed, and so joined many of his friends who had been condemned earlier.'

On 16 October 1944 he write to his wife:

'I need hardly say that my thoughts are still with life. But it is hard to write about that now, much though it might help. Looking back over the decades, one thing stands out; how rich and rare these years have been for me. The misery of the first war fades into the background, just as other memories stand out, clear and strong: the happy carefree days of my youth in the country, my ten years in the *Wandervogel*, with rambles near and far, the friendships of my youth, the happy student days in Frankfurt and Marburg, and the firm friendships that sprang from them, and then the joys and satisfaction of my teaching work; then the rare gifts of my life, my travels in Europe, America and East Asia, the four years of flying and the bird's-eye view of the world, and the days and nights of scientific work in between; and finally the richest and most precious of all: the twelve years with you and the children. How much reason to be grateful!'

WALTHER ARNDT

8 January 1891—26 June 1944

WALTHER ARNDT studied at Breslau University and, like his father, chose natural science as his subject. In 1911 he took part for the first time in an expedition abroad, and on 18 August 1914, having passed his final examinations, he received his degree as Doctor of Medicine. He subsequently volunteered for active service, was taken prisoner by the Russians on 23 October 1914, while he was a medical NCO in a field hospital, and was repatriated two and a half years later as part of an exchange of medical personnel. In May 1917 he returned to Russia with the Prisoners-of-War Welfare Commission set up by the War Office and was captured a second time, as he had predicted, and eventually returned home in 1919 by a circuitous route via Japan, the Philippines, America and Sweden. In 1920, he took the degree of Doctor of Philosophy and afterwards accepted a post with the Zoological Museum in Berlin, where he worked first as an assistant and later as a curator and professor.

Side by side with the tasks of a museum official, Walther Arndt produced and published numerous scientific works. He took an active part in the work of various scientific organisations and was always ready to take on any tasks concerned with public education which might come his way.

In the course of his various exploring expeditions he made many contacts abroad. (His address book contained, in addition to 600 German addresses, about 400 foreign addresses ranging over 47 countries). Abroad, his importance had been recognised very early : In 1929, the Peking Society of Natural History appointed him a corresponding member, and in 1932 the Bulgarian Society for Scientific Research made him an honorary member; in 1938 he became a member of the International Zoological Nomenclature Commission and in the same year he received a medal from the King of the Belgians; in 1940, he was appointed an honorary member of the German Zoological Society.

Arndt was known for his selfless and idealistic devotion to his scientific work; but in 1944 his doom was sealed by a

remark he made after an air-raid, which he had spent putting out fire bombs in his museum, and which was reported to the authorities by one of his colleagues and a girl friend of his youth. He appears to have said something like this: 'Now this is the end of the Third Reich, it only remains to bring the guilty to punishment'; and for that he was sentenced to death by the People's Court on 11 May 1944.

The notes he wrote in prison made it quite clear that he knew his fate. On 22 April 1944, for instance:

'If my life, which was so rich and happy, must now come to an end, perhaps it is according to the old saying "They whom the Gods love, die young". But wherever I may come to rest in the great universe, my soul will always turn towards our home.'

Before his death on 26 June 1944 he wrote to his sister:

'I've just been given the chance to send you a few lines. I think it's really better for all three of us that these days of waiting are coming to an end today, though there have been some good hours among them . . . and now I feel rather like Faust: the hand moves, time stands still, the hour has come. . . .

'How often have I opened the hymn book at the hymns we sang at father's funeral—I shall do so again today—and said them or sung them to myself. And I've just thought of his motto: "Be true until death . . .".'

His last words, before the sentence was carried out, on 26 June 1944 were: 'My sister, my own part of the country, and my scientific work were the loves of my life.'

The following is an extract from the obituary which appears in the *Archiv für Hydrobiologie, 1947*, volume XII, pp. 614-621:

Now, as I try to recapture the delightful personality of my unforgettable friend, in all its simple greatness and its absolute integrity, the conviction grows on me that all the characteristics which we loved and admired in him, sprang from three sources. The one which we may well regard as the main spring of his whole nature was human kindness, and the other two were an absolute love of truth and an unselfish devotion to duty.

If I say that human kindness was his main characteristic I must add that it did not take the form of mere benevolence towards his fellow creatures: it was rather a case of active and positive kindness. I must give myself the pleasure of mentioning at least one concrete example: I remember how I once asked him when he thought he would be promoted to the post of Curator of the Berlin Museum. 'Well,' he said, 'a vacancy has just occurred, and it would be my turn according to seniority. But I have decided to step down in favour of X, because he is a married man and so needs the security of a permanent post.'

In his capacity as a research worker, however, it was not his kindness which took first place, but his absolute love of truth and objectivity, and his real devotion to his work. One could always rely absolutely on any statement which might appear in one of Arndt's publications; his method of compiling the relevant data from his reading, and the facts gathered by observation, was exemplary; never did he deviate by a hair's breadth, for the sake of a theory or for the purpose of more effective presentation, from what he regarded as the strongest probability on the strength of the proven facts.

The very quality which distinguished both him and his work was, finally, also the cause of his early and terrible death. In a time and circumstance where hate was preached as a virtue, a man whose whole being was inspired by kindness to his fellow men and by an unshakable love of truth, was bound to come to grief sooner or later. Maybe there was nothing so particularly admirable in his frankness with people whom he believed he could trust; but none can fail to admire the great courage which Arndt displayed before his 'judges'; that is to say, in the face of certain death. With the help of the innumerable references and petitions handed in on his behalf, he might possibly have saved his life. The fact that he did not withdraw or qualify his assertion that he would sooner sacrifice his life in support of truth, than save it by denial, denotes a greatness of mind before which we must bow in admiration and gratitude.

But for the men like Arndt, the avowed lovers of truth, one might despair of scientific objectivity. He did not die in vain. For this man who was condemned by the court as being 'for ever without honour', died in fact for the honour of the German people, for the honour of science and for the honour of the human race.

PROFESSOR ERNST MATTHES,
Museo e Laboratorio Zoologico da Universidade Coimbra.

3 FRIENDSHIP

UNDER totalitarian rule, uniformity is everything and individuality counts for nothing. If the individual pits his will against the state, his will must be broken.

One chapter in the history of resistance to National Socialism concerns the simple stories of help to friends and neighbours, help which is normally taken for granted but which takes on a special significance when it involves grave personal risk. People were hidden and people were warned. Money was collected by the neighbours and friends of the man who was in trouble and, as unobtrusively as possible, put at the disposal of his family. The hunted and the persecuted found refuge in the homes of their friends, who at risk of their own lives hid them for weeks and months on end. People who lived near the frontiers, fishermen and mountaineers, smuggled those under pressure out of the country. There were employers who took on men and women in need of protection, officials and soldiers who failed exactly to observe the regulations and thousands of people, of all kinds—from the market woman who gave food, to the civil servant who falsified papers—who stood by citizens of Jewish origin, in stark opposition to those who did not. When such actions were discovered, the wrath of the authorities did not descend only on the 'guilty' man; he had always to reckon that his family would also be involved, and the infamous *Sippenhaft* (family arrest) spared neither children nor old people.

There was also a smaller band of people, which should not be forgotten, who believed that they would by dying ease the fate of others; and no-one will ever know how many took their own lives while under arrest in order to take their secrets with them.

Personal stories are legion, but the following is typical of many: Dr Philipp Schaefer, a 45-year-old scientist, was executed on 13 May 1943, after proceedings against the Harro Schulze-Boysen group. He had wanted to rescue an old Jewish couple and had tried to climb into their flat, where they had turned on the gas taps, by a rope. But the rope broke. He was badly hurt and was taken to hospital, where he was arrested. During the trial he was accused of having failed to report his friends to the Gestapo. He replied: 'Gentlemen, I have been asked why I did not report this affair. I can only say that I am not a police odd-job man.'

JOACHIM GOTTSCHALK

I N the Stahnsdorf cemetery in Berlin there lies at rest an actor and his family. On the gravestone, put up by friends, are engraved their names, their dates of birth and the day of their common death:

JOACHIM GOTTSCHALK
Born 10 April 1904

META GOTTSCHALK
Born 13 August 1902

MICHAEL GOTTSCHALK
Born 19 February 1933

Died 6 November 1941

Hugo Gau-Hamm, who was in the same company as Gottschalk during the years in question, gives the following account of the events which lie behind this inscription:

Joachim Gottschalk, the son of a doctor, had been at sea for three years when he decided to go on the stage. He built up a reputation in Leipzig and Frankfurt-am-Main and then signed a contract with Eugen Klöpfer for the 1938-39 season in the Bülowplatz Theatre in Berlin, which was by that time only nominally connected with the People's Theatre Company, meanwhile disbanded by the Nazis.

Gottschalk's first rôle was Fiesko, which he played with great success. His talent aroused justifiable expectations, he was very popular and his upright, straightforward character was a symbol of loyalty at a time when personal relationships were often very strained. He was known as 'Joschi' to his friends and colleagues. To his great circle of admirers he seemed young, happy and successful, and only a few people knew that a dark shadow hung over the life and being of this quiet, unostentatious actor; but among his closest friends the fact that his wife was a Jewess was often discussed.

Gottschalk knew that so long as Gustaf Gründgens directed the state theatres in Berlin, actors with Jewish wives would be able, with special permission, to carry on. But his was a special

Photo by Atelier Ruth Wilhelmi

case: his ability, his success on the stage and his youth had attracted the attention of those responsible for making 'politically valuable' films. He won respect as a film actor in his first two parts and after his appearance with Paula Wessely in *Ein Leben lang* his natural wish for success was fully realised, and he achieved widespread popularity.

The popularity of an artist who was married to a Jewess and who, as it appeared, could not be persuaded to separate from his wife, created difficulties for the Minister of Propaganda of the Third Reich. 'I can no longer bear the sight of him. . . .' Goebbels' well-known intimation was readily understood, indeed it had to be understood, by his willing minions: Gottschalk was not wanted, he would not be allowed to continue to practise his profession in the 'cultural' sphere, he would be banned from the stage, from films and from broadcasting . . . unless, of course, he would yield to the demand, repeatedly made and as often refused, that he should leave his wife.

If on the other hand all sources of income were stopped, he would be unable to fulfil the many obligations he had incurred while he was receiving a substantial income from his film work. When he made this point, it was suggested to him that he should go on tour with the so-called 'Strength-through-Joy' organisation. Gottschalk was strongly opposed to such a dangerous offer: if he had to leave his wife and child alone, then he would do so only as a soldier, since the wife and child of a soldier must be protected from persecution. But when he volunteered for military service his offer was refused.

The strain increased, and became torture. The day came when a rehearsal at the Hebbel Theatre could not begin because Gottschalk was missing. Then it was announced in an atmosphere of emotion, in flat, broken sentences full of shock and grief, that the Gottschalk family had chosen suicide.

His wife and child were first lulled to sleep with veronal, then Gottschalk arranged everything exactly as he had agreed with his wife a little earlier, and finally he himself took leave of the world and his friends. 'Think of the words of Kleist,' he wrote in his last letter to his sister Ulrike. 'The truth is that there was no help for me on this earth.'

The actor Ernst Sattler laid a wreath on their graves on behalf of all his colleagues. No word of remembrance was permitted, but the old grey-haired priest spoke courageously on that dismal November day, in spite of the presence of Nazi 'supervisors'. He rejected the reproaches of those who had described the Gottschalk's action in killing their child as irresponsible, saying that in his opinion they were on the contrary prompted by a high sense of responsibility, in that they had decided not to leave their child alone in such a barbaric world.

So much is easily forgotten. Today, when one reflects on the sudden death of the Gottschalk family, one can see that it probably helped to save many other people, living under a similar strain, from a greater misery; and so one can find some sense, ironical though it may be, in this tragic story.

Gottschalk was a man of high principle and, for what it is

worth, some of his friends believe that such considerations, the possibility that others who were in similar distress might be helped, played no small part in his decision to die.

5. November 1941

Farewell message from Meta and Joachim Gottschalk, written a few hours before their suicide.

(*Translation*)

5 November 1941.

Fanny my dear,

Take this brooch as a souvenir, and goodbye. Thank you for your true friendship, you know what I wish for you!

My love to you all, and you must not mourn for us, you know we are happy. Thank you for everything,

and good luck,

META

About the money that you lent me. I have communicated with my sister.

Greetings,
JOACHIM

LILO GLOEDEN

19 December 1903—30 November 1944

THE death register for 1944 includes under the numbers 3078/80 the following names: Erich Gloeden, Architect, born 23 August 1888, Berlin. Elisabeth Charlotte Gloeden, born 19 December 1903, Cologne. Elisabeth Kusnitzky, born 21 January 1878, Strasbourg.

Their crime is given as treason; the penalty, death; the date of conviction, 27 November 1944; the date and place of execution, 30 November 1944, Berlin. A short note states that the condemned had hidden Fritz Lindemann, a former general, in their home for six weeks, while aware of his being guilty of treason.

Dr Lilo Gloeden was the daughter of a Cologne doctor, named Kusnitzky, and of his wife, formerly Baroness von Liliencron. In 1938 she married Erich Gloeden, an architect. She was known as a woman with many artistic leanings and as a charming and conscientious wife and daughter. Her mother, who had settled in Berlin after the death of her husband, spent most of her time with her.

Lilo was a woman of great integrity with a deep sense of justice. She and her husband found the conditions of those days quite unbearable, and were passionate opponents of the Nazi dictatorship. Whenever they could, they helped people who were oppressed; and in particular they concealed victims of anti-Jewish and political persecution (among others Dr Goerdeler is said to have hidden for a while in their home).

Soon after 20 July a friend of Erich Gloeden's, from Dresden, brought to their house a General Lindemann, whom they did not know before, and for whose arrest the Gestapo had issued a warrant and offered a reward of half a million Reichmarks. He stayed longer than had been agreed, for it was obviously impossible for him to find other accommodation. On 3 September a strong contingent of police seized him at the flat, and shot him. Erich, Lilo and her mother were arrested, and subjected by the Gestapo to terrible interrogation.

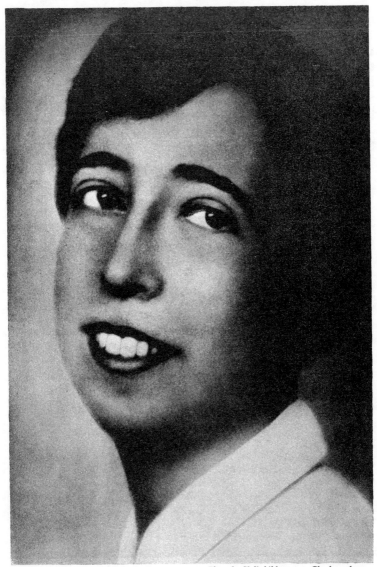

Some years after the war, when the informer was on trial, fellow prisoners revealed that Gloeden had, in the autumn of 1944, tried until the end to protect the two women. He had maintained that they did not know that it was Lindemann who was living with them; the General, he explained, had been introduced under a false name. But when the death sentence was passed on her husband, Lilo Gloeden declared that she had from the start known the identity of the man they had sheltered, and that she wanted to die with her husband. Then old Mrs Kusnitzky said that she too was aware of her son-in-law's and daughter's complicity, and that life would have no further meaning for her after their death.

At intervals of two minutes, man, wife and mother were beheaded in Plötzensee prison.

LOTHAR ERDMANN

12 October 1888—18 September 1939

LOTHAR ERDMANN spent his childhood in Halle, where
his father was a professor of philosophy. He matriculated
in Bonn in 1905, studied history and philosophy at Freiburg
University and then went to London for a post-graduate
course. There he came in contact with the Fabians, and so

Photo by Atelier Augenstein

began his allegiance to socialism. He volunteered in 1914 and later became a company commander on the western front. After the war he worked for the Trade Union International in Amsterdam and simultaneously held a post with Wolff Telegraph Office. From 1924 to 1933 he was secretary of the German Trade Union Council in Berlin and during that time became editor of *Die Arbeit.*

When the National Socialists took possession of the Trade Union offices, on 2 May 1933, Lothar Erdmann was among those who were reprimanded: but the new régime were at pains to win him over to their side. He consistently rejected their advances, including the request that he should contribute to the *Arbeitsfront,* the Nazi press organ, in spite of threats that he would otherwise be handed over to the SS. During the next few years he tried to keep going as a freelance journalist, contributing to papers like *Die Hilfe,* but he and his family lived in very reduced circumstances.

In a letter dated 19 July 1934, he wrote to his son:

'Many older people demand of the young enthusiasm, devotion, faith and obedience. Enthusiasm? Yes, but only for men and ideas which one can support with passion and conviction after one has subjected them to every test. Faith? Certainly, but only in men worthy of trust, and in thoughts which emanate from truth and which need no justification, which are in themselves convincing, positive and realistic. The wares which are to-day peddled in the market places are suspiciously reminiscent of a bargain basement stocked with cheap and shoddy goods.

'Obedience? Yes, but only when a simple purpose demands a definite chain of command—in the army for instance. In other situations obedience may lead us to abandon our own future, and that of the nation, to the accidents of history and to blind historical chance, which often enough places leadership in the hands of a group, under whom passive obedience amounts to a crime against this and all future generations.

'No, the duty to keep our heads above water, critically to examine people and opinions, and freely and objectively to decide what can be done, was never so pressing as it is in these obscure times. For true faith comes only through responsible and individual thinking: it is better that you keep your enthusiasms to yourself, than that your judgment be influenced by other people.'

At the outbreak of war, on 1 September 1939, Lothar Erdmann was arrested by the Gestapo for 'preventive reasons'. A week later, he was sent to the Sachsenhausen concentration camp.

On the way to the camp, a fellow prisoner stumbled and was beaten by the guards. Lothar Erdmann protested against this treatment, telling the SS that such behaviour was impossible. At this the SS guards struck him also, and on arrival at the camp took him to the Commandant. To the question whether he knew why he was in a concentration came, Erdmann replied: 'As an opponent of National Socialism'; and to the Commandant's second question, whether he knew what obedience meant, he retorted that there were various kinds of obedience; he himself had been an officer during the first world war, and his two sons were now serving at the front.

Lothar was sentenced to punishment by drilling, which was to be increased by an hour each day. On the sixth day he broke down. This was labelled mutiny; so he was bound to a pole for three hours, to be beaten and kicked. The results were broken ribs, torn neck tendons and internal injuries. On 18 September 1939, death put an end to his suffering.

GERTRUD SEELE

22 September 1917—12 January 1945

'Michaela, my dearest little daughter, today your mother must die ... I have a great favour to ask of you, my child: you must be brave and sensible and try to make your grandparents happy. Your father is .... and was born on 5 March 1907, in Leipzig. You will find out the rest from your grandparents. You have all my dearest wishes for your life, and please love me always and never forget me. My heart weeps for you and for my parents. Do be nice to them and give them joy, by growing up to be able and good. I picture you in my arms, I press you to my heart and kiss you——
Goodbye, my darling little daughter
from your despairing MOTHER.'

Deine verzweifelte Mutti

(The missing parts were censored by the authorities of the People's Court. The editors have not thought fit to publish the name of the father.)

GERTRUD SEELE was tried before the People's Court in Potsdam on 6 December 1944, and was sentenced to death. An amnesty was refused. Her last wish, 'I only want to see my child once more,' was ignored. The sentence was carried out at Plötzensee, Berlin.

The events which led up to this death sentence were—as Michaela's guardianship documents show—investigated and established seven years later, through regular court proceedings.

Gertrud Seele, a talented child from a working-class family in Berlin, went to a secondary school for two years. On leaving the elementary school she worked in the Labour Service and at the age of 18 entered a nursing school. After completing her training she took a special course in public health and social welfare service, and finally took up work in that field. Her daughter Michaela was born on 11 September 1941. In 1942 mother and daughter were evacuated to Merke Niederlausitz, but returned to Berlin in 1943.

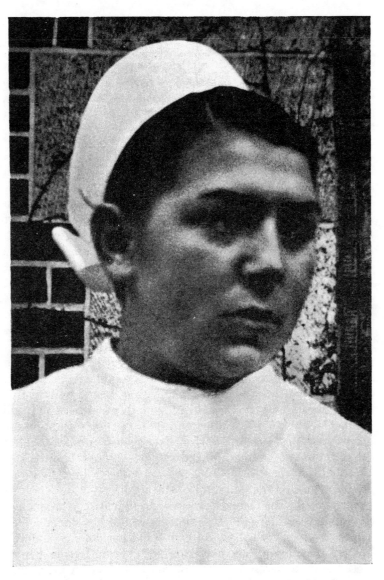

Gertrud's mother, Luise Seele, who has since died, wrote in a letter dated 27 August 1951:

'Once at a party in Merke people were complaining about the Nazis. Gertrud had a healthy sense of justice and fair play, so she was a passionate opponent of the Nazis, and during the conversation she expressed her indignation against them in no uncertain terms. During the war she repeatedly helped Jews and other persecuted people. And so at a time when other people were praising Hitler and the Nazis, she developed a loathing for them. She had left her belongings in Merke and went there in January to make sure they were all right, having not the slightest idea that she was in danger. In Merke she was arrested, taken to an investigation centre in Frankfurt-on-Oder and later moved to Berlin.'

On 22 December 1951, Luise Seele, acting in the interests of her granddaughter Michaela, submitted an application under the law passed on 5 January 1951 (giving victims of the criminal law of the National Socialists the right to claim compensation) to the Public Prosecutor of the District Court of Berlin, asking for the cancellation of the previous judgment passed against her daughter by the People's Court. She wrote at the time: 'The papers concerning the judgment then passed were handed to the solicitor, but as he cannot now be traced, I am unable to quote file numbers.'

In a letter dated 15 January 1952, she was informed by the Public Prosecutor of the District Court: 'I can find no trace of the case you raise in the court records, and the documents are no longer available. I must ask you to let me know the names of all the prisons where your daughter was kept in connection with the sentence in question. In the light of this information I will try to find out something about the case.'

On 17 October 1952, after painstaking efforts and endless correspondence the previous sentence was quashed by the 4th Criminal Chamber of the Berlin District Court. The Court Order recording this decision states: 'Investigations have shown that the daughter of the applicant was sentenced because she had made so-called defeatist statements, designed to undermine the fighting morale of the people.' These remarks, according to the notes of her defence counsel, formed the basis of the sentence designating her as a 'convicted and recognised enemy of the state.' The verdict was confirmed in communications forwarded by the Public Prosecutor to the People's Court and dated 21 November 1944, and 10 January 1945, respectively, the original texts of which may be found in the records of the chamber.

It is also confirmed by the duplicate copies of two documents of the President of the 5th Senate of the People's Court, dated 20 November 1944. These papers were attached to the records of the court by the defence counsel, Dr Ernst Falck, together with a convincing supplementary statement in a letter dated 2 September 1952.

It is thus quite clear that the decision of the former People's Court was made on purely political grounds.

ERNST HEILMANN

13 April 1881—3 April 1940

'THIS case is subject to the personal decision of the Reichs-führer of the SS.' From 1933 till 1940, this was the inevitable answer to every effort to mitigate the fate of Ernst Heilmann as he lay in prison; with this reference to Heinrich Himmler's order, the Gestapo officials evaded all attempts to avert the unwritten death sentence which was finally executed in the seventh year of Heilmann's unparalleled martyrdom.

Before 1933 Heilmann's Social Democrat friends jokingly called him the 'Uncrowned King of Prussia'. In 1924 they had elected him chairman of their party group in the Prussian Diet, of which he had been a member since 1919. This office, as spokesman and leader of the strongest party in the parliament of the largest German *Land*, imposed on its bearer a large and truly royal measure of responsibility, risk and influence. Within the legal framework of a modern democracy, Ernst Heilmann's work can be said to have played a large part in determining the fate of Prussia.

Heilmann's constructive work, and his influence in the fruitful years of the coalition of Social Democrats, the Catholic Centre Party and the Democratic Party, was the central pillar on which rested the stability of the Prussian government under Braun and Severing, and indeed in the days of the so-called 'Little Weimar Coalition', 1924-32, when Heilmann steered the government through all difficulties and dangers. His success must be attributed to his friendship with the leader of the parliamentary group of the Centre Party, Dr Hess, to his great intelligence and to his remarkable political ability.

Ernst Heilmann was the son of middle-class Jewish parents in Berlin. While he was still a student and before he passed his law examinations in 1903, he joined the Social Democratic Party. But in the Royal Prussia of those days, a political decision of this kind was a bar to the further government-controlled legal training which was necessary for the final examinations; so Heilmann had to sacrifice his chosen career for his political convictions. At first he became a stenographer

in Parliament, later a free lance journalist, and finally chief
editor of the *Chemnitzer Volksstimme*. Later he also edited
Social Democrat information bulletins and periodicals. In
the second year of his war service he lost the sight of his
right eye.

After the first war Ernst Heilmann was one of the most
energetic, and therefore to his totalitarian enemies one of the
best hated, defenders of the young republic in parliament;
he opposed all the revolutionary attempts of the communists:

in the parliamentary committee set up to investigate communist disturbances in central Germany in 1921, in the sessions of the Prussian Diet (where he called them 'moles trained by Moscow to undermine democracy'), and in all organisations concerned with attacking the existence of the democratic state.

The National Socialists found in Heilmann's views on foreign affairs, which were based on understanding with former enemies, reason enough to consider him their archenemy; and this developed into unbounded hatred for the influential democratic politician of Jewish origin against whom they had to contend not only in the Prussian Diet, but also after 1928 in the *Reichstag*. In 1933, for all that, Heilmann stayed in Berlin. He made this decision, at the risk of his life, in the conviction that he fought for the greatest cause in the world; and even after Parliament had been dissolved and a ban imposed on political parties, he did not want to leave Germany, although he knew quite well what the future held in store. Ernst Heilmann's journey through the famous Gestapo prison Columbiahaus, the Plötzensee Prison, the concentration camps of Oranienburg, Papenburg-Börgermoor, Dachau and Buchenwald was even more cruel than the fate of most of his friends and fellow victims; and, by its very duration, inflicted on him an ever greater despair.

Walter Poller, author of the report *A Doctor's Secretary at Buchenwald* describes among other humiliations how an SS Officer named Roedl had trained bloodhounds to attack Heilmann to amuse his guests. The dogs mangled his arms and hands. Earlier, at Papenburg-Börgermoor, Heilmann had tried to end his life by pretending to escape and thereby inciting the guards to shoot, but they only shot him in the right leg, and what followed was worse than death.

But for all the agony, even though he was disfigured almost past recognition, Heilmann still proudly acknowledged his past, by whispering almost imperceptibly 'And still I did what was right.'

He also retained his political judgment. Late in 1938 he told one of his fellow prisoners (the doctor's secretary at Buchenwald), 'There will be war. You "Aryans" will still have a chance because they will need you. But they will kill all of us Jews', and during the first winter in the war he said: 'Germany cannot win this war'.

In spring 1940 Ernst Heilmann lay in the camp mortuary; his body was enveloped in wrapping paper, but brave witnesses discovered that there was a fresh incision near the veins in the crook of his right arm.

His wife and daughter were among the few who ever received permission to go to Buchenwald for a last farewell to their dead husband and father. An SS-Officer read in the presence of the widow a medical report of the illness which had, allegedly, led to Heilmann's death, and the report ended with the words '. . . consequently a clear case of weakness and old age'.

WILLI HÄUSSLER

18 April 1907—22 March 1945

A YOUNG labourer from Hamburg represents thousands of
honest opponents and victims of the Nazi régime. Willi
Häussler was born on 18 April 1907 in Hamburg, and one
might almost say that he grew up in the Labour movement,
through the influence of his family; he was a member of the
Kinderfreunde and of the *Arbeiterjugend* before he joined
the *Reichsbanner Schwarz-Rot-Gold* and the Social Democratic Party, in 1925. He worked for the Hamburg Warehouse
Company, but lost his job in the summer of 1933 because of
his 'hostile attitude towards the state'.

In the *Reichsbanner*, Willi Häussler belonged to the 10th
Hamburg Defence Company (Barmbek); and in Barmbek
the illegal work of the Hamburg Defence Companies started
in 1933. Political friends in danger, from all parts of
Germany, were helped across the borders; inscriptions
appeared on the walls of houses, in particular the three
arrows of the *Eiserne Front*, a symbol of the determination
of the workers to fight the Nazi dictatorship; leaflets and
handbills, calling for uncompromising and steadfast resistance to the system of slavery were passed from hand to hand.
One of the handbills read:

> 'We are not concerned with the elimination of a political
> party and the ambitious clique who lead them, much as they
> may deserve it; we are concerned with the fate of the whole
> German nation, which is once again in danger of being led
> into peril by its unscrupulous leaders. Our own future is at
> stake . . . The disappointed masses who long to turn away from
> Hitler will now find that a new political force is coming into
> existence.'

In October 1934 the first wave of arrests hit the men of the
Reichsbanner at Hamburg and about a hundred people in
ten groups were sentenced by the courts; and when, soon
afterwards, the new leaders of the resistance groups of the
Reichsbanner were also arrested, Willi Häussler, without a
moment's hesitation, stepped into their place.

Frau Mimi Häussler has written the story:

In summer we lived in a little shack in our allotment, outside the city. A few days before my husband was arrested (13 June 1936) we went to our home in Pestalozzistrasse and were told by our neighbours that the Gestapo had been in our flat the night before. After this my husband tried to hide.

The Gestapo came to me night after night to get me to tell them where they could find him. In fact, my husband had somehow managed to obtain all necessary documents and tickets so that he could escape to Denmark. But two hours before his departure he was arrested. The Gestapo ordered me not to mention to anybody the fact of his arrest or the events that led to it. But I warned our friends, and some of them were able to escape.

Our daughter was five years old when all this happened. Later, at school, the following statement appeared in her file: 'Father detained for political reasons'.

The state Welfare Organisation were prepared to grant financial aid to Frau Häussler only on condition that she divorced her husband, and so she was compelled to work for 75 Pfennige per day. The Labour Office also turned her away when the Director of Personnel learned that her husband was detained on political grounds. Finally, she found a job as a shop assistant.

Friends who tried to help the families of people who had been arrested were able for a time to put money under her door-mat; then the danger involved became too great, and this too became impossible.

Arrest followed arrest; forty-five people were involved in the 'Häussler case' in court, and many of them did not live to see the end of those hard days, but the Nazis never really succeeded in destroying their solidarity.

On 13 June 1938 Willi Häussler was sentenced to seven years' imprisonment. One year of the time he had been held pending investigations was to be deducted. He was imprisoned first in Hamburg-Fuhlsbüttel, and later at Bremen-Oslebshausen.

He served his sentence, but he was not released. Instead, he was sent back to Fuhlsbüttel in 'protective custody'. From there he was transferred to the camp for foreigners at Hamburg-Wilhelmsburg.

Frau Häussler writes:

I was able to see my husband only very seldom. While he was in prison, only every four months. A permit was necessary for each visit. Then I could talk to him for five minutes. In Fuhlsbüttel and in the camp at Wilhelmsburg I was however allowed to bring him clean clothes. Two weeks before his death I saw him for the last time. On recent visits I had secretly provided him with money, some ration coupons, and identity papers which somebody had procured for me. Among the prisoners too it was no secret that the war was nearly over and, should he hear any word of his 'liquidation', my husband intended to escape.

The death certificate, which was sent to me, read: 'Killed by enemy action at Wilhelmsburg Camp on 22 March 1945'. The body was, however, not released for burial, in spite of my application.

HEINRICH JASPER

21 August 1875—19 February 1945

On 19 February 1945 Dr Heinrich Jasper was found dead in
the grounds of Bergen-Belsen concentration camp by one of
his fellow prisoners. At nine o'clock the next morning his
body was thrown on a funeral pyre to be burnt. The day
before, he had been whipped by the notorious Commandant
Kramer. A few months later, in Brunswick, there were many
people who, for all the differences of opinion they had had
with him in the past, were saying: 'If only Heinrich Jasper
were here!'

Who then was this man whose powers of leadership were
so clearly recognised?

He was born on 21 August 1875 at Dingelbe, not far from
Brunswick, and was the son of well-to-do parents; he was a
Doctor of Law at the age of twenty-five, practised as a solicitor
and, three years later, became a Social Democrat member of
the municipal council; after the last elections before the first
world war (still under the *Dreiklassenwahlrecht*), he became
a member of the *Landtag* of the Duchy of Brunswick.

True to his political convictions, Dr Jasper served as a
private throughout the 1914-18 war. In 1918 the government
of the Duchy of Brunswick, faced with administrative chaos,
asked him to return, and in 1919 he was elected President of
the *Landtag* by unanimous vote. He was also a member of
the National Assembly at Weimar. From the end of the war
until 1921 and again from 1922-24 and from 1927-30, he led
the Brunswick State Government.

In a speech dedicated to the memory of Heinrich Jasper,
Prof. Dr von Frankenberg said of him:

> His unselfishness knew no bounds. Whoever knew him well
> knows how strict he was with himself, how unyielding was his
> sense of duty, how modest his way of life, almost to the point
> of absurdity. The simplicity of his clothing was proverbial, and
> he even refused to use a car and went about his official
> business by tram and train; for all that, he gave generously
> and freely if ever he saw a friend in need, and no-one will ever
> know how many people he helped in private. . . .

The election of 5 September 1930 brought to Brunswick a tragic distinction, for it became the second German *Land* to have a National Socialist Minister in its government: and with the coming of Dietrich Klagges, all hell was let loose. The so-called *Machtübernahme* (assumption of power) when the Nazis came in, was, for Heinrich Jasper and for hundreds of people who thought and felt as he did, the beginning of fearful suffering and sorrow.

Dr Jasper was arrested in the street and taken to the *Volksfreund* building and there, like so many others, terribly maltreated. At first nobody knew where he was, and Klagges refused to answer questions: in fact, Jasper had been so horribly beaten up that his face was hardly recognisable; in the evening he had collapsed, and the next day slowly regained consciousness and heard the clocks strike twelve. For all that time he had lain in the dirt in his own blood.

At pistol point, he was forced to clear up the mess. He was then taken to another room and asked whether he knew how to use firearms:

'Yes, of course.'

'Well then, we don't want to find you alive when we come back, otherwise we'll see to it ourselves.' Jasper quite calmly replied: 'You can wait as long as you like, but that is a favour which I shall not grant you.'

That afternoon he was handed over to the county prison near the Rennelberg; but a few weeks later he was suddenly released. His political friends then begged him to emigrate at once, but this was something he would not do. Soon afterwards he was arrested for the second time.

After two years of solitary confinement, Jasper was taken to Dachau, and later to Oranienburg. He was kept there for nearly five years and meanwhile Klagges managed to keep at bay all attempts to have him released.

But finally, in 1939, he was released. He was not allowed to resume his practice as a solicitor, and the Gestapo had taken over the library which he had collected with so much care and love, and only a few law books were left. But Heinrich Jasper's mind did not rest, and one could see him in those days in the Brunswick State Library, bending low over old records and documents, passionately absorbed in some scholarly work.

When the end was in sight, in 1943 and 1944, many people saw in Heinrich Jasper one of their hopes for the reconstruction of Germany. But this did not escape the men in power, who saw to it that he too was swept away in the great wave of arrests that followed 20 July 1944.

On 22 August, the day after his birthday, Jasper was hauled from his bed and taken to Camp 21, near Hallendorf; and from there he trod his weary way back to Oranienburg, and finally on 4 February 1945 on to Bergen-Belsen. A fortnight later the flames of the funeral pyre completed the story.

HANS SCHIFTAN

8 December 1899—3 November 1941

Office of the
Secret State Police
-IV C2- H.- Nr.Sch.9788-

Berlin SW 11
Prinz Albrecht Strasse 8
22 May 1941

Order of Protective Custody

Surname, Christian name: Schiftan, Hans
Date and Place of Birth: 8 December 1899, Schöneberg
Profession: Clerk
Marital Status: Married
Citizenship: German
Religious Denomination: None
Race: (to be mentioned in cases of Non-Aryans)
Place of Residence: Berlin Neukölln, Zietenstrasse 27
is taken into protective custory.
Reasons:
Information obtained by the State Police reveals that his con-
duct is such as to constitute a danger to the nation and to

public security, because his political record leads to the belief that he would, after serving a two-year sentence for plotting high treason, again take part in activities of a Marxist character.

Signed: HEYDRICH   *Witnessed:* ROTTAN

HANS SCHIFTAN married at the age of 26, while he was working in a radio business, for thanks to hard work and his own ability he had already achieved independence and a middle-class standard of living. His youngest daughter has described his fate:

> We had a happy family life, gay and carefree. There were for instance expeditions in paddle-boats with a huge and ancient tent, the beginning, for us three children, of long weeks of delight. . . .
>
> But all this stopped with a bang when my father was arrested. I was only ten years old at the time, and for me it was all rather incomprehensible, meaningless and painful. But gradually I began to fit the pieces together and to understand things which, at that age and at that time, I should never normally have taken in.
>
> My father was a member of the German Social Democratic Party. His personal ties to the party were strong, and he was above all aware of his responsibilities and obligations to his friends. After 1933 he kept in touch with party friends who had emigrated to Czechoslovakia; there were secret visits which I was not to mention to anybody, and he was in fact the key-man of an underground group on this side of the frontier.
>
> When Hitler marched into Czechoslovakia in 1939, most of my father's friends were arrested, and his own arrest followed on 13 April 1939. In the legal proceedings that followed he was sentenced to two years' imprisonment for plotting high treason. During those years, and indeed in the years to come, my mother (although suffering from a disease of the kidneys), looked after us with incredible energy, courage and love. Then, on 20 April 1941, a telegram came: 'Arriving 8.37 p.m. at Lehrter Station—Father'.
>
> For this last meeting with my father I have to thank a technical blunder on the part of the Gestapo. Having completed his sentence, my father was sent home. The order for 'protective custody' by which he was to have been transferred to a concentration camp, as soon as his term of imprisonment was over, had arrived too late, probably because of the birthday celebrations for the *Führer* which took place that day; and my father was already on his way home. He was with us from

Sunday night until Tuesday morning. On Monday he took me to school, because I found it so hard to go at all now that he was home at last. On Tuesday my mother could no longer stay away from work, so my father and I were alone together until he went to report to police headquarters in the Alexanderplatz, as he had been told to do. He did not want to go, although he had no premonition of what was in store for him. He would not allow me to wave good-bye from the window, because he was afraid I might fall out in my excitement. So I watched him secretly until he disappeared round the corner. At Police Headquarters he was immediately arrested again. That was on 22 April 1941.

A month later Hans Schiftan was sent to the Mauthausen Concentration Camp. On 10 November 1941 his family received a notice from the camp authorities saying that he had died from septicaemia on 3 November 1941 in the 'local hospital'.

JOHANNA KIRCHNER

24 April 1889—9 June 1944

JOHANNA KIRCHNER'S life had been ruled by her readiness to help other people and to stand up for her ideals. Her daughter tells her story:

She was born on 24 April 1889, and came from an old Social Democrat family in Frankfurt-am-Main. From the age of 14 she belonged to the Socialist Labour Youth Organisation; and so from her youth she was bound to the Social Democrat movement, by tradition and experience, and these ties grew all the stronger when she married Karl Kirchner, a Social Democrat expert on local government who was much respected in Frankfurt. My mother worked at his side as press officer at party and trade union congresses, in party headquarters and, with particular devotion, for the 'Labour Welfare Organisation'. She organised a mutual-aid plan under which Frankfurt families looked after the children of workers who were locked out during the Ruhr strike, and she was deeply involved in the scheme for sending German children to Switzerland during the inflation.

When the Nazis came to power in 1933 my mother continued with undaunted energy to work for her ideals. She was never tired of helping people who were arrested, and continually devised new ways and means of escape. At one point in her efforts to secure the release of Carlo Mierendorff from Gestapo hands, she had to go to Geneva. Then it became clear that she herself could no longer stay in Frankfurt, and she decided to emigrate to avoid arrest.

Until January 1935, she lived in the Saar, where she took part in the preparations for the plebiscite, but she then had to take flight again. She wanted to stay as near as possible to her beloved Germany, and therefore settled in Forbach, in France, where she stayed until the war broke out, in very close touch with the German resistance movement and its struggle against Hitler. She helped in relief work among German emigrants and German volunteers in the Spanish Civil War, and in work for the 'underground' in Germany. 'Die Hanna', as she was called, became a symbol of refuge.

After the outbreak of war she was arrested by the French Government and interned in a French camp. Members of the French resistance eventually succeeded in freeing her from

the camp at Gurs, but freedom did not last long, for after the occupation of France the Vichy régime complied with a demand from the Hitler government for her extradition. In this she shared the fate of Rudolf Hilferding, a former German Minister of Finance, and of Rudolf Breitscheid, a former member of the *Reichstag*, who had always worked for Franco-German understanding, and of many others who held the same convictions.

On 9 June 1942, the ordeal began which led her through the inferno of Gestapo interrogations, and in May 1943 the People's Court sentenced her to ten years' imprisonment. But at Cottbus prison, where she spent one year of her sentence, she partly recovered from her experiences with the Gestapo, thanks to the care and friendship of her fellow prisoners, and in spite of her imprisonment, regained hope and happiness.

Early in 1944, the proceedings against Johanna Kirchner were re-opened and on 20 April 1944, the Court, with the notorious Freisler as Presiding Judge, sentenced her to death after a 30 minutes' session.

She received her sentence calmly and with courage, and spent her last days quietly, confident that the rule of terror would soon end. Her last letter was strong and brave:

'We have to part now. My love and my blessings will always be with you and I shall set out on my last journey without fear or despair. My last wish is that you too will be brave and undismayed. Don't let yourself be overcome by grief, remember the words of Goethe: "Stirb und werde".

'Always hold together in love and friendship; it is a great comfort to me to know that you are united. Thank you for all you have done for me, I know that circumstances were stronger than your love. Please, please do not mourn and weep for me . . . Your love and braveness are my great consolation in my last hours.

'May peace soon unite you in happines . . . be happy and be brave, the future will be better . . .'

Pastor Buchholz who saw my mother shortly before her death, wrote that she had met her cruel fate with rare self-control and calm, and had kept her dignity and her composure until the very end, setting an example to us all and revealing to the full the strength and maturity of her personality and the greatness of her soul.

Johanna Kirchner was executed at Berlin—Plötzensee Prison on 9 June 1944.

WILHELM LEUSCHNER

15 June 1888—29 September 1944

WILHELM LEUSCHNER grew up at Bayreuth and became an engraver. At the age 17 he went to Darmstadt, where he soon proved himself in the trade union movement. He was a

Photograph taken in the People's Court

member of the Municipal Council of Darmstadt for many years and of the *Landtag* of Hessen. He became Minister of the Interior for Hessen in 1929 and Deputy Chairman of the German Trade Unions Association in 1932.

'The National Socialists will use slander, insult and accusation in their election campaign, but never serious discussion. We demand of our leaders and national representatives greater truthfulness, better morals, and higher intelligence than do the Nazis or the Communists.

'Our fight is directed just as much against Communists as against National Socialists, because if they did not split the vote, National Socialism could not play the part it is now playing in Germany. We want to reunite all the workers in one party. Thus we fight against Fascism and against Communism; and for a strong parliament in the *Land* of Hesse, and a strong social democracy.'

These were the final words of Wilhelm Leuschner's speech before the *Landtag* elections in Hesse on 30 May 1932.

A year later he found himself in the hands of the SA, after the National Socialists arrested him in the trade union headquarters in the course of their occupation of trade union centres. Before they left the headquarters, Robert Ley, under cover of an SA Order, questioned every one of those arrested and gave orders as to what should be done with them. Bruno Gleitze, who was arrested with Leuschner and detained in the cellar of the Anti-War Museum in the Parochialstrasse in Berlin, described how Leuschner was subjected for several days and nights to the brutalities of the SA, and was then transferred to a cell in the block next to the executioner's building at Plötzensee Prison. Quite surprisingly, he was released again and forced to go with Robert Ley to Geneva to attend the International Labour Conference, thus giving some credence to the claim of the German 'Workers' Front' to a seat at the conference.

Leuschner did not speak in the Assembly. The General Secretary of the International Confederation of Trade Unions, I. H. Oldenbroek, and the Secretary of the European Regional Organisation, W. Schevenels, still remember how deeply the delegates were impressed by this 'brave silence', and needless to say, in the discussions which followed the meetings, he left no doubt that he had never changed his views.

On his return to Germany, Leuschner knew that the Gestapo would be waiting for him at the frontier; and two years in concentration camps were the punishment for the opinions he had expressed in Geneva.

After his release Leuschner succeeded in taking over the management of a factory in Berlin. Here he employed almost exclusively political friends from the trade union movement; and he used the opportunities offered by extensive business trips to make contact with old friends and other opponents of the régime, and to prepare a network of resistance groups to cover the whole of Germany.

On 20 August 1939 he wrote to a friend abroad: 'I am afraid there will be war this autumn and that it will last for years. France and Britain have only recently begun to prepare themselves for it. Tell our friends there, particularly Walter Citrine (then General Secretary of the British Trades Union Council), that we still think as we did before. But we are quite unable to prevent this disaster: we are the inmates of a huge prison. To rebel would be suicide, just as surely as it is suicide for prisoners to revolt against their heavily armed guards.'

During the war Leuschner concentrated on preparations for the tasks of 'the day after', and in this he worked with all the trade union groups and with representatives of the different political views of the past. He co-operated with Beck in the plan to overthrow the government before the catastrophe had reached its height, and helped Goerdeler in preparations for an interim government which would follow the overthrow of Hitler, and in which he himself was to become Vice-Chancellor.

Professor Dr Ludwig Bergsträsser has described meetings with Leuschner at the time:

'When I visited him in Berlin I was surprised at how well informed he was, and equally surprised to note the intelligence, calmness and objectivity with which he followed developments and drew his conclusions. During the war he saw clearly how far the situation had worsened, and he knew that the war would mean the end of Hitler's dictatorship and that this end ought to come soon to avoid unspeakable suffering.

'In these reflections he rose above the level of narrow party opinion—if he had not done so long before. Indeed he felt strongly the need to do so, just as he felt the need to unite

105

all the workers so that the situation in which there were too many trade unions, with too many divergent aims, would not arise once more after the collapse of the Hitler Government.

'Although he himself had found his place and career in the Social Democrat Party, he was convinced that now the disaster of dictatorship had fallen on Germany, all men of goodwill who would fight for freedom, honesty and justice must work together.'

Until the very end Leuschner worked with friends who shared his views to solve the detailed problems of a new order in society which could be created neither 'by the recipes of a bygone age nor by reviving democracy as it had been after 1918'.

He was particularly concerned with German youth. Just before 20 July, when the organisation of a future Labour Youth Organisation was being discussed, Leuschner insisted that the educational standard should be improved, that vocational training should be extended and that the main task should be to 'educate German youth to be first-class human beings'.

It was certainly not by chance that one of the people who worked in Leuschner's factory in Berlin was Hermann Maass, who had come from the youth movement and had been secretary of the Association of German Youth Movements until 1933. He too had to pay the final penalty, and so did another close friend of Leuschner's, Ludwig Schwamb, a former Councillor of State and an untiring and devoted negotiator.

Wilhelm Leuschner was a man with a strong instinct for the essential, and his great aim was to unite all sympathetic forces for the next step. On his way out to the gallows on 29 September 1944 he made one sign to his friends, a sign that meant: Unity.

BERNHARD LETTERHAUS

10 July 1894—14 November 1944

BERNHARD LETTERHAUS served his industrial apprenticeship in the Rhineland and later attended the Prussian
College for Textile workers. He served in the 1914-18 war and
was awarded the Iron Cross (1st Class). He was severely

Photograph taken in the People's Court

wounded towards the end of the war and recovered very slowly; he made use of this time to continue his education.

During the 1914-18 war, Bernhard Letterhaus decided to devote himself to the Catholic Labour Organisation. In a letter dated 4 August 1940 he writes about this decision:

'Profession and calling are interrelated concepts. I was called to what I have done in the past and I shall be called to what I have to do in the future. By whom? Christians know their answer: by God. In the last war my heart heard His voice and I followed it, and therefore I have no right to be cast down if my way leads me through shadows. I should lose the struggle only if I did not follow His voice.'

Letterhaus worked for the Association of Christian Textile Workers from 1921 to 1927 and later found in the Catholic Workers' Associations a field of activity which strongly appealed to him. As secretary of the Council of West German Workers' Associations he had scope not only for administration, but for educational work. He was much admired as a teacher of economics, sociology and statistics. He was a gifted speaker. Heinrich Brüning, a former Reichs Chancellor who had been a close friend of Bernhard Letterhaus for many years, wrote in a letter to Frau Letterhaus on 15 August 1946:

'I know of nobody who had so many positive qualities as your husband; the ability calmly to consider the facts of a case or to decide quickly if necessary; a clear and definite judgment of other people, accompanied by great kindness; a rare political instinct; the patience to wait without being stung into some useless activity; courage in danger and a passion for justice, honesty and order in his beloved country. Against all intrigues and incapable of indulging in them himself, he was also quick to recognise them before they became effective, and knew how to fight them calmly and surely when they first appeared.'

Bernhard Letterhaus was appointed by the Centre Party first to the *Landtag* of the Rhineland and then, in 1928, to the *Landtag* of Prussia, and he soon saw the danger of Hitler. At this time he said:

'Should this demagogue ever succeed in becoming leader of Germany, that would be the beginning of the end, there would certainly be a war as well. We must stem this tide by every means in our power.'

In 1931 as Vice-President of the Catholic Rally in Münster he spoke almost prophetically of the difficulties to come, and after 1933 he and his friends worked incessantly to foster resistance among members of the Catholic Church. Frequent trips abroad enabled him to keep in touch with representatives of the international labour movement. But these journeys did not pass unnoticed by the Gestapo, and the result was endless interrogation.

When Letterhaus was called up for active service in 1939 he used his position in the *Wehrmacht* High Command, where he was a Captain in the Defence Department, to strengthen the resistance forces by giving them information, his views on the situation, and by using his connections for their purposes. Soon he was working with leaders of the resistance movement, and was considered for a post in the new government.

Bernhard Letterhaus was arrested immediately after the plot of 20 July 1944. After that he had no news from his wife and child. He spent the last months of his life helping some of his friends with whom he had fought and suffered. Undismayed and fearless, a deeply convinced Catholic, he was sentenced to death in the People's Court on 13 November 1944. The next day he and two Catholic friends were hanged.

Franz Leuninger, a former General Secretary of the Christian Metal Workers' Union, was also executed shortly before the end of the war. Heinrich Körner, another colleague and the former Secretary of the Christian Trade Unions, was shot in front of Plötzensee Prison on 25 April 1945. With the help of these men, Jacob Kaiser, later to become a Minister in the Federal Republic, had brought about the union with the Social Democratic trade union leaders. Max Habermann of the *Deutschnationaler Handlungsgehilfenverband* was also a member of the group. After 20 July 1944 Max Habermann was hidden by friends, but was discovered and arrested on 30 October 1944. In prison, Habermann committed suicide because he 'did not want to give away those who had given him asylum'.

4 THE STATE AND THE LAW

THE burning of the *Reichstag*, four weeks after the National Socialists came to power, was their first major act of violence. It was represented as a Communist plot, in an attempt to rally the people to the new rulers by producing a common enemy; and it was used as a pretext for the persecution of large numbers of leading citizens. The Chief of the Berlin Fire Brigade was the first of the experts to question the theory of Communist arson. He was retired from his post at short notice and later 'removed' as a troublesome witness. There were many similar cases.

The National Socialists' concern to preserve the legal façade, to transform democracy into dictatorship by ostensibly lawful means, was evident with each move. New laws were made as and when necessary, bogus democratic resolutions were produced, national crises were staged and exploited, always in a manner calculated to show that the law was on the side of the authorities. Thus the 'Enabling Act' was wrested from the *Reichstag* against the background of a wave of terror: the debating chamber was filled and surrounded by SS and SA units and Hitler was prepared to have as many deputies arrested as was necessary to ensure the two-thirds majority. Soon after this the 'Law concerning the Re-instatement of the Professionally-trained Civil Service' was applied to secure the dismissal of all politically tiresome or non-aryan civil servants 'who, in view of their previous political activities, do not appear to be strong supporters of the National Socialist state'. As time went on, politicians who were not Nazis lost all influence and even the 'Enabling Act', though it delegated almost unlimited power to Hitler, was overstepped and, like the Weimar Constitution, sank into oblivion.

There remained the President of Germany, the highest authority, constitutionally elected, who stood between the nation and extreme arbitrary power. But he was old and ill and had retired to his estate in East Prussia. He was cut off from political life and surrounded by devoted servants of the *Führer*. At first, his very existence was an asset to the Third Reich, but he soon ceased to count. By the time he died, in 1934, the mass arrests and the arbitrary shootings had made it plain to everyone that the law had become Hitler's tool and plaything. The abuse of the law continued, and the climax came when members of the armed services and civil servants were ordered to swear the Oath of Allegiance to Hitler: this oath, taking the name of the Lord in vain, put them in the position where they were technically breaking the law each time they opposed Hitler or his policies, and was as wicked as it was unconstitutional. The figure of the raging Freisler, the Nazi judge who finally presided over the highest court in Germany, became the incarnation of the lawless state.

Many people, either voluntarily or under duress, accepted the new order. But there were others who did not, who deplored the growing confusion between tyranny and justice and for whom conscience, and not the law, became the determining factor. Most of them did not find it easy to take the law into their own hands, but they died in the conviction that Hitler, by subjecting the law to the state, had shaken to its foundations the common life of the people.

WALTER GEMPP

13 September 1878—2 May 1939

AFTER his matriculation Walter Gempp studied mechanical and electrical engineering at the *Technische Hochschule* in Karlsruhe (Baden) and also had some practical engineering experience. He obtained his diploma and then worked for three years as a designer with Siemens-Schuckert in Berlin. In 1906 he was entrusted with the expansion of the Berlin Fire Brigade and was in particular concerned with the experimental branch of the mobile detachment. The first motorised unit was put into service in 1908, in the station in the Schönlanker Strasse, and by 1914 there were eleven more motorised fire brigade units of the same type. Gempp was later promoted to Technical Director and in 1923 was appointed Chief of the Berlin Fire Service. In this capacity he further contributed to the expansion and general organisation of the Berlin Fire Brigade and to the spirit of co-operation within its ranks.

With the burning of the *Reichstag* on 27 February 1933, Gempp, who had a high reputation both in Germany and abroad and was respected as an excellent engineer and a loyal civil servant, was confronted with a situation which was to prove decisive for his life and work. For well over a quarter of a century he had been working to perfect the instrument which on that notable occasion so ably stood the test. But this fire was more than a technical problem. It was a political event. The circumstances of the alarm, the manner of the immediate enquiries and above all the subsequent political persecutions which were launched all over Germany, only a few days before the *Reichstag* elections of 5 March, made this clear. And Gempp was not only a technical expert and an able civil servant, he was also a man of conscience and integrity. All this led him, at a meeting of the fire brigade inspectors and officers, to correct the official reports. He stated that the Fire Brigade had been warned too late and had met Storm Troopers at the scene of the fire; and moreover that the acting Minister of the Interior, Göring, had at first expressly forbidden him either to call in all

112

available help or to make full use of the firemen at his disposal; and finally that enough fire-raising material to fill a lorry had been found in the undamaged rooms of the closely cordoned building; facts which all went to disprove the theory of communist arson. Thus Gempp became a troublesome witness of the terrorist tactics used by the National Socialists, for whom the burning of the *Reichstag* was only a prelude to the suppression and removal of all their political enemies.

Four weeks later, Walter Gempp fell victim to the purge which was carried through under cover of a so-called reform of the civil service. Although Hindenburg, the President of Germany, had repeatedly acknowledged his confidence in him and even Hitler, shortly before the incident, had expressed his particular thanks and warm appreciation for his 'conscientious leadership', Gempp, a member of the Democratic Party, was now accused of 'marxist and communist subversive and inflammatory activities' and of passing over 'national-minded Fire Service officials'.

There was great consternation. The *Vossische Zeitung* wrote on 25 March 1933:

The motives of the State Commissioner in suspending the invaluable Chief of the Berlin Fire Brigade, who has been in the service of the city for 27 years, are not known. What is well known is the fact that Gempp, who is 55, has made the Berlin Fire Brigade the protector of the Berlin people. Thousands of foreigners have studied the Berlin fire system with envy and have recognised and appreciated his work . . .'

Gempp repeated his statements during the *Reichstag* Trial, which lasted from September to December 1933.

But even his final discharge did not satisfy the new dictators, and there followed defamation of the worst kind, cross examinations and arrest. Finally, in September 1937, he was again committed for trial. Carefully planned proceedings accusing him of so-called official malpractice resulted in his conviction, against which, with the support of outside lawyers, he appealed. On 2 May 1939, shortly before the beginning of the new trial, Walter Gempp was found dead in his cell. He had been strangled.

MARTIN GAUGER

4 August 1905—14 July 1941

MARTIN GAUGER, fourth son in the large family of a parson in Wuppertal, was unusually gifted, full of vitality, critical and fully aware of the problems of his day. Even as a student he was moved and worried by the social cleavages in Germany; in his own immediate circle in the *Boberhaus* he tried to do something about the problem by organising the first voluntary labour camps where workers and students (of Professor Rosenstock of Breslau) worked together. From this there developed his friendship with the Kreisau circle, particularly with Helmuth von Moltke and Carl Dietrich von Trotha. It was there that he found the courage to believe in himself and came to the conclusion that every man can fashion his own life and that each must exert his influence in public affairs. He studied political economy and law and also spent some time at the London School of Economics, finally emerging with a Diploma in Political Economy, success in his law finals and the degree of Doctor of Law.

In 1934 he became an assessor in the office of the public prosecutor in München-Gladbach. With his gifts, his education, his humour and his ability to get on well with people, his future looked promising. But he saw clearly what was going on around him. He witnessed the unjust removal of his father from his post (as an editor) and the imprisonment which followed, and he suffered under the increasing lawlessness of the Nazi dictatorship. The official explanation given by the Minister of Justice after the murders on 30 June 1934 deeply horrified him, and he thereupon refused to submit to the demand that all officials should swear an Oath of Allegiance to Hitler. As a lawyer he realised the full implications of the oath, and his conscience forbade him to take it.

For this reason he left the civil service. Sometime later he became legal adviser with the provisional administration of the German Protestant Church and then with the Lutheran Council in Berlin. Here, guided by Christian ethics, he learnt where his task lay; and with no thought for his own life did what was humanly possible to help members of the clergy in their struggle with the authorities. His greatest joy was the release of seven pastors from Lübeck from a concentration camp, which was largely his own doing.

In his opposition to the Nazi régime he was above all concerned to protect the Church and to enable it to survive the Third Reich. He devoted his energy to this arduous task, although he fully realised that 'we are regarded by the authorities as enemies of the state. That leaves us undismayed, because we have a clear conscience and good grounds for believing that it is we who are in fact the patriots.'

Martin Gauger wrote these words in a letter in 1938. In the same year he turned down the offer of a professorship at the Christian College of Madras, India, explaining: 'So long as it is possible for me to work at all, I cannot run away from my post here.'

As well as numerous articles in the Protestant weekly, *Licht und Leben*, and in the Gotthard-letters, he wrote in the years before the war *Notes on the Rights of the Protestant Press in Germany* and the pamphlets, *Confession and Church Policy* (Wuppertal, 1936). Both books were immediately confiscated by the Gestapo. When the war began, Gauger was offered a job with the Red Cross in Geneva. But, true to his own work, he again refused. Then in April 1940 he was called up. At this time he wrote:

'For a time I thought I could bear this war if I did not have to serve as a soldier myself, but that is taking a very false and narrow view, and a view that is essentially cowardly. I now believe that one should not serve in the war at all, certainly not in this war, because it is not a defensive war . . . for a time I thought the answer was a job on the supply side, when at least I would not have to serve at the front. But then I asked myself: Why? Is there any difference between actually fighting and equipping and supplying those who are fighting? No. There's no difference at all. And I cannot and will not support this war or help to spread this sea of blood and tears to other countries.

This was his answer when friends tried to give him a way out by offering him an administrative job. He still felt unable to take the Oath of Allegiance to Hitler, but his refusal endangered his work, his family and himself.

Gauger finally decided to flee to Holland and early in May
1940 he swam across the icy waters of the Rhine. But soon
after he crossed the frontier into neutral territory, Hitler's
SS troops marched in. Gauger was seriously wounded and
then captured, and after passing through several prisons
ended up in the civil jail in Düsseldorf. There he spent one
year, while his case was investigated by the Gestapo. In

June 1941 he was transferred to Buchenwald concentration camp. One night when he and ninety other prisoners were taken away under special security precautions, he knew that his end had come.

HANS von DOHNANYI

1 January 1902—8 April 1945

'INSTIGATOR and guiding spirit of the movement to eliminate the *Führer*': thus the Gestapo described Dohnanyi after the investigation into the events of 20 July 1944 had revealed the part he had played for many years in the plans to overthrow the Hitler régime.

After his arrest the Gestapo took special precautions, of which there is evidence in the memoirs of Harald Poelchau:

'It must have been in July or August 1944. I had taken over temporary duties at the Military Prison Hospital at Buch, and enquired which of the prisoners had registered for visits by the Chaplain of the garrison. A number of names were mentioned and then, with slight hesitation, they said:
"A Colonel Z has also registered."
"Colonel Z? Who is that?"
"We don't know either."
'When I was alone with Colonel Z and introduced myself, he said: "I know about you, I am Dohnanyi."
'Physically, he was suffering, but he was quite composed, a man of strength and personality for whom I could do very little.'

Dohnanyi was born on 1 January 1902 in Vienna and grew up in close contact with the Bonhoeffer, Delbrück and Harnack families. After he had taken his law examinations in 1929 he obtained a post in the Reich Ministry of Justice, worked in the Departments of International, Constitutional and Administrative Law, which also dealt with questions of High Treason, and was later private secretary to several Ministers of Justice. This position gave him an early insight into the true character of National Socialism. Already under Brüning, whom he had got to know while attending cabinet meetings as a young legal adviser, he argued that the nationalist radicals should be strictly forbidden to wear uniform.

After the *Reichstag* fire Dohnanyi tried to organise a public inquiry by the German judges into the growing rule of terror. But his appeal to the President of the Supreme Court of the Reich met with no success. In discussions with Reich Minister of Justice, Gürtner, in particular on the occasion of the *Reichstag* fire, Dohnanyi left no doubt as to his views. In spite of this he became head of the Minister's private office and thus saw even more of the working of the government machinery, and made many important contacts. He constantly used his connections with people in public life to work for the protection of the persecuted, but he realised after many useless onslaughts at the highest level, the futility of all legal protests against the system of concentration camps. And so he decided on active resistance.

As early as 1933, Dohnanyi began to keep a secret record of crimes committed by the Nazi régime and of those who were responsible for them. The material for this record, which was to be used and published when the day of reckoning with Hitler's dictatorship arrived, came from the secret files of the Ministry of Justice.

Soon Dohnanyi became the pivot of various civilian resistance groups. By reason of his position in Gürtner's office he was always well informed on what went on in government circles, and he came into close touch with Popitz and Goerdeler. The unwavering courage with which he faced the powerful party leaders also enabled him for five years to scotch the constant intrigues of Freisler, at that time Permanent Secretary in the Ministry of Justice, even though he was not a member of the *Rechtswahrerbund* ('The Association of the Guardians of Justice', a Nazi organisation for members of the legal profession). During the trial of General Fritsch, Dohnanyi got to know Beck and Oster, who held a key position under Canaris in the Military Intelligence Service. This friendship was of vital importance in all subsequent planning.

Dohnanyi's position, in view of the fact that he was not a National Socialist, was soon 'not acceptable', and Gürtner, under pressure from Freisler and Bormann was finally forced to post him as *Reichsgerichtsrat* to the Supreme Court at Leipzig. But Dohnanyi managed to continue weaving his web, even after a plot against Hitler had failed in 1938, because his duties frequently took him to Berlin. When war broke out Beck saw to it that Dohnanyi went to Canaris' staff in Military Intelligence, and there he worked in Oster's

department as head of the Office of Political Affairs. The plan to end the war during the winter of 1939-40 was largely the result of his illegal work in the Military Intelligence Service; as intermediary between Beck and Leuschner he helped to synchronise resistance activities, and no less important were the negotiations with the Vatican which he opened through Josef Müller. Their result—a clear offer of peace—was submitted to the leading generals, before the victorious French campaign wrecked the project. But Dohnanyi continued his effort. In March 1943 he flew to the headquarters of the Middle Army Group on the eastern front to co-ordinate the plans for Hitler's assassination worked out by Tresckow and Schlabrendorff with the political preparations in Berlin; but this plan also went awry when the bomb in Hitler's plane failed to explode.

On 5 April 1943 Dohnanyi, Josef Müller and Dietrich Bonhoeffer were arrested, quite unexpectedly. One of their agents had indulged in irregular currency transactions and so drawn attention to Oster's staff; and this at last gave Himmler's Security Service the pretext to intervene in the affairs of the otherwise independent Military Intelligence Service. Persistent questioning, to which Dohnanyi was then subjected, completely failed to produce any conclusive evidence of the suspected resistance activities in the Military Intelligence Service; but one of the main centres of the conspirators had been destroyed.

After 20 July 1944 Dohnanyi's past rôle could no longer be disguised, but with all his legal experience he was able to put up a steadfast and skilful defence which defeated all attempts of the Gestapo to prove his guilt, although they left no stone unturned. There were therefore no legal proceedings, and no conviction.

Dohnanyi is believed to have died on 8 April 1945 in Sachsenhausen concentration camp, but no-one knows exactly what happened.

MARIA TERWIEL

7 June 1910—5 August 1943

MARIA TERWIEL was the daughter of a senior civil servant and was born at Boppard. She passed her matriculation in 1929 and, as was her great wish, studied law.

Her mother was of Jewish descent and consequently the Nuremberg Laws of 1935, against the Jews, made it impossible for Maria to take a university examination, and she finally had to abandon her law studies. Her father, a Social

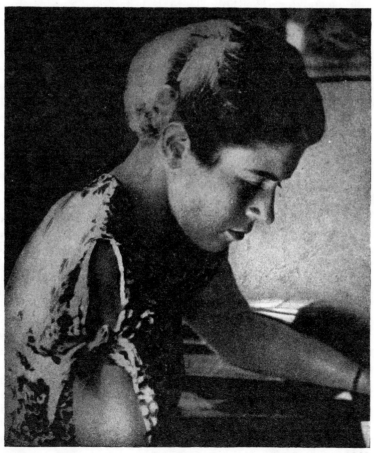

123

Democrat and a Roman Catholic, was dismissed from his office at Stettin in 1933 and took his family to Berlin. There Maria found work as a secretary in a Swiss textile factory.

When war broke out she shrewdly managed to obtain permission for a French director of the firm, then treated as a prisoner of war, to carry out his compulsory labour with his own old firm.

Later, when the opportunity came her way, she made contact with Captain Schulze-Boysen's group and used it to distribute copies of Bishop von Galen's sermons and to provide Jews in danger of persecution with passports.

She was sentenced to death by the *Reichskriegsgericht* in January 1943, together with her fiancé, Helmut Himpel. The sentence was carried out on 5 August 1943. Maria Terwiel died a convinced Catholic. Her father had died a year before, and her mother and brother were killed in an air-raid on 17 December 1943.

Maria Terwiel, the girl whose wish to follow the legal profession had been denied her, worked up to the end as the secret advocate of those who had been outlawed by the Nazis. A Polish girl, of whom we know only that she was sent from Moabit to the Leipzig prison for women, talked of her in a letter, which found its way to Maria Terwiel's family.

Berlin-Moabit, 15 September, 1943

'. . . Meeting her for the first time, one could not guess the depth of feeling which lay behind her clear and honest features. Only her eyes spoke for themselves.

'She had been alone in the cell until I joined her there. At first we were all very closely guarded and watched. There was always an SS-man outside in the corridor, who looked through the spy-hole every other minute, and the lights were on all night. All this was intended to frustrate any attempt to commit suicide. Maria could not sleep, her bed was full of vermin, she kept pacing up and down the cell. During the daytime she did piano exercises on a piece of wood and stood at the window for hours whistling all kinds of tunes. One day I was pushed into her cell by a female guard, and she at once took me under her protection.

'At that time I was a newcomer to the prison, straight from Warsaw. I was separated from my Polish friends for the first time, afraid, and very near to tears. But with Maria a stiff upper lip was the order of the day.

'At first she did not think that a death sentence was in store

124

for her. Only with time and experience—no more news, except of new death sentences; after a retrospective law came out and all the other girls, Cato Bantjes van Beek, Eva Buch and the rest, were given death sentences—only then did we understand that there was also no hope for us.

'Then Maria became very restless, she worried about Helmut . . . Before the Gestapo she tried to take all blame on herself. Of course Helmut did the same thing!

'We were both hungry and cold and shared the narrow bed. During those endless winter evenings Maria whistled her most beautiful melodies for me and I had to tell her Polish fairy tales. Of course I could do that only very slowly and haltingly because I knew so little German. Later, in January, came the days when Maria went into Court, while her case was heard. Outwardly she was completely calm and showed much courage and composure. When the police brought her back to the prison after she had received her death sentence I thought at first all had gone well—at the door of the cell she was still talking to the guards with a smile. I could hardly believe it when she told me that she and Helmut . . .

'After the death sentence we stayed together for two more weeks, then I was sent to Moabit and Maria shared a cell with another Polish girl with the same name as mine, Christina Katowiz. The other Christina and Maria got on very well too and Maria saved her life because she told Christina again and again that she should admit nothing. That she did, and instead of being brought up before the Court, with the certainty of a death sentence, she was sent to a camp. Not only I and the other Christina, but also many other Polish girls will never forget Maria. She was always willing to help and she wrote the petitions for pardon for many of us, first of course for me. She often said: "It is a pity that I could not defend you in court. You know I could have done very well!" When I saw her again in Moabit, in the rest hour, my heart leapt for joy. We tried at once to get together again but it could not be arranged. The Court had ruled that Maria was to be kept in solitary confinement and on top of that I, being a Pole, was not allowed to share a room with her.

'Here at Moabit her health began to fail and she really needed a nurse. At first she had a rash on her back and could not endure wearing the prison clothing. We made a little slip for her from my pillow case, which was much softer and more comfortable. Later she often could not digest the soup we had for lunch, after a few spoonfuls she had pains and was sick. But the worst thing was her finger. She suffered so much that

125

she could not sleep at night and kept walking up and down her cell. I don't know how she managed to dress and undress, wash and comb her hair. She could only write with her left hand in quaint clumsy little letters. She said that by her finger she had atoned for her sins of next year, and tried bravely to smile when we met in our free time. I would have given so much to be able to help her. Months spent together in prison bind people together more closely than long years of freedom . . .

'I have seen so many splendid people die that I wondered after Helmut's and Maria's death, whether there were any left.

'With all my kindest regards,

Yours,
CHRISTINE.'

['I have absolutely no fear of death and certainly none of heavenly justice; that at least we don't have to fear.

'Stay true to your principles and always stick together.

Your sister MARIA.

From the last will of Maria Terwiel, dated 29 January, 1943.]

ERNST von HARNACK

15 July 1888—3 March 1945

ERNST VON HARNACK was the son of Adolf von Harnack, a religious historian. He grew up in Berlin, studied in Marburg and Berlin and fought in the 1914-18 war.

After passing his law examinations, he worked in the Prussian Ministry of Education, in the *Land* administration in Hersfeld, as Vice-President of the administrative Council of Hanover and Cologne, and as President of the Council in Merseburg. From 1919 onwards he was a member of the Social Democratic Party. The steps taken by von Papen against Prussia led to von Harnack's temporary retirement, and Hitler's re-organisation of the civil service in 1933 brought about his final discharge. Finally his efforts to instigate enquiries into the murder of Stelling, after a night of slaughter in Köpenick, landed him in prison for a few weeks, for the first time but not for the last.

Fundamentally, Ernst von Harnack was a man of a gay, frank and optimistic temperament, full of vitality and remarkably gifted; the trait which his sister Elisabeth particularly mentions was his strong sense of justice, which inevitably led him to side with the oppressed and underprivileged. Oblivious to public opinion or personal safety, he was guided in all the important decisions of his life by his Protestant faith, and answerable only to God and to his own conscience.

The Prussian administration had become part of his life, and when he was forced into premature retirement he felt the urge to write of his experiences in the profession he loved. In his book *The Practice of Public Administration* (1936) he brought to light in his own inimitable style the inner workings of the administrative machine, so much so that the book was banned immediately on publication.

Although a civil servant by inclination and truly devoted to his work, Harnack had about him little of the typical government official. He was too much of an individualist for that, and because of his artistic interests and talents, which he indulged and developed all his life, he was at home in

127

many other settings. There was in particular his love of music. As a schoolboy he founded an orchestra, he played the flute very well indeed and was well versed in the history of music, as in the history of literature and art. He had learned bookbinding, his drawing was a delight, and his skill in other arts and crafts were a source of much pleasure to his children and his friends.

Von Harnack was by nature gregarious, in fact social life in all its manifestations, small talk, anecdote, conversation and argument, was for him an almost passionate necessity. His natural sympathy gave him an intense interest in the personal fate of his friends and acquaintances, and indeed in their practical problems and decisions; and of course in current political and religious questions. But politics were his burning interest, and the conversations which really attracted him were those whereby he might clarify his own mind about motives, aims, relationships and behaviour; and this whether he was concerned, often at the risk of his life, in helping the persecuted and the pursued, or in saving their possessions, or whether he was engaged in resisting the 'government without goodness or grace', as he called the Hitler régime. This he did both openly and in secret, but often, as both his sons were at the front, with a heavy heart.

Hendrik de Man's daughter tells of a visit which she and her husband paid to Harnack in the winter of 1941-42, and of his efforts to establish contacts abroad:

'We met in a big room on the first floor. Its tall windows looked on to an inner courtyard which lay silent and mysterious in the half-light of a November afternoon. The room looked rather like an artist's studio, and the furniture bore silent witness to the break between the past life of its owner, and the present.

'Ernst von Harnack, aristocrat, former government official, Socialist, had lost his high position through the Hitler régime and was now working as a traveller for a cloth factory, but the war had so seriously restricted the textile market that he was looking for another job. In the second year of the war he found a most unusual one. Under instructions from the Berlin City Council he had to draw up lists of the graves of famous men which were scattered over the cemeteries of the city.

'From the very start it was evident that Ernst von Harnack had no illusions about our attitude to the German political leaders of the time. He spoke quite openly, although with some

caution. The purpose of our visits to his office or to his lovely
house could always be concealed under the pretext of our
common love of music, and his *collegium musicum,* as he called
it, provided excellent cover for his dealings with people "not in
step" with the régime.

'To questions about the dangers of the secret resistance work
he gave a reply worth recording: I asked him if the Gestapo,

with whom we were just beginning to come to grips in Belgium, did not make the whole illegal business very difficult.

'Ernst von Harnack replied with a smile: "Since the German armies occupied most of Europe, they have gone away from here, and we have some peace at last". And it was a fact that the police vice which had gripped Germany so tightly since 1933 was by 1941 much looser. Perhaps the brown-shirted rulers thought that military success would suffice to remove all thought of a plot against them.

'But Ernst von Harnack saw further than the rulers. I remember in particular two of his lines of thought:

'"The most important thing is," he said to me, "that the régime should be destroyed at one fell swoop, rather as one opens a zip-fastener. All preparations must be completed in advance, so that there is no danger of a general demoralisation of the nation. That is the reason why this slow work of undermining is so important. The opposition must spin their web through the whole machinery of the régime, and at the same time try to make contact abroad."

'Ernst von Harnack undertook the important task of informing countries abroad, and particularly Belgium, at that time a political backwater, about the secret forces working to bring about the downfall of the Hitler régime. He therefore wanted without mentioning names of other conspirators, to give Hendrik de Man some idea of the nature of the resistance.

'As soon as we returned to Brussels, in March 1942, I lost no time in giving my father an exact report. He was very interested indeed and impressed upon me the need for secrecy, saying I must tell no-one else about these conversations. It is a strange thing that barely a fortnight later, he heard of similar plans from a former S.P.D. member of the *Reichstag*, Carlo Mierendorff, whom he met in Paris.'

Two years later things began to move. Von Harnack had been away from Berlin on business and returned just after 20 July 1944. Although he must have known of his peril, and although relations and friends tried to persuade him to hide in some out-of-the-way place, he remained in Berlin and in the next few days tried with the help of the Catholic Church to find the children of his friend Julius Leber, who had been arrested in accordance with the Nazi practice of punishing not only the man, but his family as well.

On 1 February 1945 the People's Court sentenced von Harnack to death, and the sentence was carried out on

3 March. In the weeks before his death, he remarked to another political prisoner: 'The most important thing is not to achieve one's end, but to find the right means for the attempt'.

A silhouette torn from black-out paper with the point of a nail—one of von Harnack's occupations between his trial and his death.

FRITZ ELSAS

11 July 1890—4 January 1945

FRITZ ELSAS, the son of a factory owner, was born at Cannstatt in Württemberg. After his matriculation he studied law, and soon made a name for himself by his untiring work in public administration.

Conspiracy was alien to his character, for he was a man who dealt in sober and concrete terms. Not that he lacked political enthusiasm, and family tradition alone had brought him in contact with the democratic circles in Swabia (where he grew up) at an early stage in his life; but he had no political ambition, and was more concerned to see order resulting from good administration and the inviolability of justice in the state. His boyhood dreams had been academic, and he never abandoned them. He was first legal adviser to the City of Stuttgart, became President of the *Deutscher Städtetag* (Association of Municipal Councils) in 1926, at the early age of 36, and then Mayor of Berlin in 1931, but in addition to his official tasks he still continued important research work on economic and social aspects of municipal policy.

The year 1933 wrecked his career in public life because of his Jewish descent. But five years in the *Städtetag* had won him respect in political circles of both Left and Right, and also much personal friendship and confidence. Many who waited for a turn of the tide in politics always remembered him, and so in the long years of darkness were comforted by the hope that plans and drafts prepared for the future would yet come into their own. He had no illusions about the dangers that threatened his own life. Several months of imprisonment in 1937 (for giving legal advice to emigrants) had been intended to bring him to heel. That had not worked, and there were still independent judges in Berlin . . . but for how long would this be the case? He was arrested for the second time in August 1944. A few months later friends found in his empty house (his family had already been taken away into *Sippenhaft*, preventive custody of family members)—a note among his papers that had escaped

the careless search made by the Gestapo. This note was to
tell his wife to whom she should turn after he had disappeared: the names were Goerdeler, Popitz, Zarden and
Heuss.

Theodor Heuss, who with Eberhard Wildermuth had
formed the nucleus of an intimate circle in Swabia, occasionally tells of his last talks with Fritz Elsas in Berlin. Heuss
himself had moved to the south of Germany in August 1943.
He tells how after a talk with Goerdeler, he asked Elsas,
whom he knew to be a close friend of Goerdeler's, whether

133

Goerdeler might not be persuaded to go about his business rather more quietly. He had then discussed Goerdeler's plans with this man whom he hardly knew, but who was as honest as he was un-political; and finally Elsas had laughed and said: 'Perhaps you are right. But a noiseless motor has not yet been invented and Goerdeler is the motor that drives all who hesitate.' There was nothing more to be said.

After the failure of the plot of 20 July 1944 Karl Goerdeler came to Elsas's house in Patschkauer Weg, Berlin-Dahlem, where he had so often been before. It is hardly likely that his coming was as happy as it used to be, but since he was actually there he found a friendly reception, on 27 July and again on 31 July—anything else would have been quite contrary to Elsas' nature. The community of thought between him and Goerdeler had always spelt danger, and did so all the more at this critical juncture. Frau Elsas said later that they had been 'very careless and on one occasion walked in the garden'. People who are really made for conspiracy would probably take more care. In any case it is assumed that Goerdeler was recognised by someone in the neighbourhood on this occasion. That meant that the fate of Fritz Elsas was also sealed.

His case never went before a court. Apparently all the maltreatment and questioning failed to reveal any substantial evidence against him which could have been used in court, and although he could on occasion lose his temper, it was always in such critical moments well under control. It was apparently impossible to accuse someone of Jewish descent of so noble a sentiment as 'human loyalty'.

He never knew that his whole family was in *Sippenhaft*. Late in October he succeeded in smuggling a letter out of the Gestapo prison in Lehrter Strasse, but friends who entered his deserted house found it in the letter-box. No one knows who had brought it there. He wrote this letter with great effort, left handed, 'but the abscesses on my right hand [probably the result of torture] are healing'. There were questions about this and that, how was the garden getting on and was there enough coal in the house? He wished his family 'strength and health to master everyday life'. And then come the reflections: 'Time will always put new and unknown claims on different men in turn. Hölderlin's letters to Diotima show how man can gain strength in spite of suffering and need. So even suffering in love is a source of strength'. But his words never reached their destination.

Late in December Fritz Elsas was transferred to Sachsen-hausen. Once, he was taken to Berlin for one day to be questioned again. In accordance with 'simplified procedure' he was shot by the SS on 4 January 1945 in the so-called *Industriehof* at Sachsenhausen.

JOSEPH WIRMER

19 March 1901—8 September 1944

DURING his trial before the People's Court, Joseph Wirmer made one remark which is in itself proof of his courage and confidence: 'If I am hanged, Herr President,' he said, 'then you will be the one who is afraid, not I.'

His confidence was unaffected by his gamble with death, and he was absolute master of the situation. In character as in appearance, he was upright and forceful . . . and so the natural enemy of National Socialism. On 1 May 1933 he heard the broadcast of Hitler's speech at the Tempelhofer Feld, among friends who were all too easily carried away; and announced with religious solemnity: 'I shall be Hitler's enemy.' The hour in which this enmity was born was in fact the hour of Hitler's first public appearance after he came to power, and at that moment Wirmer understood the nature of his enemy and knew that he must oppose the anti-Christ, if necessary at the risk of his life. He saw from the start that Hitler threatened the ethics, the Christianity and the culture which were part of his own being, the basis of his life as man, as a father, as a responsible citizen and as a member of the legal profession.

Of Wirmer's sense of justice his brother Otto has written:

'He believed he could best retain his independence in the practice of his profession as a solicitor, although the rigid rules and regulations were an anathema to him and an outrage to his feeling for individual responsibility. For all his legal training and inclination, he regarded laws which took no account of facts or circumstances as so much nonsense; the thesis *autoritas non veritas facit legem'*, he dismissed as Jesus dismissed the tempter in the desert, and he was in the end deeply convinced that law must emerge from the order established by historical evolution, and must itself and by that virtue continually evolve. He thus believed that by defeating the formal law introduced by a dictatorship he was in fact serving on a much higher plane the cause of justice to which he had dedicated his life. The fact that Freisler attacked him with particular venom was a sure sign that the régime regarded him as one of its most dangerous enemies, and therefore as one to be eliminated. Just

Photograph taken in the People's Court

as they had thrown him out of the *Rechtswahrerbund* (a Nazi
organisation for members of the legal profession), years before,
for his fearless defence of victims of racial persecution.'

*   *   *

'My brother Joseph had got to know Karl Goerdeler through
Jakob Kaiser, now a Minister in the Federal Republic. I
remember meeting Goerdeler, frequently, at my brother's office
in Berlin, and in his flat in Lichterfelde I also met Julius Leber.
Joseph also knew Ulrich von Hassell and Klaus Bonhoeffer

137

and spent much of his time with Max Habermann, but above all he worked with Bernhard Letterhaus. He was in touch with resistance in the Services through Claus von Stauffenberg.'

Joseph Wirmer was sentenced to death by the People's Court, under the presidency of Freisler, on 8 September, 1944, as one of the principals in the attempt of 20 July 1944. He was hanged the same day.

BERTHOLD SCHENK GRAF von STAUFFENBERG

15 March 1905—10 August 1944

BERTHOLD SCHENK GRAF VON STAUFFENBERG
studied at the universities of Heidelberg, Jena, Berlin and

Photograph taken in the People's Court

Tübingen, and after taking the degree of Doctor of Law in 1927 worked as an official at the Institute of International Law in Berlin. At the age of 26 he was sent to the Court of International Justice at The Hague, and in 1933 he was recalled to Berlin to take over a department of the Institute of International Law. At the beginning of the war, because of his special knowledge of Maritime Law, the Navy asked for his services. Until 20 July 1944 he worked as legal adviser in the Naval Operations Headquarters. He was sentenced to death on 10 August 1944 by the People's Court, and the sentence was carried out the same day.

*   *   *

Berthold von Stauffenberg and his brother Claus had been close friends ever since they were children: they were very much dependent on each other during their years at school and at university. Both were members of the *Georg-Kreis* and, in spite of their different careers, they kept in touch to the end of their lives. They spent the evening of 19 July 1944 together, and together they met their death for the same cause.

On 14 July 1944 Berthold said to his wife: 'The worst thing is knowing that we cannot succeed, and yet that we have to do it, for our country and for our children.' These words illustrate both his own character and the contrast between him and his brother Claus, the man of action. Werner Traber, Berthold's closest friend for many years, has written of him:

'Should one want to fashion a statue to integrity, kindness and the sense of justice, one should use Berthold Stauffenberg as the model. He knew by instinct what was right, often far sooner than other people who later had to acknowledge his judgment.

'Berthold himself was not a man of action and had no interest in power and glory. He studied and taught law. The problems of law and justice in the international field were his work and became also his interest and concern, and so far as he could he went on with his work during the war, when he was a senior official in the OKW (Supreme Command of the Navy). Speech and writing were the media which suited him best, poetry and art were part of his life, by tradition and inclination.

'All this made him a natural enemy of the National Socialist system of government, but the step from the thought to the deed was too great for many people, and the course which he took was completely out of character. He saw the crimes which Germany had committed, in which her leaders daily involved her more deeply. Therefore he rose to the terrible situation, and with clear conviction made the sacrifice demanded of him by Germany and by the cause of justice.'

ERWIN PLANCK

12 March 1893—23 January 1945

ERWIN PLANCK, the son of Max Planck, the internationally well known physicist, was born in Berlin. After passing his matriculation he joined a Fusilier Regiment in Schleswig-Holstein, as a cadet, and was later commissioned. He then studied medicine for several terms and when war broke out in 1914 went to the front, but in the same year he was severely wounded and taken prisoner by the French; he was exchanged by way of Switzerland in 1917.

He remained in the army and in 1923 was attached to the Reich Chancellory as liaison officer, and later, after his transfer to the civil service, he worked in the same office as a civilian. He became an Under-Secretary in 1932, under von Schleicher, but resigned when Hitler came to power in 1933.

He travelled for a time in East Asia, and as his political convictions made it difficult for him to find a post he could accept, he spent the next few years in private studies in economics, political science and history, until he finally accepted a post with the Otto Wolff Company in Cologne.

Erwin Planck had taken a keen interest in politics and political science ever since the first war. In his military and later in his civil career he tried always to penetrate more deeply into these problems, and to find in history lessons for his own work in the service of the state. He soon became convinced that moral principles also apply to politics, and said more than once: 'It never pays to use immoral means in politics.' After his recovery from an illness which struck him down when he was about 30, he wrote in his diary, on 20 July, 1924: 'The only thing of value that remains when I venture into shadows, be it of pain or death, is character. Why should I imperil or neglect it on the off chance of some sort of material profit?'

Hans, Baron von Kress has written a sketch of his friend:

'People who were often in his house will remember him holding some book close to his eyes and allowing nothing in his surroundings to disturb him while he was reading; always searching for an answer or learning something new.

'He had the rare gift of being able to listen and to bide his time, and he was always reserved and modest; but once he joined in a conversation he immediately evoked an atmosphere of interest and intimacy. Erwin Planck was a friendly and tolerant man, always careful in forming an opinion, always at pains to avoid hurting other people's feelings. He was no revolutionary and certainly no adventurer, and he had no great love of taking risks. But where brutality and evil were concerned he was always ready to resist.

'Until 1933, Erwin Planck had taken pleasure and a personal

143

interest in his civil service work, but when Hitler seized power he realised at once that the new policies were irreconcilable with his principles and that the new régime meant the end of his professional career. During the era of the Third Reich he watched the course of events closely, tried always to search his own conscience, to encourage other people to search theirs and to keep alive to the demands of justice and humanity. He also, with his wife, helped wherever he could, and he knew it was no longer a question of politics, but of a fight against evil. The spread of injustice grieved him more and more and he came to the conclusion that disapproval was not enough, and to the belief that he would have to offer positive resistance, even at the risk of his life. Some time before his arrest he said:

‘ "Atonement must be made for the injustice that has been done"; and in this spirit he accepted his fate.'

Erwin Planck was arrested on 23 July 1944, described by Freisler as a traitor to his country, sentenced to death on 23 October and executed in Berlin-Plötzensee on 23 January 1945.

KLAUS BONHOEFFER

5 January 1901—23 April 1945

KLAUS BONHOEFFER was born in Breslau, the son of a university professor. He was admitted to the bar in 1930 and became legal adviser to the German *Lufthansa* in 1936.

Klaus Bonhoeffer grew up among two elder and five younger brothers and sisters, but soon, according to his brother Karl Friedrich, created a world of his own in their midst. He had a good sense of fun, but was not on the whole easy-going; good natured as he was, he could be obstinate if handled the wrong way. He was an excellent judge of character and uninfluenced by either rank or age.

When he was 16 or 17 he began to concern himself with the question that was to absorb him always, the problem of individual relationships in human society. He was intensely interested in men and nations, customs and characteristics. He liked travelling and his journeys took him from Finland to North Africa and from England to Greece and Turkey; but it was the Latin and the French speaking countries that drew him most.

In his law studies the human and social implications of the law held his attention, rather than legal formalities and abstractions, an attitude which is best illustrated in his thesis *Über die Grundformen des Rechtes* (The Basis of Law), published in the periodical *Weisse Blätter*, in which he challenges the legality of a totalitarian state, and compares it with communities whose development has been natural and organic.

It goes without saying that he saw through National Socialism from the start, and refused to be hoodwinked or intimidated when the Nazis came to power. His passionate respect for justice and human dignity immediately led him into the fray, and 'Principiis obsta'—nip evil in the bud—was his motto even before 1933. When this had failed, he was quite unable to sit by and see all that made life worth living—justice, culture and national honour—squandered by a mob of mediocre tyrants, and he began to search for ways and means of overthrowing Hitler.

He was soon in touch with the various resistance groups, with Beck and Goerdeler through his brother-in-law Hans von Dohnanyi, with the Social Democrats and the trade unions through his wife's cousin Ernst von Harnack, and with the Confessional Church and the Ecumenical Council through his brother Dietrich.

When he knew that his arrest was imminent, he made no attempt to run away, for he did not want to incriminate his relatives and friends. He was sentenced to death by the People's Court on 2 February 1945, and wrote a farewell letter to his children which has been published in the book *Auf dem Wege zur Freiheit* (On the Road to Freedom). In this he said:

'Ask a lot of yourselves and your friends. The search for fame and popularity will enslave you, unless you can equally well do without them, and in this few succeed. Don't listen to cheap applause.

'But when you meet other people take them as they are. It is a mistake to jump on what you don't like or what seems odd to you, try always to see the good sides. This way you will not only judge more fairly, but you will prevent yourselves becoming narrow-minded. It takes all sorts of flowers to make a garden, the tulip is beautiful to behold but has no scent, and even the rose has thorns; and whoever is truly observant also enjoys the less spectacular green. It's just the same with people, one generally discovers all sorts of hidden qualities if one can just put oneself in the person's position. Self-centred people never realise this. But do please believe me. You will not begin to discover what life is about until you learn to think of other people. If you only listen to one instrument, or worse still try all the time just to hear your own, the music will pass you by, but if you have any real feeling for music you are only interested in yourself as part of the orchestra. If you can just develop the same attitude to your life, you will find it infinitely rewarding. It is not just a case of helping people now and again; that's usually a great pleasure, but you often give pleasure by receiving—graciously—help from other people. There are other things too—give other people their due, take an interest in their doings, never indulge in sour grapes. Courtesy goes without saying, and will always endear you to other people. Cultivate courtesy, it is a fine art. If you can walk with kings and keep your virtue, so much the better, and it is merely crude to despise the ways of the world. If you can't, then keep very quiet. But you have plenty of time. I am only talking like this now because I won't be with you later on.

'I hope time and circumstance will allow you to develop mentally and each in his own way, so that you will experience the great joy of a genuine education. But don't imagine the main purpose of education to be the high position for which it may fit you; the main purpose is the individual dignity and freedom which it can bestow. It widens your horizon in time and eternity, and contact with the great and noble things of life gives their true value to decency, judgment and feeling; fires enthusiasm and makes sense of everyday life.

'That way you can be the kings of the earth. And one more thing—self-control, for thereby you can not only develop your talents and become able and efficient, but also, if circumstances permit, come to be judged not only for what you do, but for what you are.'

Klaus Bonhoeffer was shot by the SS during the night of 22-23 April 1945, while the Russians were entering Berlin.

RÜDIGER SCHLEICHER

14 January 1895—23 April 1945

RÜDIGER SCHLEICHER was the son of a civil servant in Württemberg. He was seriously wounded in the first world war and later studied at Tübingen University. He passed his law examinations and obtained his Doctor's degree in 1923

with a thesis on aviation law. He continued his work in this field, and wrote more on the same subject for the Ministry of Transport and Communications and later for the Air Ministry. After 1939 he held a part-time job as chief of the Institute for Aviation Law at Berlin University.

In a petition for mercy filed in January 1945, Dr Brandenburg, the Director of the Aviation Department of the Ministry of Transport and Communications, wrote of Rüdiger Schleicher:

'I and my colleagues have always regarded Dr Schleicher as a man of great individuality. His frankness and his love of truth had no limits and he seemed to be quite unaware of intrigues and of the sordid side of life. He was invariably successful in his work, and as often his success went unnoticed; but it was always achieved by the fairest of means. In fun I sometimes called him "Our Parsifal". Lies and deception were not in his nature, his trust in people was profound and he was in fear of no man because he had absolute faith in the existence and reality of "right". For him the word had a deeply religious meaning, and all his life he had had scruples as to whether his own ideas were really "right", and worried in case anyone might be hurt and whether he was really expressing himself honestly. He could be most disarming, by suddenly opposing his own theory. Under the surface he was always fighting with himself.'

Schleicher was a scientist, a teacher and a civil servant, and at heart always remained a Swabian democrat, but his acute sense of justice was bound before long to bring him into irreconcilable conflict with the demands of dictatorship. His superiors often warned him against continuing his interventions on behalf of Jews and concentration camp prisoners. In 1939 he refused a court martial case because he would not help to convict anyone whose attitude he himself approved. Time and again he came to grips with the basic principles of law and in 1942, for instance, made a speech on 'Right and Law', the publication of which was forbidden. In prison, he was still absorbed in legal problems.

Owing to its position, his Institute for Aviation Law on the Leipziger Platz became a meeting-place for the opposition, and here liaison men were able to get in touch with the various resistance groups without attracting attention. Under cover of bogus scientific missions, Schleicher enabled his assistant Hans John to visit fellow conspirators in other cities, and after the arrest of his brothers-in-law, Hans von Dohnanyi and Dietrich Bonhoeffer, such opportunities took on an even greater significance. Schleicher continued through his ministry to send information to the inner circle of conspirators and at the same time worked on problems dealing with civil flying in the event of Hitler's overthrow.

After the 20 July uprising Hans John and, on 4 October, Rüdiger Schleicher, were held in the Lehrterstrasse prison. He and his friends were sentenced to death on 2 February 1945, and the case against them was based on the Emergency Decrees of 28 February 1933, for which the *Reichstag* fire had been the original justification.

In spite of his war wound, Rüdiger Schleicher was kept in chains, and spent the last months of his life in the same prison as his brother-in-law and son-in-law. During the night of 22-23 April he was shot by an SS firing squad near the Lehrter Station, together with Hans John, Klaus Bonhoeffer, Justus Perels, Albrecht Haushofer and other prisoners.

On 3 February 1945, Rüdiger Schleicher's brother, a doctor, was on his way to the People's Court with a Petition for mercy, and had to take shelter in the underground station on the Potsdamer Platz during an air-raid. From there he was summoned to the burning building of the People's Court and told that the President of the Court, Freisler, had been seriously hurt.

When he arrived, Freisler was dead. Rolf Schleicher was asked to certify his death. He refused, because Freisler had sentenced his brother to death the day before.

5 TRADITION

WHEN in October 1931, at Bad Harzburg, a number of well-known Conservatives made common cause with the National Socialists, many people lost their political bearings. Some of them seem to have thought not only that National Socialism would improve economic and social conditions but also that it would strengthen patriotic feeling and revive the political and intellectual traditions of the past; and as time went on and the disaster became apparent, the whole question of tradition and its meaning came into dispute.

Many of the traditional Conservatives, men whose views and standards were determined by their birth, education, upbringing and profession, were at first wholly deceived as to Hitler's real intentions and were able to rid themselves of the illusion of a 'national renaissance' only after great struggles with their own consciences and after they had had solid proof of the destructive character of the new régime. Many of them placed their confidence in the *Wehrmacht*, which appeared to have retained its independence and was in their eyes the pillar of old and valuable traditions.

The *Wehrmacht* did not justify this confidence. This was probably due less to the character of the senior officers of the day than to the past history of the German army and in particular to its development after 1918, when many officers who were bound in strict allegiance to the Kaiser found it impossible after the German collapse to come to terms with the young democracy. They saw the Weimar Republic as the offspring of the left-wing groups who had opposed the army bills before 1914 and disapproved of Ludendorff's policy during the war. The military profession continued its old tradition and resisted the influence of the new democracy. The *Reichswehr* remained a reliable instrument in the hands of the commanders-in-chief, but it was out of sympathy with the state it served.

The National Socialists were at first no more able to influence the *Wehrmacht* than were the Weimer politicians. The discipline and control of the army contrasted too strikingly with the boisterous behaviour of the party and its Storm Troopers. But things changed after the seizure of power and the proclamation of military sovereignty. Hitler's measures to increase the size and power of the *Wehrmacht* naturally met with approval in military circles, even if the influx of fanatical National Socialists did not, and though some senior officers may have had a secret antipathy towards the new rulers and their brutality, they did not interfere. They offered no opposition to the events of 30 June 1934. But when after Hindenburg's death the *Wehrmacht* swore the Oath of Allegiance to Hitler, and he made use of his new authority drastically to curtail the freedom of the officer corps and to challenge their right to use their own judgment, he found that tradition was a double-edged weapon.

The rival conceptions of obedience and responsibility were bound to cause conflict between Hitler and the service chiefs. The generals, for instance, believed that a violent solution of the *Lebensraum* problem by aggression would stir up a world war which would result in utter defeat for Germany. They warned him against each successive annexation: and on military matters they were not accustomed to having their advice ignored. The first military revolt was planned in the summer of 1938, and thereafter many senior officers toyed with the idea of a *coup d'état*.

Opposition sprang from many sources: some of it was inspired by military rather than ethical considerations, by the belief that Hitler would bring Germany to military disaster, but there were many cases where fundamental convictions lay behind military motives, and others where military considerations were the starting point to much deeper understanding. In the summer of 1938 General Beck, the Chief of the General Staff, resigned from his post, and there began the story which was to end with many German officers actively supporting the resistance movement, and many more unable any longer to bring themselves to hope for a German victory, even if one had been possible.

Tradition implants values as well as views. Representatives of the aristocracy, senior civil servants, monarchists, moved in the same direction as the officers. The Bavarian royalist who pleaded for a patriarchal (but constitutional) state, the landowner who considered it his duty to look after 'his' people, the mayor, the father of the city, who would not stand by and see the systematic destruction of local government and the manipulation of public life; the old-world

ADOLF von HARNIER

14 April 1903—12 May 1945

ADOLF VON HARNIER, Freiherr von Regendorf, was the third son of a landowner who was also Chamberlain at the Bavarian Court. He became a Doctor of Law in 1934. Thereafter he settled in Munich as a solicitor, believing that it was

out of the question under the Nazis to follow his own inclinations and to engage in politics or in some more ambitious legal activity. Nazi Germany was the antithesis of his conception of a just and ordered state and he sharply rejected Hitler from the moment in 1923 when he had been an eye-witness of the *Putsch* and of Hitler's subsequent appearance in a trial for high treason.

Adolf von Harnier was always concerned with religious and philosophical questions and was converted to Catholicism in 1934.

On 12 May 1945, after six years in prison, he died of typhoid due to starvation and general physical weakness. He did not live long enough to regain his freedom, for he died on the day that the Americans, who had meanwhile occupied the prison, had arranged to release him. This was the news which met his wife when she finally reached the prison at Straubing, six days after his death.

*   *   *

Adolf von Harnier never swerved from the course he believed to be right. He rejected force as an instrument of politics and was convinced that Nazism must destroy itself. He therefore concentrated on preparations of a Christian, legal and democratic character, for the time after the Nazi collapse.

One day a Gestapo informer succeeded in gaining admittance to a meeting held in the home of the town surveyor, Josef Zott—also one of the victims of those years. In August 1939 the whole group was arrested and Harnier as the leading figure was remanded for five years while enquiries were carried out. In 1944, after a trial for treason, he was sentenced to ten years in prison and ten years' loss of civil rights.

During his years in prison he remained just as strong as he had always been in his predictions of the catastrophic end of the Third Reich, just as dauntless as he had been in his defence of clergymen, and in his legal assistance to persecuted Jews. Many of his fellow-sufferers found him a great moral support.

His friend, Erich Chrambach, tells us:

'I was often shocked when we met for brief moments between questioning or in the gloomy prison yard. Deathly white, his dark eyes shining from deep caverns, he was the very picture of suffering. And yet no word of complaint ever crossed his lips, and often enough he made use of the few means of communication that were left to give us a word of consolation and encouragement.'

The notes which Adolf von Harnier made for his defence illustrate both his own attitude and the background to the accusations.

The following are extracts:

'I am a true servant of my King and country, not only as a dutiful subject but also because I am a convinced monarchist, politically and intellectually. I mean by that, that quite apart from myself and my relationship to my Bavarian and German fatherland, I believe monarchy to be the most successful form of government that the history of mankind has known.

'As an adult, tax-paying citizen, I have the right and even the obligation to take an active part in public affairs. Such activity can be restricted only by constitutional decrees or other legislation and only in individual cases, never in principle.

'The legal situation in Germany after 1933 led to very severe restrictions of the political activities of the citizen. But theoretically, and even in practice, such activity has not been entirely eliminated. Since 1933 there have been plebiscites and elections in which the people were supposed to express their approval or disapproval of individual political acts and even of the entire policy of their government. . . .

'I have never encouraged anyone to enter or to undermine party organisations. On the contrary, I have always considered it the duty of people of character to forego membership of political parties if such membership was against their own convictions, even if the refusal meant loss of privilege and persecution. This is the passive resistance which a man of honour must offer, regardless of the system under which he lives. . . .

'The most I can have said about Hitler's origins is that it has always been the custom for State officials to be drawn from all classes of the people. I cannot possibly have spoken of better or worse races, let alone mentioned "the worst" races, because on principle I consider it immoral to believe that one race is better than another. I have the same attitude to the mixing of blood, of which I myself am a product. For the very reason that I oppose the Nazi programme of racial discrimination, I protest that I cannot have said anything about Hitler's ancestry, about which I in any case know nothing. . . .

'I have never intended "to tip the scales with my ideas"; I intended quite simply to give help and advice to a circle of simple, decent, helpless friends who thought as I did, in so far as they asked me to do so. That was simply a social duty, but at the same time it gave me cause to search my own conscience. Nothing is so difficult as to stand the test of conscience before a group of uneducated but critical and intelligent working men, with their unerring instinct for character. . . .'

OTTO KARL KIEP

7 July 1886—26 August 1944

OTTO KARL KIEP was born in Saltcoats, Scotland, and was the son of a German Consul; he continued the family tradition and won respect in international diplomacy for his many-sided work in the German Foreign Service.

He was arrested by the Gestapo on 16 January 1944, condemned to death on 1 July, and executed in Berlin-Plötzensee on 26 August.

*   *   *

Otto Kiep studied law in Germany, received his Doctorate of Law at the University of London, served in the 1914-18 war and then entered the Foreign Office. He first took part in conferences concerning reparations. His service as a diplomat was interrupted by a term as Head of the Imperial Press Department under the Luther Cabinet, but he was appointed Counsellor at the German Embassy in Washington in 1927 and Consul General in New York in 1930; by his own wish he was recalled to Germany in 1933. He has given the reasons for his resignation in notes which he wrote for his children during his imprisonment. Bearing in mind that the letter had to go through the National Socialist Censorship, he wrote in these words:

> 'In Germany there were six million unemployed, in the U.S.A. twelve million, so that the German New Order was regarded by the Americans with more understanding than one might have expected, considering its fight against democracy and Liberalism. But this favourable atmosphere vanished as soon as the anti-Jewish measures were taken in Germany. . . . Albert Einstein, who was staying in America at the time, giving lectures, became a central figure in the Jewish reaction, and was more or less elevated to the position of one of the martyrs of international Jewry, and his presence in the United States represented as an escape from persecution in Germany.
>
> 'I had been staying in Florida for a fortnight to get rid of a cold. On my return I found that my deputy, Schwarz, had accepted on my behalf an invitation to a banquet to be held in Einstein's honour by the city of New York and several cultural

societies there. My decision to go to this banquet later involved me in all kinds of difficulties and led to my resignation from the active list. . . ."

In his notes, Kiep then gave details of the warnings and threatening letters addressed to Einstein, which gave rise to the fear that he would be set upon by hysterical German exchange students before his return to Germany. Kiep felt that this made his own presence at the banquet more necessary than ever, if he was not to be identified with the official German attitude. He then writes: 'I was given many interesting diplomatic posts later on, but whenever the question of promotion to a legation or embassy arose, I met with the objection that the "Einstein case" had done me too much harm.'

The German Foreign Office recalled him from New York in 1933, at his own request. And since, as they told him, there was no other post immediately available, he was given extended leave. He mentions this move also in the notes he wrote in prison:

'This decision also gave me some headaches, but considering that the policy which I had publicly represented in America in the past year had been completely reversed, I felt that it was essential that a new man should replace me. Though some of my friends and acquaintances condemned my attitude I realise, in retrospect, that I was absolutely right.'

Otto Kiep then led a trade delegation to South America, in 1934, and to East Asia in 1935. From 1937 to 1939 he was the German representative on the London Non-Intervention Committee for Spain. In 1939, instead of staying in England, which would have meant internment, he chose to return to Germany and entered the Foreign Department of the Armed Forces Headquarters, which became one of the key positions for resistance activities against Hitler, as a reserve-officer. He managed to keep his activities secret until the day when a tea-time conversation at Elisabeth von Thadden's flat, about the war situation and the collapse of the eastern front, was betrayed to the Gestapo. On 28 September 1943, Otto Kiep visited his sister Ida and confided to her, as she wrote after his death:

'I have been thinking seriously about this matter for a long

160

time. If we don't do something soon to change course we'll all be on the rocks for certain. I had always hoped that as in 1813 a Yorck would appear among the generals to put things into reverse on his own responsibility . . . if they're on my tail now it's only because of what I said at the tea-party. Naturally they try to liquidate everybody who sees through the party and its machinations, or has any political vision. I am confiding in you because it is very likely that after I am arrested they will arrest my wife too. That is what happens now.

'I must ask you to look after the children for me and to tell my brothers, if anything happens to me, that I send them a fond farewell and that they should think of my death as if I had been killed in the front line.'

After this visit Otto Kiep went back to Berlin. On 16 January, three SS men came to his home and took him away. Two criminal investigation officials remained in the house to guard his 16-year-old son, Albrecht. A few days later his wife Hanna was arrested, and while the parents were imprisoned in the concentration camp at Ravensbrück, separated from one another by a wall, Albrecht, by then just 17, was called up on 1 April 1944, for service with the Navy at Stralsund.

After the execution of Otto Kiep, his wife was released. Three months later his son was reported missing after his ship was sunk off the Finnish coast.

KARL FRIEDRICH GOERDELER

31 July 1884—2 February 1945

KARL GOERDELER came from a conservative Prussian family with a long tradition in the Civil Service. He studied law and later had some experience of commerce and banking.

Photograph taken in the People's Court

He served in the 1914-18 war, and from 1920 to 1930, a time
when his sympathies were with the German National Party,
he was Deputy *Bürgermeister* of Königsberg. From 1930 to
1937 he was *Oberbürgermeister* in Leipzig, and in his spare
time worked under Brüning as Commissioner for price regu-
lation. He put his many connections and his reputation in local
government at the service of the resistance movement and
became one of its leading figures. He was condemned to
death on 7 September 1944, and was executed after imprisonment and torture, on 2 February 1945.

*   *   *

The German opposition to Hitler had to contend with
endless difficulties and set-backs, and in such circumstances
the personality of Karl Friedrich Goerdeler, with his iron
nerve and his indomitable will, was a powerful asset. Above
all he had an unshakable belief that by virtue of human
reason and vision, good would finally prevail. He was convinced that a system which lives 'from financial folly,
economic compulsion, political terror, lawlessness and
amorality' could not last long. Sooner or later collapse was
certain, 'by the laws of Nature and of God'.

A secret circular letter which Goerdeler sent to the generals
in March 1943 makes his attitude clear:

> 'It is no good whitewashing the facts or burying our con-
> science, for that will not absolve us from the duty of averting
> this disaster before it is too late. 1918 should have taught us to
> know when the time has come. If one is seriously convinced
> that the war cannot be won and that a better opportunity for
> negotiation will not arise, then one must substitute political for
> military action; and if the government of the day stands in the
> way, the Government must fall, as governments have fallen
> throughout history; all the more so when it dominates the scene
> and has gone far to exclude everyone else from their share of
> responsibility. If such a government does not seek its obvious
> duty to put the fate of the people before it's own, then the
> lesson must be brought home.
>
> 'I see no risk at all in embarking on negotiations. How is it
> possible that a decent people can put up with such an unbear-
> able system for so long? The explanation is simple: only
> because all infringements of justice and decency are protected
> by secrecy and terrorism. But all this can change at one blow if
> these impossible conditions are brought out into the light of

day. The German people should be told out loud of what they already know and discuss in secret, of the consequences of incompetent military leadership, of the excess of corruption and of the countless crimes, which are quite incompatible with honour. They should then be asked to declare in public whether they are prepared to defend this state of affairs, and which of them can justify it. I guarantee that no-one in the world, not even a born criminal, would publicly associate himself with such a criminal system.

'It is a great mistake to assume that the moral force of the German people is exhausted; the fact is merely that it has been deliberately weakened. The only hope of salvation is to sweep away the secrecy and terror, to restore justice and decent government and so to pave the way to a great moral revival. We must not be shaken in our belief that the German people want in the future, as in the past, justice, honesty and truthfulness. And as in the past too, the few degenerate elements who do not so wish must be kept in check by the legal power of the state.

'The practical solution is to bring about the conditions, even if only for twenty-four hours, in which the truth can be told, to restore confidence in the resolve that justice and good government shall again prevail.'

EWALD von KLEIST-SCHMENZIN

22 March 1890—9 April 1945

EWALD VON KLEIST-SCHMENZIN grew up on his parents' estate at Dubberow in Pomerania. He was a lawyer and landowner, chairman of the District Employers' Association and a member of the provincial Synod. Politically, he was in sympathy with the *Deutschnationale Volkspartei* (the National Party); and with the Stahlhelm movement. In 1933 he came into collision with Hugenberg over the formation of a coalition Cabinet of the Nationalists and the National Socialists.

He was first arrested on 1 May 1933, and kept in prison for a few days by the Belgard police; on 21 June he was arrested again and taken to Schievelbein for three weeks.

His third arrest was the result of his connection with various resistance groups involved in the 20 July rising and of their meetings at Schmenzin, his country house. On 21 July, the Security Service and the military requisitioned his estate and Ewald von Kleist-Schmenzin was taken, via Köslin, to Stettin, and from there on 18 August to the Gestapo controlled prison in the Lehrterstrasse in Berlin. He was beheaded in Plötzensee on 9 April 1945.

The following extracts from a pamphlet he published in 1932 bear witness to his lucid appraisal of the political situation and to his early rejection of National Socialism:

'Now a new faith is rammed down our throats; we are asked to believe that National Socialism and Hitler, and they alone, have power to bring us joy and salvation; a belief which demands a fantastic quota of gullibility. In villages, for instance, where the German Nationalists and Social Democrats have for all their differences lived in peace, there is now war to the knife between the Nationalists and the Nazis. . . .

'National Socialism is purely destructive, and gives itself away at every turn. Fanatical party members feel no loyalty but to the Party itself, and so completely disregard the advice or decisions of even quite unpolitical bodies or organisations. Officials neglect their normal duties and, in short, the basic principles of both private and public life are destroyed. . . .

'It is not merely a question of the open National Socialist agitation, which breaks all bounds for sheer unscrupulous pro-

Photo by Atelier Bieber

vocation . . . but the whispering campaign is even more vicious. Even among respectable citizens the idea is gaining currency that after the National Socialists have seized power, any man will be allowed to attack, without fear of punishment, whoever may displease him. I am continually amazed at how few people recognise the danger, or even want to recognise it.

'National Socialism would never have gained such a flying start if normal and patriotic citizens had openly come out

167

against it. The attitude that National Socialism is a respectable national movement which happens to have a few passing defects, an attitude which we have condoned, has placed our whole future in jeopardy; and it will take all our strength to avert the danger.

'The promise of the *Reichslandbundes*, of the V.V.V., of the Crown Prince and others, at the second Presidential election, although perhaps excusable on grounds of ignorance of the facts, were completely lacking in political instinct and drove hundreds of thousands of respectable people over to Hitler; and so paved the way to the devil. The German National Party also made mistakes, and it was quite clear after Harzburg or when candidates for the first Presidential election were nominated, that a working arrangement with Hitler and National Socialism would never be possible.

'Religion alone stands between us and National Socialism, and always will. We believe that faith in God and obedience to His Word must permeate our public life; National Socialism holds a fundamentally different view, and let me say that questions of dogma have nothing to do with it.

'What it comes to is that Hitler regards as the basis of policy —the fact that he may occasionally say something else does not alter the case—the race and its demands. This is a crude form of materialism, and quite incompatible with Christianity. According to his theories, it is the duty of the state to encourage not ability, but racial characteristics. He reduces the state to the level of a cattle-breeder, and shows that he is quite incapable of understanding its character and obligations. He does not recognise the fact that every race has shortcomings, which the state must mitigate. Hitler's first concern is the breeding of healthy bodies. He deliberately states that the forming of character is only a secondary matter. There is no point of contact with this sort of attitude.

'In my opinion we can no longer tolerate the fiction that National Socialism is a national movement. This lunacy must be exposed, and so must the completely false picture of Hitler which has been built up. Apart from that I would like to ask: What have we in common, spiritually, with National Socialism?

'In the last resort we must recognise that it is the downfall of our nation and the deadly enemy of our way of life. Any decent elements there may be within its ranks will have less and less say. The end of a National Socialist government will be the same as the end of the Rienzi—chaos.'

Ewald von Kleist-Schmenzin was as good as his word, and after the Nazis came to power refused absolutely to compromise. He retired from all public affairs and lived on his estate. He was a deeply religious man and had no fear of death. Just before his execution he wrote: 'Who is the greater, who has achieved more for humanity, Caesar, or a simple, conscientious genuine working man, whose whole life has been an example of faith? I think it is the working man. It is worth thinking about.'

LUDWIG BECK

29 June 1880—20 July 1944

LUDWIG BECK was born in the small town of Biberach, on the Rhine. His father had broken the military tradition of his family by becoming an industrialist. But Ludwig Beck, after passing his matriculation, chose an army career. In 1911 he was attached to the General Staff and after the 1914-18 war he held several commands in the *Reichswehr*. In 1932, as a Lieutenant-General, he commanded a Cavalry Division, and a year later the *Truppenamt*.

From 1935 to 1938 General Beck was Chief of the Army General Staff. The General Staff, the élite of the German Army, was responsible for the preparation and conduct of all land warfare and he, as their Chief, was entitled and in duty bound to take a major part in all important military decisions.

On 30 May 1938, Hitler made known his 'unalterable decision' to conquer Czechoslovakia by military action in the foreseeable future. General Beck strongly protested. The Army was quite unprepared to deal with the general war which would be the inevitable consequence of this action, nor could it be sufficiently strengthened in time, particularly in the unsatisfactory economic conditions which then existed. If the Army was to engage in war, the political leaders of Germany must take into account the opinions of the military experts. 'Differences about the relation between politics and war, and discrepancies between political objectives and military potentiality, may well be the decisive step in losing the war itself. Not for nothing do historians tell us of wars which were won or lost before they began; and in the last resort politics were nearly always to blame.'

General Beck's opposition to the attack on Czechoslovakia was not founded only on his recognition of the fact that it would lead to a world war and a German defeat. He was also angered that war should be undertaken so lightly and so casually at a time when there was no good reason for it. He knew too much about it to be able to condone a policy which set out to solve the 'space problem' by force.

Beck strongly opposed Ludendorff's belief in total war.
170

Photo by Atelier Bieber

Ludendorff based this belief on his experiences in 1914-18 when, as he saw it, life had been torn asunder by the holocaust of military action and political factors had ceased to count; when, in the end, every effort was directed towards the complete annihilation of the enemy. Ludendorff therefore regarded a modern war as one of annihilation between two whole peoples—total war. His politics were conducted in this spirit and were fundamentally belligerent.

General Beck refused to support total war on the grounds that it excludes 'any moderate political objective' and cannot therefore lead to a 'satisfactory peace in the Bismarckian sense.' He was convinced that even modern war can be limited and controlled, 'not by technical or military measures, but through a policy based on moral principles which should prevail in all circumstances, so that war should be a political instrument and subordinate to politics; and by a new sense of morality and idealism which would govern the state and its relations with other nations.' It was also necessary 'that the political leader should be a man of integrity who must in the last resort be subject to his personal moral law, his conscience.'

With this attitude Beck was bound to reject a policy which depended on the reckless use of force to its own ends and on ruthless indifference to the rights of other nations, which ultimately brought about a world-wide war of annihilation.

At first, in 1938, he tried to organise a unanimous condemnation of Hitler's policy by the Chiefs of Staff, who were to demand under threat of mass resignation that the war plans be abandoned. When this failed, because the Commander-in-Chief of the army rejected it, Beck, on 18 August, resigned his position as Chief of the General Staff, and was released from the Service three days later by Hitler, who kept the whole matter secret. In the following years he played a leading part in German resistance and was the recognised leader of the conspirators. On 20 July 1944 he stood at their head, ready to act. In the War Office in the Bendlerstrasse, on the evening of the day the rising had failed, he ended his own life.

HANS OSTER

9 August 1888—9 April 1945

THE life story of Hans Oster begins in the security of a Calvinist parsonage on the banks of the Elbe. His early career was typical of the professional soldier. He was educated at the Humanistisches Gymnasium zum Heiligen Kreuz in Dresden, entered a Saxon artillery regiment and in 1917, after distinguished service at the front, was appointed to the General Staff. After the war the General Staff and a certain number of troops were deployed in Dresden, Mecklenburg and Westphalia. From 1933 onwards Oster, in the normal course of his career, worked in the Ministry of Defence, and later in the Army High Command, in its important but to some extent misunderstood section, the *Abwehr*. From there he chose a course which from 1943 onwards brought him into great personal danger and, on 21 July 1944, into the clutches of the Gestapo. He died in the Flossenbürg concentration camp four days before Allied troops marched in.

The story of his life is a good illustration of the manner in which conscience may react to events in the modern world. Oster was a gentle child whose great loves were first his garden and later on the 'cello. In the army, it was horses and riding, his great passion until the end of his life. After the 1914-18 war, when he was a gay and elegant General Staff Officer, he was moved by the inevitable distress and misery of the post-war years. In the streets of Dresden he saw hungry men, with their women and children, and the Communist agitation among them. He was a witness to the murder of the Saxon War Minister, himself a working man, who was thrown into the Elbe by a raging mob, and drowned. The *Reichswehr* often had to open fire, but soldiers and the Salvation Army also brought first aid, and field kitchens stood on the street corners. Oster took part in all this and it was then, according to his son Achim, that he came to two important conclusions: that 'the professional soldier should be a convinced pacifist, because he knows war and therefore also understands the responsibility it entails', and secondly

173

that 'the army should never be placed in a position in which it has to open fire on its own countrymen'.

In the Catholic city of Münster, during the thirties, Oster watched the growth of the right-wing radicals and formed the conviction that National Socialism was no solution. His hopes lay with the steps taken by the Reich Chancellor, von Schleicher, to thwart Hitler. Two years later, on 30 June 1934 von Schleicher was murdered, and Oster then decided to resist the Hitler régime in every possible way and as time went he even made use of the *Abwehr* to shield and protect the oppressed.

When General von Fritsch was marked down as 'undesirable' to the Nazis, early in 1938, Oster knew no rest until he had obtained for General Beck, then Chief of Staff, the facts of the slanderous campaign against him. From then on Oster and Beck worked together, and so another professional soldier became an open rebel.

On one occasion he reproachfully asked a senior officer of the Austrian Army, later to become his friend, who reported to him after the German Army had marched into Austria: 'Why didn't the Austrian Army shoot when we marched in? Don't you know you have been trapped by a criminal?'

From this conviction there developed in the autumn of 1938 a carefully prepared plan: the British were advised to stand fast on the question of Czechoslovakia, enquiries were made to ascertain which military commanders were ready to fight for freedom and peace; a special force was formed to deal with the Reich leaders; foreign countries were sounded to find out how a bid to re-establish justice would be received; and contact was made with trade unionists and with representatives of the Social Democrats so that the people might be prepared for future events.

But everything was in vain. With the peace after Munich the opposition in the Army had no hope. Hans Oster, like so many others, believed that all hope of frustrating Hitler had gone. The day war broke out in Poland he greeted a friend in the street with the words *'Finis Germaniae'*!

Events demanded desperate decisions. It became clear that disaster could no longer be controlled from within, but that outside influences might still have some effect. When the deadline had been decided for the invasion by German

174

troops of the neutral countries whose peace and security
had been guaranteed by the *Führer*, Oster, believing in a
duty greater than patriotism, warned his friends in those
countries. He hoped that news of the violation would be
broadcast from there before it actually took place, and that
this would serve as an appeal to the honour of the German
soldier, which would drive him to decisive action. But this
hope was also vain.

During the war years Oster took it upon himself to jog

the conscience of the Army General Staff. Whether it was a question of the shooting of Jews, of party orders, of euthanasia or the murder of hostages, he was determined that no-one should be able to say that he did not know what was going on. On the contrary, that they should be reminded time and again what kind of régime they served, what responsibility they took upon themselves if they did not work for the restoration of justice. He did not take advantage of the chances he had to save his own son, who was defending a hopeless position before Stalingrad, saying that 'suffering and distress must be equally shared by all'.

The last year of his life was only an echo of the past, for he saw no way by which the fate of his country could be divorced from its insane leadership. He still tried to help and conceal his friends and to make good use of his position, and through his efforts to help Dohnanyi after his arrest, he himself was removed from office and banished to Berlin. But it was not until 20 July 1944 that the Gestapo became fully aware of Oster's true rôle in the resistance.

HENNING von TRESCKOW

10 January 1901—21 July 1944

HENNING VON TRESCKOW was born in Magdeburg. He came from a family with a long military tradition. In the 1914-18 war, when 17, he became a lieutenant in the

1st Regiment Foot Guards, and after the war transferred to the regular army. In the early twenties he interrupted his military career to learn banking, and spent some time abroad. He returned to his regiment, spent several years of regimental soldiering, attended a staff course and was finally appointed to the General Staff. At the outbreak of war in 1939 he was Chief General Staff Officer of an East Prussian infantry division. Later, after a long period as Chief General Staff Officer of the High Command of the Middle Army Group, he commanded an infantry regiment on the eastern front and saw some very heavy fighting. After this he became a Major-General and Chief of the General Staff of the 2nd Army, which he extracted from the Pripet marshes in a classic retreat after the collapse of the Middle Army Group on the Dnieper.

Tresckow was one of the most impressive personalities in the military resistance movement. Simultaneously with his important command on the eastern front he worked unceasingly with those who were trying to arouse a group of officers to resist the growing abuse of the *Wehrmacht*, and who planned the repeated attempts on Hitler's life. After the failure of the attempt on 20 July, he committed suicide.

*   *   *

According to Bernd von Kleist, Tresckow grew up to be a God-fearing man with a strong sense of duty and a great respect for tradition. He was modest and loyal, and combined these qualities with a clear grasp of affairs which went beyond the military field and which was all the stronger for his years in civilian life and for the time he spent abroad.

If Tresckow had any illusions about Hitler's solemn vows that the 'national revolt' would proceed along the path of right and honour, they were quickly dispelled at the Potsdam meeting of March 1933. For a man of his kind there were no half measures, and so he was to be found in the resistance camp at a very early stage.

It soon became clear that Tresckow was in a unique position to take a leading part in the work of the military Fronde and to convert others to its cause. The decisive factors were his own principles which, consistently as he might follow any course he had chosen, he never betrayed in the fight against the enemy, either internal or external. For this

178

reason the personal decisions which the ominous situation demanded of him were particularly hard, for he struggled with them alone, preferring not to burden others with his problems.

But he often talked with trusted friends in the Middle Army Group at Smolensk about the possibilities of freeing his country. In all these discussions, anxiety about the position on the eastern front was confused with the fundamental political tension. There existed always the conflict of conscience with which a soldier must contend if he opposes his government during a war; if, in fact, he has the high moral sense which in the final analysis leaves him no choice in the struggle between his honour as a soldier and his sense of responsibility for the future of his country.

Tresckow was well aware of the risk involved in the attempt to overthrow Hitler, but he was uninfluenced by current opinion or by the chance of success. His conduct was governed by his sense of historical responsibility and by the belief that he was called upon to help his country in an hour of need. After the failure of the attempt on Hitler's life and in spite of Nazi propaganda against the men of 20 July, his former subordinates stood by him, down to the youngest soldier, their love and respect unchanged. A strong argument for their belief in his integrity.

'In spite of, and perhaps because of, the demands he made of people, Henning von Tresckow was a wonderful friend,' declared the former Colonel von Gersdorff: 'He asked a lot of his subordinates and was capable of severe reprimand, but he gave to everyone with whom he had dealings a feeling of security, for he seemed to know all their needs, public and private. He was always aware of other people's feelings and was incapable of hurting their dignity'.

Schlabrendorff, in his book *Offiziere gegen Hitler* (Officers against Hitler) records Tresckow's words on the night before his death: 'God once promised Abraham that he would not destroy Sodom if there were but ten just men in it. I hope that God will not destroy Germany. We cannot complain about our death. Those who joined us were prepared to face death. The moral strength of a man begins at the point at which he is ready to give up his life for his convictions'.

179

ULRICH-WILHELM GRAF
SCHWERIN von SCHWANENFELD

21 December 1902—8 September 1944

ULRICH-WILHELM GRAF SCHWERIN VON SCHWANENFELD
was born in Copenhagen, the son of a German diplomat. He
inherited land in Mecklenburg and in West Prussia. As an
officer he served in the war from 1939 until 8 September 1944
when he stood before the People's Court and told Freisler
that he had become an opponent of the system on account 'of
all the murders inside and outside Germany'.

*   *   *

Ulrich-Wilhelm Schwerin was studying at the Institute of
Technology in Munich at the time of the Hitler *Putsch* in
1923. He took an active part in the fight against *Putschisten*
and from then on had no use for National Socialism. With
the same determination he refused to join a student *Korps*.
Later on he studied at Breslau University, where he took
his diploma in 1925, and it was there that he came across
three former school friends, Peter Graf von Yorck, Albrecht
von Kessel and Botho von Wussow, who were concerned, as
he was, to see political reform on a basis of Christianity and
social justice.

As the years went on Schwerin became increasingly
interested in politics. In 1932 he expressed grave doubts
about the re-election of Hindenburg as President of the
Reich and about the mounting radicalism of the Nationalists.
When Hitler came to power he had no doubt about the
coming catastrophe and with the friends who shared his
convictions, men like Adam von Trott zu Solz, Eduard
Brücklmeier and Josias von Rantzau, was determined to do
everything possible to avert it. As early as 1935 Schwerin
was of the opinion 'that the only hope for the liberation of
Germany from the National Socialists is the death of Hitler,
which must be brought about by force'.

From then on he made every effort to contact other resistance groups and was soon in touch with Oster, Dohnanyi
and their circle; he was a great personal friend of Witzleben

180

Photograph taken in the People's Court

and of other officers in the military resistance, and during the
Sudeten crisis he, a civilian, became the main link between
the military and civilian groups that wished to overthrow
Hitler. His son, Christian, writes:

'Shortly before Chamberlain went to Munich a last meeting
took place in our house at Göhren, when the final directives for
the overthrow of Hitler were settled, but Chamberlain's surpris-

ing flight to Munich made it impossible for us to put the plan into action. In spite of their great disappointment my father and his friends started work on new plans. My father was also involved in the scheme to remove Hitler on the occasion of his visit to the Siegfried Line early in 1939.

'At the outbreak of the war, he was called up and took part in the Polish campaign. When it was over he became Assistant Adjutant to Witzleben and continued his political activities by serving as liaison between Witzleben and other generals.

'My father, Oster and other close friends worked out the plan for the attempt on Hitler's life in the spring of 1942, but after Witzleben's dismissal he too lost his post because he was "not sufficiently reliable from a political point of view". He went to Utrecht for a time but soon moved to Berlin, at Oster's request, where in various capacities he gave all his energies to preparation for the overthrow of the régime. His work at that time brought him into close touch with Leber, Leuschner and Mierendorff.

'During the final months of preparation, immediately before 20 July 1944, my father was quite conscious of the fact that the removal by force of the National Socialist régime could no longer ward off catastrophe for Germany. But in spite of that he believed that, even if the plan should miscarry, the attempt would at least prove there were men for whom no sacrifice was too high to be rid of the spiritual disease of National Socialism.'

Graf Schwerin's letter to one of his sons on his confirmation, dated 6 April 1944, is characteristic:

'In such times of suffering and general confusion we all need an anchor, and great inner strength, and there is no doubt that the teachings of Christ, which have been valid for nearly 2,000 years, give us that inner strength. Every day and every hour, demands are made on us and we must do our duty, but it is not always easy to decide where our duty lies. When you are faced with a choice, choose always the harder course and you may be sure that you have chosen right. You see, it is very hard to do one's duty, no matter if it is the duty of a boy or a soldier, of a professional man or a housewife. Today, in the war, the final sacrifice is demanded every day, for every day it is the duty of the soldier to give up the best he has to give, his life. But it would be wrong to regard duty only as a burden. I want you to remember something your grandfather often said, that duty was his pleasure. Whoever looks upon duty in that light will, whatever the circumstances, be able to draw from it great strength'.

On the evening of 20 July 1944, when Ulrich-Wilhelm Schwerin was led away from the Bendlerstrasse, handcuffed to Eugen Gerstenmaier, he said to him: 'In the last resort, what more can we do than die for our cause?' He was sentenced to death, and executed later in the day.

PETER GRAF YORCK von WARTENBURG

13 November 1904—8 August 1944

THE name of Yorck conjures up the Napoleonic wars. On 30 December 1812, General Hans David Ludwig von Yorck, an officer who had always and obediently served his king, acted quite without the king's consent and led the Auxiliary Corps which he commanded away from the ranks of the Napoleonic troops which were then streaming back from Russia; then on his own responsibility Yorck concluded the Convention of Tauroggen with the Russian enemy, an act which became the signal for the national war of independence.

On 7 and 8 August 1944, his great-grandson, Peter Yorck, stood before the People's Court in Berlin to answer the charge of taking part in the revolutionary attempt of 20 July. He spoke up fearlessly and told the Court what had been the reason for his conflict with National Socialism : 'The main thing was the tyrannical demand of the state on the citizen, which totally ignored his religious and moral obligations towards God.'

*   *   *

Peter Graf Yorck von Wartenburg was born on 13 November 1904 at Klein-Oels, in Silesia. He studied law and political science in Bonn and Breslau, began his career as legal adviser to the Breslau Administration and later became an official with the Commissioner for Price Control in Berlin. In the war he took part in the Polish campaign and after 1942 was employed in a government office in a job which gave him good opportunities to make many new contacts for the German opposition, both in Berlin and on the various trips he had to make in the course of his duties. He was one of the founders of the Kreisau group and a close friend of Helmuth Moltke, and he worked on plans for a future reorganisation of the state, based on greater de-centralisation and more responsibility for the *Länder*. On 20 July, Yorck was among the group which went to work in the War Office

Photograph taken in the People's Court

in the Bendlerstrasse. He was also among the first to be arrested and executed on 8 August 1944.

In the last few hours of his life he wrote to his mother:

'At the end of a life which was more than blessed with love and friendship, I feel only gratitude towards God and humility in bowing to His will. It is a great sorrow to me that I am causing you this pain after all you have had to suffer. I beg you to forgive me. I have had more than two weeks in which to put myself and my actions before God and I believe I shall find in Him a merciful Judge. People who are wrapped up in

185

other convictions which I cannot share, will never understand the spiritual suffering that people like myself have had to undergo in the past few years. But may I assure you that not a single ambitious thought, no lust for power has influenced me in what I have done? It was solely my feeling for my country, the anxiety I felt for the Germany that has emerged from the past 2,000 years, concern for her development, external and internal, that prompted my actions. That is why I can look my ancestors, and my father and brothers, in the face. Perhaps the day will come when our actions will be judged differently, when we shall be looked upon not as scoundrels but as patriots who uttered the warning cry. I pray that this wonderful call to action may be our chance to do honour to God.'

He also wrote to his wife:

'We have probably reached the end of our beautiful, rich life together. Tomorrow the People's Court will sit in judgment over me and the others. I hear that the Army has cast us out; well, they can strip us of our uniform but they can't kill the spirit that moved us. And in it I feel at one with our ancestors, relations and friends. This must be regarded as one of God's inscrutable decisions which I myself accept in all humility. I believe I have gone some way to atone for the guilt which is our heritage, and that is why I am confident of finding God a merciful Judge. When we came away from our last Communion, I was aware of an almost uncanny sense of revelation, I might even call it nearness to Christ. Looking back, it seems like a call.

'I hope my death will also atone for all my sins, that it will be a sacrifice for what we have all had to bear. May it contribute to God becoming a little less remote in these days. I too, am dying for my country, and even if it seems to all appearances a very inglorious and disgraceful death, I shall hold up my head and I only hope that you will not believe this to be from pride or delusion. We wished to light the torch of life and now we stand in a sea of flames.'

6 CHRISTIANITY

THE individual steps forward from the ranks to sacrifice himself for others: this is the theme which emerges from the photographs taken at the trial, which underlies this whole story of resistance to tyranny, which is the embodiment of the Christian spirit and which finds expression in the great part played by the Christian Churches in the struggle with National Socialism.

The Protestant Church was itself rent by the conflict from the beginning, for in 1932 a movement known as the 'Protestant National Socialists' or alternatively as the 'German Christians' was formed within its framework. This was an attempt to adapt Church teaching to political attitudes, and to the same ends the Nazis tried to establish a Protestant National Church, to which the 28 *Land* churches would be 'co-ordinated'. In the event the struggle for the establishment of a national Church was synonymous with the struggle for the true doctrine.

The fact that many people felt the need for unification among the Protestant Churches in Germany was an initial asset to the National Socialists, and their avowal of 'positive Christianity' had some effect. But it soon became clear that they regarded the Churches as useless bourgeois institutions and merely hoped to exploit them for their own purposes and to present the picture of the progressive assumption of power in a pseudo-Christian frame. The ceremonial opening of the new *Reichstag*, after an election campaign of state-organised terror, took place in the Garrison Church in Potsdam, on 21 March 1933. In May 1934, at a synod in Barmen, the Confessional Church was founded. This was not a territorial Church, but a movement within the Protestant Church to counter the false doctrines which threatened it. At this point the régime dropped even the 'German Christians' and from then on state measures were directed not at the reconciliation of the Church with the National Socialist *Weltanschauung*, but at the subordination of all things Christian.

The attempt to oppress the Catholic Church was at first a little more circumspect and the negotiations which followed the Reich Concordat of 1933 gave some protection for the time being. But attacks on the Church, and the persecution of those who professed allegiance to it, steadily increased; and the Papal Encyclical *With grave Concern,* which was read to the faithful from the pulpits in 1937, was tantamount to a declaration of war. Both Churches suffered confiscation, restriction and persecution, and both challenged the policies and ideologies of the state. They opposed the biological creeds and the idolising of the German people. They protested against the Oath of Allegiance and its claim to impose unconditional obedience not to God, but to man, and against the anti-Christian teaching given to the young, the arbitrary methods of the Gestapo, the horrors of the concentration camps and the ill-treatment of the population of occupied territories. They also protested most violently against the murder of incurables.

Many individual clergy and priests became widely known. The outspoken sermons of Father Rupert Mayer sent him to a concentration camp as early as 1936; today, he is honoured as a Saint in Bavaria; he died in 1945, soon after his liberation while taking a service. Pastor Schneider Dickenschied, the 'preacher of Buchenwald', never ceased to protest against the crimes of the régime, right up to the time of his death after many years in a concentration camp. Father Franz Reinisch, an Austrian, who was denied his calling first by the Gestapo ban on preaching in 1940 and then by his conscription into the army, refused to swear an Oath of Allegiance to Hitler and was executed in 1942. Pastor Niemöller's sermons in the Dahlem Church in Berlin, for which he had to spend eight years in a concentration camp, will never be forgotten. Nor will the sermons in Münster of Bishop Graf von Galen, who maintained from the pulpit that Christianity was an integral part of the German character and of German history, and laid bare the hollow nationalism of the Nazis:

'Grow strong. Stand firm. Remain steadfast. Like the anvil under the blows of the hammer. It may be that obedience to God and loyalty to conscience will cost you or me our lives, our freedom or our home. But let us rather die than sin. May the mercy of God, without which we can do nothing give us that strength.'

In the trial of strength, theologians were bound to re-examine the problems of Christianity in practice. In particular the Protestant Church, which up to 1918 was closely tied to the state, had to revise its attitude on the proper relation between them. One of its theologians, Dietrich Bonhoeffer, went so far as to approve active resistance until the tyrant had been deposed:

'Any person in a responsible position who takes the blame upon himself, and no responsible person can do otherwise, must ascribe the guilt to himself and to no-one else. Must accept absolute responsibility, not out of wanton revelry in his own power, but knowing that he is bound to make this choice and that in so doing he can rely only on mercy. He can justify himself to other men on grounds of necessity; in judging himself, his own conscience will acquit him; but before God he can but hope for mercy.'

ERICH KLAUSENER

25 January 1885—30 June 1934

LIKE his father Erich Klausener went into the Prussian Civil Service, and became a *Regierungsassessor* in the Ministry of Commerce. On 1 August 1914, when he had just been married, he went to the front. He was recalled in 1917 to take over the office of Chairman of the District Council in Adenau (Eifel). In 1919 he became Chairman of the industrial district of Recklinghausen, in 1924 head of a department in the Ministry for Welfare in Berlin, and in 1926 Chief of the Police Department of the Prussian Ministry of the Interior.

He had meanwhile become well known for his work in the Catholic Lay Movement and had been leader of the Catholic Action in the diocese of Berlin since 1928. On 2 February 1933, he was forced to resign his office. He was then employed in the Reich Ministry of Transport.

By 25 June 1933, National Socialism had already encroached upon the freedom of the Churches, had labelled the Catholic Workers' Association as 'subversive' and had cast doubts on the purpose of all and any Catholic societies. Even so, 45,000 people came to the vast stadium in Berlin—and they came without swastikas.

In the next edition of the *Völkischen Beobachters*, Alfred Rosenberg wrote in a leading article: 'As in the past, the Roman Catholic Conference in Berlin was a tremendous success; and had it been nothing more than an ecclesiastical convention, we should have had no cause to criticise.'

But there was one sentence in Dr Klausener's speech which Rosenberg considered 'intolerable': 'If the revolution of national revival is not accompanied by an inner, spiritual revival, then all strength and all efforts have been in vain.'

Rosenberg had understood the meaning of the words and replied to them: 'So the member of the Centre Party, Dr Klausener, regards Adolf Hitler's fourteen years of struggle and the great uprising of the people, the like of which is seen among nations only once in four hundred years, as a movement based on insufficient spiritual inspiration.'

Erich Klausener was one of those men who, in his anxiety

to avoid national disunity, was prepared to give the benefit of the doubt to some of the plans of the National Socialists; but he had no doubt at all that a spirit other than that of National Socialism would have to create a new and much-needed moral basis. His speech at the Catholic Conference illustrates his attitude:

'Nothing could be worse than for Germany, and particularly

the younger generation, to swing from liberalism to the other extreme, to submit to the indifferent and thoughtless regimentation of a system based on the supremacy of the state' and 'let this therefore be our vow this day: our lives must derive their inspiration from the Eucharist, and this inspiration must spread into the farthest corners.'

Klausener went on to say:

'Though the Church opens up to us a prospect extending far beyond the frontiers of our country, though her cathedral roof stretches out over all lands and peoples, over all races and both sexes, it is not some vague international movement that opposes national wishes, thoughts and feelings. The Catholic Church is universal. It espouses every people on earth. The aim and purpose of our Catholic organisations is to foster and preserve spiritual strength in Catholic citizens, and it is for this reason that we so passionately want them to remain in being.'

The same evening, the telephone rang in Klausener's flat. Was it true, the enquirer asked, that Klausener had been arrested? He himself laughed about the incident. He could not bring himself to believe that the age of justice was past.

A year passed. The work in the Catholic Action continued. New methods were considered for extending its work and for increasing the individual's power of resistance against outside pressure. Erich Klausener, in his new position as chief of the shipping department in the Ministry of Transport, was a dynamo of efficiency whom even the National Socialists were unwilling and unable to do without.

Then came 24 June 1934. This time there were 60,000 people at the Catholic Conference in the Hoppegarten, again without swastikas, but with a steadfast faith and a clear will to profess it.

At the end, influenced perhaps by the atmosphere of the moment, but also by the tensions of the time, Erich Klausener spoke a few words which were not on the programme, but which found an echo far beyond the 60,000 there assembled. For they were the unmistakable Catholic protest against growing political pressure, the racial policy and national arrogance.

On the following Saturday, at 1.15 p.m., Erich Klausener was shot dead in his office. This was 30 June 1934, the day of the 'great purge', the day on which Hitler set out to
192

eliminate the potential of further resistance to his power, on the excuse of the so-called Röhm revolt in Bavaria.

Who was the murderer? Göring, who 17 years later at the preliminary hearing in Nuremberg, admitted that he had wanted to meet Klausener, the Catholic leader? Heydrich, who sent an SS Leader to the Reich Ministry of Transport with clear-cut orders? Or the SS man who carried out the orders and recalled at his trial in 1952 in Berlin that he had been given the 'Klausener assignment' 17 years earlier?

And what sort of a man had he killed? A note was found on his desk with a few words in his own handwriting: 'Keep your word. Do not indulge in false pride. Be angry in a good cause, but never show your anger. Be straight in all your dealings.'

From the preface to the Catholic Conference, 1933:

'Suffering and death were followed by the glorious resurrection. That is why the Cross of suffering has become the Cross of victory. There must be some power in this wood that sends forth life from the cross from which death has departed. This power is divine power. By its virtue the world will recover, the Easter of the resurrection will follow the bearing of the Cross. But only if we follow Christ in humility and obedience, only if we take up our Cross and show ourselves worthy of the name we bear.'

(signed) Dr Klausener

KARL FRIEDRICH STELLBRINK

28 October 1894—10 November 1943

KARL FRIEDRICH STELLBRINK was the son of a customs official. After passing his matriculation he entered a *Land* Theological College and, after an interval in which he took part in the 1914-18 war, returning in 1917 with a crippled hand, passed his final examinations in 1920. For a short time he was curate at Barkhausen and in 1921 was ordained for ecclesiastical office in the overseas foreign service of the Protestant *Land* Church of Prussia. He then spent eight years among German settlers and their families in Brazil, returned to Germany with his own family in 1929 and after passing an oral examination, became Pastor of Steinsdorf, in Thuringia. On 1 June 1934, he was appointed to the Lutheran Church in Lübeck.

Stoldt, a personal friend of his, and a Prior of the Evangelical Church, wrote after his death:

'He was a man with a deep insight into life and affairs, and with strong instinctive powers. Although he was not an intellectual in the true sense of the word, he was a man of great knowledge and quickness of mind, well informed and spiritually more impressive than many of his clerical colleagues with an academic training. When we were sitting together in my country rectory or at his home, he loved to talk of his years in Brazil and of his many and varied experiences there. He often longed to return to the sun and freedom of that blessed land, to the absence of frustration in his daily life and work, to the wide open spaces which invited useful activity. He hated nothing more than the restriction of word or deed. . . . He was a fanatical lover of truth, who took real pleasure in getting down to the point and in speaking his mind; and he was a practical man, always at home and able to adapt himself to anything, with the sole exception of the Third Reich. His character was such, that any initial attempts to adapt himself to the new system or to serve it were doomed to failure . . . and so it was inevitable that the day would come when the Gestapo began to take an interest in him.'[1]

[1] From *Wo seine Zeugen starben ist sein Reich*, Hansa Verlag Josef Toth, Hamburg.

194

Pastor Stellbrink was arrested by the Gestapo on 7 April 1942. Three Catholic chaplains, Johannes Prassek, Hermann Lange and Eduard Müller were arrested soon afterwards. On 24 June 1943, Stellbrink stood with these three before the People's Court, which had come from Berlin to Lübeck to pronounce the death sentence, in camera, on these four ministers of religion. The following day there took place the trial of a large group of Christian laymen, of whom eighteen,

195

some of them soldiers, were sentenced to long periods of imprisonment.

The impetus to this trial of Christians had been given by one of Pastor Stellbrink's sermons, on 29 May 1942, the day after a bad air-raid on Lübeck, when he called on Christians to listen to the word of God and obey it. His words attracted the attention of the Gestapo, who thereupon established the facts of his rôle in the dissemination of the letters of Bishop von Galen and of the spiritual unity of the clergy, of both confessions, against National Socialism.

On 25 July 1943, while in prison, Hermann Lange wrote on this point: 'The common sufferings of the past few years have brought about a *rapprochement* of the two Churches. The imprisonment of the Catholic and Protestant clergy is a symbol both of their joint suffering and of the *rapprochement.*'

Eduard Müller's comment was:

'That we, the people of today, find it so difficult to bear suffering, to take up our Cross, is because the meaning of the Cross and of suffering have been forgotten. It has all become theory; in practice we are only too ready to make conditions . . . otherwise we should glory in suffering for Christ and would willingly take upon ourselves all adversities . . . and now our Lord and Master is taking us to task, now he is giving us an idea of what it means to follow Christ.'

On 27 January 1943, also while in prison, Johannes Prassek wrote:

'In this case it is better to be out of step, to be old-fashioned, behind the times, anti-social, escapist, and all the other ridiculous propaganda words used to boost the perverted *Weltanschauung* of today. We know that our ideas and dogmas protect the security and welfare of mankind, that in these ideas of ours the law of nature is on our side, and so is the law of God. That knowledge gives us security and also the courage, if need be, to say "NO" to the age of power, though we as individuals may well be crushed by it.'

On 31 October 1943, just before his death, Karl Friedrich Stellbrink wrote to his wife:

'God condemns no man before his birth and does not take it upon Himself to harden any human heart. We are com-

196

pletely free to make our own decisions, therefore we can and must wish and choose, and God may fulfil our wishes. But He does not inspire our decisions, not even secretly; we must make them for ourselves, though He knows in advance. The compatibility of His omniscience with our free will can be explained by two principles of mathematics: 1. Parallels never intersect; 2. They intersect at infinity. These two principles are contradictory, but both are right.'

A few days later, on 10 November 1943, the four ministers of Lübeck set out on their last journey, to the place of execution in Hamburg. As convinced Christians, they went to their death with courage and fortitude.

BERNHARD LICHTENBERG

3 December 1875—3 November 1943

BERNARD LICHTENBERG, from Silesia, chose to become a priest and was ordained in 1899. He spent a short time as a curate in Neisse but from 1900 onwards worked in Berlin. During the 1914-18 war he was military chaplain to the 3rd Grenadier Guards Regiment and received the Red Cross Service Medal. After the war he became well known as a member of the Berlin City Council, on which he represented the Centre Party. In 1932 he became a Canon and in 1938 Provost of St Hedwig's Cathedral in Berlin. He lived as he preached, in apostolic poverty, strict asceticism and untiring service to his congregation.

On 28 August 1941, Bernhard Lichtenberg, Provost of St Hedwig's Cathedral in Berlin, sent off the following letter:

Dr Conti, Senior Physician
The Reich Ministry of the Interior
Unter den Linden, 72
Berlin, NW 7

'On 3 August 1941, the Bishop of Münster asserted in his sermon in the St Lamberti Church in Münster, that it had come to his knowledge that in the Reich Ministry of the Interior, in the office of Dr Conti, Senior Physician of the Reich, no secret was made of the fact that a large number of people of unsound mind in Germany had been wilfully killed, and were to be killed in future.

'If this allegation were untrue, you, Dr Conti, would have long since taken proceedings for slander against the Bishop, or the Secret State Police would have arrested him. Even though God's sacred Ten Commandments be publicly ignored, the Reich Penal Code still has the force of law. ¶211 of the Reich Penal Code provides: "Whosoever wilfully kills a person shall, if the killing be committed with malice aforethought, be sentenced to death for murder." ¶139 provides: "Whosoever receives reliable information of the intent to commit homicide . . . and neglects to inform the authorities, or the threatened person thereof, in good time shall be. . . punished."

'If the government authorities who are entrusted with prosecution and punishment see no cause to intervene here, then

every German citizen whose conscience and office urge him so to do must raise his voice.

'This I hereby do.

'A short time ago a bewildered mother came to my office. She sought my advice and help. A week before, she had received from a provincial mental hospital the news that her 38-year-old son had died of furunculosis of the lip and meningitis, and had been cremated. He had only been in this institution for a week. He had been moved there from another institution, which was merely a collecting point for "those under sentence of death". He had spent 18 years in yet another mental home, and a month before the doctor there had offered to allow him to go home. As soon as he heard this information, on his wife's return from a visit to the hospital, the patient's father had sent a registered letter agreeing to the release of his son, but this letter arrived too late, as the son had already been moved to the collecting point. A second registered letter, to the collecting point, also arrived too late, for the son had already been moved to the "place of execution". The mother went after him and persistently demanded her son, as agreed with the doctor at the first mental hospital. The doctor refused to release him, and the mother went home. The father, in another registered letter, then again demanded that the son should be handed over immediately. In answer he received a few days later news of the son's death and the information that the ashes would be made available. Only God knows how many thousands or tens of thousands of times such cases have been repeated. The public is not allowed to know and the relatives as in this case are afraid to make a public protest lest they lose their freedom or their lives.

'The burden of being an accessory after the fact to a crime that violates both the moral code and the laws of the state weigh heavily on my priestly soul. But though I am but one individual, I, as a human being, a Christian, a priest and a German, demand of you, the Chief Physician of the Reich, that you answer for the crimes that have been perpetrated at your bidding or with your consent, and which will call forth the vengeance of the Lord on the heads of the German people.

'I am sending copies of this letter to the Reich Chancellery, to the Reich Ministries and to the Secret State Police.'

(signed) BERNHARD LICHTENBERG

A further letter, which Provost Lichtenberg drafted for the Chairman of the Fulda Episcopal Conference, Cardinal Bertram, in answer to a letter from one of the Ministers of the Reich, did not reach its destination. The Gestapo found and confiscated it while searching Lichtenberg's home. The following is an extract from that letter:

'In your letter of 4 August 1941, to His Eminence the Cardinal, you find in the joint pastoral letter of the German bishops cause to express the extreme surprise of the Reich Government at the conduct of all German bishops who took part in the Fulda Episcopal Conference from 24 to 26 June, on the grounds that the bishops did not restrict themselves, as would in your opinion have befitted them, to notifying the Government of their anxieties, justified or unjustified, in a memorandum. You add that, had they done this, you would have been quite prepared to let the Cardinal (and thus all the German bishops) know the Government's reactions, and their opinion as to whether the individual points were worthy of consideration.

'Herr Reichsminister, there is a sphere in which, by the will of the divine founder of the Catholic Church, Jesus Christ, the Catholic bishops require no tutelage; in which they are on the contrary the teachers and leaders and must call a grave and warning "Halt", even to the rightful governing body of the state: *In rebus fidei et morum.*

'In this case you are hearing our views through the medium of a courteous letter; but it would be a great mistake to take that as a sign of weakness. Though the bishops seldom make demands, a request from the entire episcopate *in rebus fidei et morum* is in effect a demand, all the more so when it is directed to a temporal power which has overstepped the bounds of power set by God, and that not to protect the people but to harm them.'

On 22 May 1942, Bernhard Lichtenberg, Provost and Prelate, was sentenced to two years' imprisonment by a Special Court attached to the *Land* Court, for improper use of the pulpit and offences against the Sedition Law.

The following are extracts from the Judge's Summing Up:

I

'On 29 August 1941, the defendant held evensong in St Hedwig's Church, before a large congregation. He closed the service with a prayer in which he said, among other things: "Let us now pray for the Jews and for the wretched prisoners in the concentration camps, above all for my fellow clergy". Two women students who happened to be in church were offended by this and reported it. The charge is therefore that he, as a minister of religion and in the course of his duties in a Church, pronounced upon various affairs of state in a manner calculated to cause a breach of the peace. The defendant admits having made the aforementioned statements in the course of the evening prayer from the pulpit of St Hedwig's Church . . . He states that he has included the Jews in his prayers ever since the synagogues were first set on fire and Jewish businesses closed. He was at the time outraged by such vandalism and had therefore resolved to include the Jews in his prayers every evening.

II

'About the middle of October 1941, the defendant found a printed pamphlet on his desk . . . It was a copy of a pamphlet recently produced on instructions from the Reichsminister for Propaganda and distributed to all German citizens by the Local Groups of the National Socialist Party. The defendant immediately resolved to come out against the contents of the pamphlet by means of a proclamation, that is to say, by an announcement during divine service on behalf of all the clergy of St Hedwig's Church. To this end he prepared the following draft, which was found when he was arrested on 23 October 1941:

"Proclamation: An inflammatory pamphlet against the Jews is being distributed from house to house in Berlin. This pamphlet asserts that every German who supports the Jews out of so-called false sentimentality, even if it is by way of a friendly meeting, is guilty of betraying his people. Do not let yourselves be led astray by un-Christian ideas, but act in accordance with the stern commandment of Jesus Christ: 'Thou shalt love thy neighbour as thyself'."

III

'In imposing the sentence it must be taken into account in his (Lichtenberg's) favour that he has no previous convictions, that he can look back on many years of useful activity as a priest, that he is honoured and respected on all sides in his diocese, and that he played his part in the Great War. . . .

Taking all these circumstances into consideration and in view of the fact that the defendant is not in the best of health and that any deprivation of liberty will therefore have a greater punitive effect on him than would normally be the case . . . a total sentence of two years' imprisonment has been laid down. pursuant to ¶74 of the Penal Code.'

Provost Bernhard Lichtenberg served his two years' imprisonment in Berlin-Tegel prison. But at the end of that time he was not released. He was moved to Dachau concentration camp on 3 November 1943, and died on the journey.

EDITH STEIN

12 October 1891—9 August 1942

E D I T H S T E I N was born in Breslau, the daughter of a timber merchant. From 1911 to 1915 Edith Stein studied philosophy, German literature and history at Breslau and Göttingen Universities; she took her degree in 1916, worked for her Doctorate of Philosophy under Husserl, the Freiburg philosopher, and afterwards became his assistant. Her philosophical studies led her from atheism to a belief in God and in 1922 she became a Catholic. From 1922 to 1931 she was a teacher at Speyer and made a reputation for herself with several significant works in the field of phenomenology and philosophy. Her work *Husserl's Phänomenologie und die Philisophie des Heiligen Thomas von Aquin* (Husserl's Phenomenology and the Philosophy of St Thomas Aquinas) bridged the gap between classical and modern philosophy. There followed *Endliches und ewiges Sein; Versuch eines Aufstiegs zum Sinn des Seins* (Everlasting Existence; an attempt to reach the Purpose of Being), and *Kreuzeswissenschaft: eine Studie über Johannes vom Kreuz* (A study of St John of the Cross). In 1932 Edith Stein was appointed lecturer at the *Deutsches Institut für wissenschaftliche Pädagogik,* but was discharged in 1933 owing to her Jewish origin. Following a long-cherished wish, she entered the Carmelite convent in Köln-Lindenthal (Cologne).

'I think I know I must still suffer much for the sake of Judaism,' she once said, and 'at last it dawned on me that God had once again asked great suffering of his people, and that the fate of that people was also my own.' She made no word of complaint when she was torn away from her work at the height of her career, and in the Convent, as Sister Benedicta, she quietly pursued her secret vocation in complete dedication to the service of God.

'Then came the great day of the final, decisive Hitler election,' writes the Mother Superior of the Convent, Sister Teresia Renata de Spiritu Sancto; and she describes how 'Your Yes for the *Führer*' was written in large letters on every lime tree in the Dürener Strasse in Lindenthal. Non-Aryans were not allowed to take part in the election, so Sister Benedicta was to remain behind while the other nuns, with archiepiscopal consent, made their pilgrimage to the polls. But that evening two men appeared in the office. They had ascertained that Dr Stein was the only nun in the Convent who had failed in her duty to vote; owing to indisposition, of course, they said; but they had a car and would be glad to drive her there and back. At that moment, Sister Benedicta had no wish to divulge her descent: 'All right,' she said simply, 'if the gentlemen attach such great importance to my voting "No", I can give them that pleasure.'

But on 10 April 1938 things looked more serious. The principles of National Socialism and of Hitler's government had so clearly shown themselves to be anti-Christian and anti-God that even the simplest German could no longer be in any doubt as to the aims of the new régime. Meanwhile the power of the rulers had degenerated into a brutal reign of terror before which everyone trembled. In the Convent in Cologne there was great uncertainty as to what attitude should be adopted. The Secret State Police had already expelled from their monasteries a number of men in Holy Orders without warning or reason, and had cast them into the street without means of support. The Convent had for some time anticipated the same fate. If they should attract the attention of the authorities during the election, surely their fate would be sealed. For this reason many of the nuns were inclined to ignore well-meant advice to boycott the election, and most of them felt that it was quite unimportant whether one voted 'Yes' or 'No', as the result had been fixed in advance by the Party and whatever happened the Nazis would alter the figures in each constituency to give the required result.

But Sister Benedicta energetically opposed this view. Otherwise so gentle and yielding, she became a completely different person and again and again implored the Sisters not to vote for Hitler, regardless of the consequences either for the individual or for the community. He was an enemy of God and would drag Germany down to destruction with him.

There was considerable doubt and confusion, which reached a peak when a delegation of the election committee was announced in the office of the Convent before 8 o'clock

Photo from Morus Verlag files

on the morning of the election, just as the first group of
Sisters were about to leave for the polls. This had never
happened before and the Mother Superior left the visitors in
no doubt of her displeasure. They excused themselves by
saying that they knew that Carmelite nuns were not allowed
to leave their seclusion and that they therefore wanted to

help by collecting the ballot papers. The Mother Superior pointed out that the poll, which the nuns had never yet evaded, was supposed to be public, but secret. Argument was useless, they had to submit. The votes were cast alphabetically.

At the end the chairman, who kept the electoral list, said: 'Not everyone has voted . . .' and then came the dreaded moment: 'And Dr Edith Stein?'

'She is not entitled to vote.'

'Of course she is, born in '91. She's certainly entitled to vote.'

The answer came with icy calm:

'She is not aryan.'

The three men started. Then one of them cried, 'Write that down, she's not aryan.' They packed up in great haste and left the Convent . . . and the events of 9 November put the finishing touches to the story.

In the quiet suburb of Lindenthal everything was more or less orderly, but news of the burning of the synagogues, the beating up of Jewish people and the excesses against them and their friends, penetrated to the Convent and filled everyone with horror.

Sister Benedicta was numbed with pain. The fear that her presence might endanger the community gave her no peace.

At the end of 1938 Edith Stein moved to a Convent at Echt, in Holland, and there she was arrested by the SS in January 1942. When she entered the Gestapo office in Maastricht, her greeting was 'Jesus Christ be praised.' Later, in a period of 'conditional freedom of movement,' during which she had to wear a yellow star to show that she was Jewish, she told the Mother Superior that she had been driven to use this greeting by the conviction that she was 'in the midst of the ancient struggle between Jesus and Lucifer.'

Her final arrest took place on 2 August 1942. Jewish eye-witnesses reported: 'Among the prisoners brought in on 5 August, Sister Benedicta attracted attention by her great calm and composure. The distress in the camp and the agitation among the new arrivals was indescribable. Sister Benedicta went around among the women, consoling, helping, calming, soothing as an angel. She immediately took over the wretched children, washed them and combed their hair, saw that they had food and attention. As long as she stayed in the camp she made of washing and cleaning a labour of love, and we were all amazed.'

Then her road led her to the east. In Auschwitz camp, on 9 August 1942, Edith Stein, No. 44074, was murdered in a gas chamber.

MAX JOSEF METZGER

3 February 1887—17 April 1944

MAX JOSEF METZGER grew up in the Black Forest. He studied theology in Freiburg, was ordained in 1911, took his Doctorate of Theology and spent some time as a curate in Mannheim, Karlsruhe and Oberhausen. He went to France in 1914 as a divisional chaplain, and then in 1916 became chaplain in charge of the People's Welfare Centre in Graz. He was deeply influenced by the war and soon became one of the leading Catholic pacifists. In 1917 he and Stratmann, a Dominican, founded the 'Peace League of German Catholics', of which he was the Secretary-General up to his death. He also played an important part in the foundation in 1938 of the 'Una Sancta Brotherhood'.

His concern for the future of Germany induced Max Josef Metzger to submit to the Protestant Archbishop of Upsala, Dr Eiden, in 1942, a memorandum on the question of a new system of government for Germany, with the request that he should intercede with the Bishops in Allied countries to use their influence to make peace. This document, in which as a precautionary measure (as it was to be sent out of Germany), 'Nordland' was used instead of Germany and 'Anti-national Party' instead of National Socialist Party, read as follows:

'Germany (the united German *Länder*) shall be a federation of democratically governed free states (Prussia, Bavaria, Saxony, etc.). Within the framework of the German Constitution each state shall enjoy independence in internal affairs and administration, and in cultural and social matters. Foreign policy is of common concern and shall be the responsibility of the Federal Government.

'The Constitution shall ensure that German policy, both domestic and foreign, shall be a sincere policy of peace based on moral truth, good faith and social justice.

'The domestic peace policy shall rest on fundamental moral laws, on the recognition and preservation of equal basic rights for all citizens, on a progressive social policy (security of work, earnings and livelihood; nationalisation of all mines, power stations, railways and of real estate, including arable land,

208

forests and lakes; a social tax policy which shall protect the weak); and a just policy in questions of nationality and race (to include self-administration for national bodies, e.g. in respect of public funds for school purposes).

'The foreign peace policy shall recognise and respect to the full the rights of foreign peoples and shall support, or effect, voluntary disarmament (except for a police force for the preservation of internal order) in favour of supra-national armed forces which, in the service of an impartial organisation of the "United States of Europe", shall take over the protection of lawful peace among the states.

'The Constitution shall guarantee to every German personal dignity and legal security, freedom of culture, language, conscience and religion; freedom of opinion and, finally, freedom in the possession and use of personal property, within the bounds necessary in the common interest, which shall be clearly and legally defined.

'All Germans who can be proved guilty of contributing towards the national disaster and of abusing their own people, in common with all persons sentenced for common crimes, shall be deprived of civil rights for a period of twenty years (voting right, the right to hold public office, etc.). The complicity of all agents of the National Socialist Party and its affiliated organisations and of their military self-protection organisation shall be presumed, until or unless their personal and political reliability can be proved. The national register of such persons shall be public.

'Until such time as the new constitution has been approved on the basis of general, free national elections, legislative power in Germany shall be vested in the German *Volkstag*. The *Volkstag* shall consist of leading representatives of all branches of public life, who shall be selected initially from the German Order of Peace, an association of such personalities from all political groups and former parties who, in defence of the moral, social and political principals of the new peace policy, have proved their worth before their people and the world, particularly by the fact that they were prepared for the sake of their convictions to suffer personal disadvantage through the disfavour of the discredited régime.

'This political programme has been drawn up for use in the event of a revolution at the end of the war, during which the continuity of justice could no longer be preserved.'

This document fell into the hands of a woman Gestapo agent; and Metzger, who had already been imprisoned for a time in 1936, was arrested by the Gestapo on 29 June 1943, and condemned for 'high treason and for assisting the enemy'. For him, of course, there was 'no room' in the Third Reich, as Freisler made quite clear before the People's Court.

Brother Paulus as Metzger called himself, after the apostle, had often spoken at the great international peace congresses of the post-war years in Berne, the Hague, Graz, Luxembourg and Constance; in 1921 he was the first German to raise his voice in Paris where he proclaimed that knowledge of Christian obligation demanded of every Christian that he live up to God's Commandments in the political sphere also. 'That is what brings peace, that spirit of final, personal sacrifice, even at the cost of one's own life, just as Christ paid the price on the Cross; self-sacrifice for truth, justice, love and peace, for the kingdom of God on earth.'

When the death sentence was pronounced on 14 October 1943, Brother Paulus replied quite calmly: 'I should like to say once more that I have a clear conscience before God and before my people and that I have only tried to serve them . . . now it is done. I am at peace, I have offered up my life to God for the peace of the world and the unity of the Church.' He was executed at Brandenburg on 17 April 1944

FRIEDRICH JUSTUS PERELS

13 November 1910—23 April 1945

FRIEDRICH JUSTUS PERELS was closely connected with the Church from his early youth. While he was a pupil of a Berlin Gymnasium he belonged to a schoolchildren's Bible class, and as a law student in Heidelberg and Berlin he was a member of the Christian Student Association. After his first law examination in 1933 he spent most of his time working for the *Pfarrernotbund* and the Confessional Church. He died a deeply convinced Christian. Owing to the *Sippenhaft* system, his father, Dr Ernst Perels, a professor at Berlin University, fell victim to the Gestapo at the same time.

*   *   *

Christianity for Friedrich Justus Perels meant that God wished to be taken at His word, and would then make his people free and mould their lives. While he was working for the Confessional Church he therefore consistently rejected 'German-Christian' interpretations of the scriptures and insisted that they should be presented unfalsified and unabridged, and that conclusions should be drawn accordingly. Martin Fischer remarks in an obituary that Perels would not allow anyone to say that it was the duty of the Church to serve the people. 'No, not the people, but God. It is all too easy for a man to claim self-justification in the service of the people, for both he and the people may have long been against God.'

Friedrich Perels rejected dishonest compromise in all its forms, exposed escapism and self-deception wherever he found them and worked with energy, intelligence and skill to bring clarity and decisiveness into the work of the Church, striving to promote unanimity within the Confessional Church and to defend it against encroachments by the state, In this and particularly in his efforts to help the persecuted, he was to some extent dependent on help from people (who were critical of the régime) in official positions, and in this way, and through his friendship with Dietrich Bonhoeffer, he came in contact with the various groups of the resistance movement—socialist, conservative and confessional. Much

212

Photo by Atelier Bieber

later, his service to the Church, in establishing this contact,
was recognised by Bishop Dibelius in the following words:

'We must remember that he was the only man we still had
in Berlin who could keep the door open to other people,
groups and powers . . . He helped us to prepare for the hour
which was bound to come and to see its approach . . . He
taught us not to let the four walls of the catacombs in which

213

we were jammed together condition our thoughts and plans for the future. . . .'

Pastor Eberhard Bethge, a close friend and later a fellow-prisoner, writes of him as a Christian in everyday life: 'When did anyone turn to Friedrich Justus Perels in vain? From morning to night he was at the service of anyone who sought his help and was often on his feet till he was on the verge of exhaustion, trying to secure freedom for prisoners, to help relatives of people in concentration camps, to advise the wives of the clergy, or to help Jews to improve their lot, to hide them or help them to escape.'

Perels was fully aware of the danger of all this work, but his own words show that he took it all as a matter of course: 'So many people fall in battle for this system. I find it better to fall in battle against it.'

His arrest soon followed, on 5 October 1944. Of his time in prison Eberhard Bethge reported:

'We came across each other for the first time at the end of November 1944, when I saw him wave to me from his cell window while I was at exercise, and every time round he again climbed on his stool so that he could wave. We had no chance to speak to each other until March 1945, when I was given a job as boilerman and passed his cell at meal times. Meanwhile we had exchanged secret messages to let each other know about our interrogations. His were particularly brutal; for weeks he had to endure physical ill-treatment, continuous threats to his family and the vilest abuse.

'I myself learnt the following facts about him: that he had belonged to the Freiburg Circle, with Ritter, Wolff, von Dietz and Bauer; that he was very closely in touch with those who took part in the attempt of 20 July; and that he was continuously involved in conspiracy with Bonhoeffer and von Dohnanyi, and knew also the chief of the Berlin Criminal Police, Nebe, a staunch opponent of the régime.

'On 2 February, he was condemned to death, nominally for having failed to report to the police. Rüdiger Schleicher, Klaus Bonhoeffer, Hans John, Hans Kloss (of Vienna) and Perels were all tried at the same time, but only Kloss escaped with as little as four years penal servitude; from him I heard later that on the day of the trial Perels had conducted an extremely able defence and that he bore himself very well.

'The condemned men were transferred to my wing and I managed to talk with them almost every day, above all with Perels. He was busy all the time sending out material and

214

suggestions to the outside world in an effort to procure a re-trial, to postpone the execution and to keep in step with those who had been condemned with him. These efforts were successful, in so far as there was by Easter reason to hope that the execution might be stayed. Nor in fact was the order ever issued. For weeks Perels had tried, through official channels, to obtain permission to receive Holy Communion, but all efforts were fruitless and with the assistance of one of the guards I administered the last sacrament to him in secret on Easter Sunday. The wine came from the cell of Ernst von Harnack, who had been executed earlier, the wafers were given to us by the Jesuit Provincial Father Roesch, another prisoner.

'The Allies were now approaching and the tension was almost unbearable; all the more so when on 21 April 1945, while the first artillery shells were falling on Berlin, the condemned men were handed over to the legal authorities and moved to another wing.'

During the night of 22-23 April 1945, Friedrich Justus Perels was dragged from his cell and, like those condemned with him, shot in the street by a special SS contingent.

'After the war the Church will be wiped out,' Friesler had screamed at Perels during the trial, which as it happened took place the day before he himself was killed by a bomb.

'The Church will endure,' was Perel's firm and serene reply.

Shortly before his death, Friedrich Perels wrote to his wife:

'Today, Good Friday, all the great solace of the Cross of Jesus Christ is directly before our eyes. It is a powerful and eternal truth that He was sacrificed for our sins and that by His wounds we have been saved. He gives us this certainty and thereby brings us happiness even in the midst of great trouble, and drives away fear and suffering. This I am learning here in full measure. And all of you should put your faith in this and it should rest on nothing else.'

DIETRICH BONHOEFFER

4 February 1906—5 April 1945

DIETRICH BONHOEFFER was born in Breslau and was one of a large family. His father, Karl Bonhoeffer, was a well known physicist, and all manner of people came to his house in Berlin; religious leaders, friends of Dietrich's and in particular the Dellbrücks and the Harnacks.

In April 1943, the Gestapo and officials from the Military Court came to the house to question Dietrich Bonhoeffer and to search for evidence that would incriminate him and his friends, but it was not until after the failure of the conspiracy of 20 July that the incriminating evidence fell into their hands. Dietrich Bonhoeffer had fought hard to survive, he had used great ingenuity and he was always optimistic. But he had often said to himself and to his friends, that he who lives by the sword must reckon that he may also die by it. On 5 April 1945 he was killed in the Flossenbürg concentration camp.

*   *   *

Dietrich Bonhoeffer was an intellectual, energetic and sensitive. He liked to have room to breathe and was convinced that the joys and satisfactions of life depend on a few important decisions: they might be obvious decisions or the outcome of thought and conflict, in either case no further discussion was needed. In his own life two decisions were vital; the decision to go into the Church and the choice of the Confessional Church, and the decision to take violent political action which was on the face of it so flagrantly opposed to the traditions of his Church.

Twice he was presented with tempting opportunities to evade such decisions and twice he thrust them aside. In 1935, in the midst of preparations for a journey to India, he was recalled from his position as German Pastor in England to take charge of an illegal training school for teachers in Pommerania. He was not much older than his pupils, but he became an inspiring teacher to a new generation of theologians. The personal difficulties which his work involved were not immediately evident. That changed in

1939, for by then he knew that he must engage in political as well as religious resistance, and that he must accept all the danger and loneliness which this entailed, because he could not and would not burden his Church with such things. In the summer of 1939, while on a lecture tour in the United States, he watched with anxiety and dismay the development of world affairs. He was offered a home, an office and a professorship, but he chose to return to Germany.

A passage in his diary reads: 'In everything I do I miss Germany, my own people . . . I cannot understand why I am here . . . The short prayer in which we remembered our German colleagues was almost too much for me . . . In the event of war I do not want to find myself here . . . Since I have been on board ship, I am no longer in two minds about the future.'

Later, from his cell, he wrote to his friend Eberhard Bethge: 'I reckon the fact that I sit here is part of my share in the fate of Germany, a share which I am resolved to accept.' And so with a few clear-cut decisions he committed himself beyond retreat, and in doing so found a great inner freedom. He was free to meet people of all kinds and convictions, and approached them in an encouraging, undogmatic and resourceful manner; to take holidays whenever the opportunity occurred, to lose himself in playing the music he loved best, the masters before Bach, and the great classics. He had zest for life and the capacity to impart it to others. He was a good teacher because there was nothing of the lecturer about him, a convincing talker because he never expected other people automatically to agree with him.

During his two years in prison, Bonhoeffer occupied himself with theological writings, and his profound experience found expression in his letters and poems. The following are extracts from a fragment of a letter, unpublished, which he wrote in Tegel prison in 1943:

'Even if you must scorn life in order to master it, at least do not forget to love it once you have done so. Beware of speaking too lightly of happiness and of flirting with misery: that is the negation of living, an abuse of man as he was created and as he lives his life, a poor sinner yearning for happiness as a slight sign of friendliness from God. It is not so easy to be unhappy, and he who is so does not scorn or abuse the man who is happy. There is no good reason to be willing to bear misery unless it is to make other people happy. Unhappiness comes of itself, or rather from God, and we have no need to run after it. To become unhappy is fate. But to want to be unhappy is blasphemy, and a grave spiritual illness.

'History, like nature, develops an excess of force to attain a necessary but modest goal. History adopts extravagant measures to preserve mankind and mobilises immense forces to bring home to man one single, essential truth. We see and regret what seems to us a mad disproportion between senseless sacrifice and moderate success, but we should never underestimate even the most modest achievement. It is like the one chestnut among a thousand, which quietly puts forth roots into the ground and in its turn bears fruit.

THEO HESPERS

12 December 1903—9 September 1943

THEO HESPERS' life led him from the peaceful security of a middle-class Catholic family on the Lower Rhine into the glare of the political arena, by way of the youth movement, and on to an early death. In his schooldays he was a member of the 'Quickborn' Catholic youth organisation and was an enthusiastic hiker. He passed his lower school-leaving certificate and then became a business apprentice. But the problems of the post-war generation caught and held his attention, so that his work with the youth organisation rather than his actual profession became his prime interest in life.

At the age of nineteen, out of youthful enthusiasm and patriotic sentiment, Hespers joined in the fight against the Separatists in the Ruhr and on the Rhine, and was arrested by the Belgians. Three years later he joined both the *Westmark* Boy Scouts and the Christian-Social movement, and his intense interest in fundamental social and human problems came to the fore. As a left-wing Catholic he was involved in violent disputes with the Nazis even before the seizure of power, and in 1933 he was forced to emigrate to Holland. His political work on the frontier at Roermond led to a complaint from the German authorities, and as a result he had to move to North Brabant.

The trial in Essen of the *Jungnationalen Bund* of the Youth Federation, in June 1937, caused great excitement among Netherlands youth organisations, and the climax came when Hans Böckling was sentenced to 12 years' imprisonment. This trial led to a widespread demand for support for German youth in their struggle against dictatorship, and also to the founding in Brussels and Amsterdam of the magazine *Kameradschaft*, of which Theo Hespers and Hans Ebeling were the publishers.

'Catholic youth has too high a conception of national unity and freedom to sacrifice itself and its ideas to Nazi demagogy. For them such unity does not lie in the destruction of the individuality of Churches, races and classes, but in

220

active co-operation and in mobilising all available forces for
the common task: of reviving the life of the people on a truly
ethical and social basis. It is quite clear that free-will and
not force is the pre-requisite of freedom,' was Theo Hespers'
message to German youth in 1938, in *Kameradschaft*. 'We
shall never do what is required of us if we throw in our hand
and retire into the ghetto! Terror, or fear of breaking the
law, must never deter us from our duty as Christians.'

Hespers' attitude rested on his Catholic faith, on his belief in federation, and he explains it further:

'In the German youth movement we have always been very critical of the old parties, the cultural and religious bodies. In some respects this attitude is open to criticism. Whenever we took it upon ourselves to infuse some life into the existing system, we insisted on keeping our distance, so that our personal attitude should not be compromised. It may be worth while to explain once more why we criticised and repudiated so many organisations whose aims and aspirations were probably admirable: at whom, then, was our Christianity directed? Was it the ideas or the people? We can answer unequivocally that it was both the people and the half-hearted manner in which the ideas were put into practice. We observed that socialists took no decisive action for social reform, that nationalists had before their eyes not the welfare of the nation, but personal goals, that Catholics lacked the broad view expected of the universal Church, that the representatives of Christianity were not bound by the doctrine of brotherly love. . . .

'None of the leading cultural and political groups which existed in 1933 found the strength to prevent the seizure of power by this despotic régime, or was itself able to survive. What was the fundamental reason why there was no adequate resistance to prevent the onslaught of total barbarism? Were the German people too immature, or unwilling to fight for freedom? Were too few of the right people in positions of power? No, those were not the decisive factors. What was lacking among the leaders in every sphere was conviction, the sense of responsibility and readiness to make sacrifices for their own cause. . . .

'The German people, too often deceived and betrayed and now caught up in a system of organised mistrust, are too thoroughly disillusioned to rally again from one day to the next, to some cheap slogan. So the most important and the most difficult job will be to re-establish mutual trust among Germans. But this work can be done only by people and groups who carry no guilt, past or present, and who can evoke confidence by their personal conduct and reputation.'

After German troops marched into Holland in May 1940, Hespers managed to reach Dunkirk. The British were prepared to take him with them, but not to accept responsibility for his wife and child during a military retreat. So he stayed in Belgium with his family and lived quietly in the country, under an assumed name, helped by friends in the Belgian youth movement. But in February 1942 he was recognised, arrested and taken to the Central Security Office of the Reich in Berlin. Soon afterwards, he was condemned to death.

Theo Hespers was hanged on 9 September 1943, after an air-raid on Plötzensee prison. Two hundred and fifty other condemned prisoners were put to death at the same time, as there was a shortage of space for new admissions.

ALFRED DELP

15 September 1907—2 February 1945

ALFRED DELP was the eldest of the six children of a health insurance official in Baden. He attended the elementary school, and went over to the Catholic faith at the age of fifteen. He was then prepared for a higher education by the Pastor of Lampertheim, and within three years he matriculated and entered the Jesuit Order. In 1937, he was ordained as a priest, having meanwhile obtained his Doctorate of Philosophy.

From 1937 to 1941 he did a certain amount of teaching himself and worked part-time for the *Stimmen der Zeit*. This last activity led to several weeks' imprisonment, even at that early stage.

From 1941 to 1944 he was one of the clergy at St George's Church, Munich-Bogenhausen. The papers he wrote in prison, *Im Angesicht des Todes* (In the Face of Death) round off his former works: *Tragische Existenz* (The Tragedy of Existence), *Der Mensch und die Geschichte* (Man and History), *Zur Erde entschlossen* (Earthbound) and *Der mächtige Gott* (The Power of God).

'The common fate, my personal situation, the decision of the next few days; it all adds up to one thing: surrender yourself unto your God and you will find yourself again. Now you are in the power of others; they torture and terrify you and drive you from one extremity to the other. Then the voice of freedom sings: for us death has no sting. For it is life that goes forth into infinity. . . .

'One thing I have learnt during these weeks of confinement is that the man who is not capable of vision and freedom in his own mind is at the mercy of his surroundings, of circumstances and of tyrants. Whoever is not at ease in an atmosphere of freedom, which is unaffected by outside powers and conditions, is truly lost.

'. . . The hour of the birth of human freedom is the hour of meeting with God.'

These words were written by Father Alfred Delp at the turn of the year 1944-45, while he was in prison awaiting sen-

Photograph taken in the People's Court

tence. At the wish of his provincial superior, Father Rösch, he had readily taken part in the conferences of the Kreisau circle in order to help with preparations for a new order in Germany after the collapse. His special task was the problem of a Christian social order, a subject to which he had devoted himself earlier while in charge of the sociological department of the *Stimmen der Zeit,* the Jesuit publication.

Even in prison he was still pre-occupied with these matters. The starting point in his deliberations was the god-lessness of modern man which, to his mind, could not be overcome merely by the preaching of the Gospel. 'I can preach as much as I like, and handle people skilfully or unskilfully and set them on the right path again as long as I please; so long as he is forced to live in humiliating and inhuman conditions, the average man will succumb to circumstances and neither pray nor think. A fundamental change in living conditions is necessary. Delp therefore demanded of the Church that it should not restrict itself to its religious interests, but 'concern itself with the secular needs of mankind and with humanitarian order'.

For him a healthy social order was of course only a 'basic pre-condition' to his true aim. It was merely intended to create conditions in which it would be possible to educate mankind to 'independence, responsibility, judgment and conscientiousness'. The intention was that man should thereby acquire a degree of 'spiritual alertness and personal vitality' that would render him 'able once more to comprehend the name and word of God, once more to recognise and consummate God's Holy Order'. For Delp, social reform was not an end unto itself, but a step towards the 'education of man for God'.

For his collaboration with the Kreisau circle Father Delp paid with his life. On 2 February 1945 he was killed in Berlin 'by the enemies of the faith', as they are called on his memorial tablet in the St. Blaise Jesuit College. He was always alive to his responsibility for the common lot, and this he proved in life and death.

'To profess Christianity and to aspire to be a Christian today involves readiness to accept responsibility for everything. In these times God does not expect a man to appear before him bringing only his own desires and presenting only his own private anxieties. In times in which God is at odds with man over the fundamental order of existence, the Lord our God demands a man of generous heart, of great responsibility, who can really take his place before Him and shoulder the whole heavy burden.'

HANS-BERND von HAEFTEN
18 December 1905—15 August 1944

HANS-BERND VON HAEFTEN was born in Berlin, the son of an army officer. He studied law, first in Germany and after his finals as an exchange student in Cambridge. He then worked first at the German Consulate-General in Geneva, and then as secretary of the Stresemann Foundation.

In 1933 he entered the German Foreign Service and served in Copenhagen, Berlin, Vienna and Bucharest. In 1940 he came back to the Foreign Office in Berlin, and was later appointed Counsellor in the cultural department. In those days he was in close touch with Adam von Trott zu Solz and Adolf Reichwein.

Haeften had in the past worked with the Berneuchen circle in their efforts to revive interest in the Church, and after his return to Berlin began to take part in the deliberations of the Kreisau circle.

For this, his part in resistance, he was condemned to death by the People's Court on 15 August 1944, after his brother Werner, Stauffenberg's Adjutant, had been shot on 20 July, and was executed a few hours later. The Gestapo had meanwhile taken his wife away from her five children, the youngest a baby, and she like other women and children of the men who took part in the revolt was held for several weeks.

*   *   *

'When I think of Hans-Bernd von Haeften,' writes Marion von Yorck, 'I see no very clear outline. He was a man of delicate constitution, and it was really his eyes which were arresting. They betrayed the sensitivity of soul and conscience. He had a penetrating intellect and a great gift for argument, but was at his best on paper. He was a good friend and a devoted father and I can best imagine him among his family.'

In his book *Geist der Freiheit* (Spirit of Freedom), Eberhard Zeller says of Haeften:

'What was happening in Germany was to him an onslaught from a crazy godless world, against which so much that had

seemed stable and enduring crumbled to dust, but he was for
ever concerned as to how the normal relationship between
men and their rulers might be rescued from this political
travesty. He was a tall, good-looking man, anxious always to
do what was good and right and acutely conscious both of
his own failings and of the sins of the world.'

As a convinced Christian, Hans-Bernd von Haeften
rejected National Socialism long before his co-operation with
the Kreisau circle began, and his uneasiness of conscience
comes out in a letter written to his friend Herbert Krimm in
May 1941, from which the following is an extract:

'I am entirely of your opinion that the Church should exert
an influence by its mere existence, and though it should not
itself take an active part in politics or busy itself in secular
matters, it is entirely responsible in the spiritual sphere. And
if in the order or disorder of things, events or conditions occur
which endanger the spiritual salvation of man, if politics place
citizens in situations which as Christians they cannot accept,
we come to the inevitable crossroads of Church and State;
inevitable because both deal with the same people, and because
these people cannot be split into citizen and Christian. But at
such points of intersection, which may be more or less obvious,
critical, or decisive, the Episcopate does not expect the Church
to watch in silence without lifting a finger. This is the time to
speak and to admonish. When the Christian peoples are beset
by the madness of political demons, as they are today, the
Church must be heard in public and must bear witness before
the whole world. This is a part of the nature of the Church,
that it shall by its very existence influence the world.

'But it takes more than this to make a Court Chaplain: and
this applies to all you who are learned theologians, professional
Christians so to speak. For if a man who has to deal with
worldly matters asks your advice as to how he, as a Christian,
can best solve this or that problem, then you must be capable
of giving him a useful and practical answer.

'The theologian should also be in a position to give advice
sub specie fidei christianæ, not specifically as a representative
of the Church, for the Church has to deal with unchangeable
tenets of faith and not with empirical advice on worldly affairs,
which must vary in time and space according to a thousand
chances of history. But if not only the individual but also "the
governments and principalities were created by Him and unto
Him", if, that is, the earthly Kingdom also receives its final
sanction from God; if it is the ultimate aim of politics to pre-

228

Photograph taken in the People's Court

pare for the world that is to come, to serve and to rule the people in such a manner that they shall inherit the Kingdom of Heaven, then Christian statesmen must be able to come to the Church for advice.

'It is this fusion of time and eternity, of heaven and earth, that Augustine meant when he spoke of the *civitas Dei.* Catholicism has preserved this tradition more clearly but in my own opinion, has drawn the wrong conclusions, in developing Church doctrines which are to be binding for all time, in

229

all social conditions, in every state and society; when in fact the putting into practice of the Christian faith in daily life must depend on secular institutions and the manner of doing so must vary with changing historical situations. Protestantism has a greater freedom of action and the theologians ought to be able to give an answer when laymen ask their advice on worldly matters.'

HELMUTH JAMES GRAF
von MOLTKE

11 March 1907—23 January 1945

HELMUTH JAMES GRAF VON MOLTKE was born at Kreisau on his parents' estate in Silesia. He was a lawyer and at the same time managed his estates. From 1939 to 1944

Photograph taken in the People's Court

he was the expert on martial law and international law with the Supreme Command of the Armed Forces. He was executed in Plötzensee on 23 January 1945. Shortly before his death, he wrote to his sons:

> 'All my life, even when I was at school, I have fought against narrow-mindedness and violence, against presumption, intolerance and that absolute and pitiless regimentation which is part of the German character and which has found expression in the National Socialist state. I have also dedicated myself to overcome this spirit with all the harm it brings in its train: excessive nationalism, racial persecution, unbelief and materialism.'

*　　　　*　　　　*

Before the war, Helmuth James Graf von Moltke was still of the opinion 'that belief in God was not essential' to maintain the struggle against National Socialism. But later he wrote: 'Today I know that I was wrong, absolutely and entirely wrong . . . The degree of insecurity which we must endure today and the readiness to make sacrifices that is demanded of us, pre-suppose more than sound ethical principles. . . .'

Moltke, who had been imprisoned months before 20 July, because he had warned a friend of his imminent arrest, said of himself: 'Ever since National Socialism has come to power, I have tried to mitigate its effects on its victims and to prepare the way for a change. My own conscience drove me to do this, and in the last resort it is a task worth doing.'

But at his trial before the People's Court there was no mention of the deeds to which he had been driven by his conscience. He was not charged with concrete action against the state. He stood before Freisler 'not as a Protestant, not as a country gentleman, not as an aristocrat, not as a Prussian, not as a German. . . .'

The point at issue was of quite another order. It found expression in the words that Freisler screamed at von Moltke during the trial: 'There is one thing, Herr Graf, which we National Socialists and the Christians have in common, and only one: we both demand the whole man.' This sentence goes to the root of Christian resistance. The demands of the totalitarian state penetrate the very soul of man, and so engage in indissoluble conflict with the demands of God. In this situation, in this chaos, man is ground to dust. Against

232

the voice of conscience compliance with the demands of the state is a symptom of weakness and failure, of lack of principle and deep personal bondage. But to follow the call of God calls forth a whole host of enemies.

This and this alone was what von Moltke had done. It was enough to bring about his death. Anything that might have obscured the issue, all other possible indictable points, were dropped. He stood before Freisler as 'a Christian and as absolutely nothing else'. He died for one sole thought: 'How, by what means, can Christianity best serve as an anchor in time of chaos?'

An anchor. The decision of the Christian for God does not only involve persecution and death, but also the saving of the soul from chaos, taking it from the clutches of the state into a freedom which is out of reach of worldly power, into 'absolute security'. Consciousness of this security gives the strength to cope with the 'degree of danger and readiness to sacrifice' of which von Moltke wrote.

The sense of inner freedom which inspired the Christian resistance movement emerges time and again, and above all in the cellars of the Gestapo. Von Moltke describes it: '. . . So far as I was concerned the whole hall could have shouted like Herr Freisler and the walls have trembled, it would have meant absolutely nothing to me. As Isaiah (II, 43) describes it: "When thou passest through the water, I will be with thee, and through the rivers, they shall not overflow thee; when thou walkest through the fire, thou shalt not be burned, neither shall the flame kindle upon thee".'

7 FREEDOM AND ORDER

THE resistance which culminated in the attempt of 20 July 1944, and which more nearly than any other may be described as a centrally directed opposition movement, brought together men and women of widely differing views. If the attempt had succeeded, if Hitler had been killed and the revolution had taken its course, these differences would have inevitably, and rightly, come to the fore: but not, the evidence suggests, until Germany had been re-established as a constitutional state; for the conspirators were unanimous not only in their wish to be rid of the National Socialist régime, but also in their determination to build something positive in its place.

Professor Max Braubach wrote in a report based on long research: 'Anyone who examines closely the personalities of such people as Beck, Goerdeler and Stauffenberg, who reads Hassell's diaries, Schlabrendorff's reports or Moltke's last letters, will come to the conclusion that whatever the influence of human fears and longings, they were moved primarily by moral indignation against injustice and inhumanity.'

In a memorandum that was sent to the Bishop of Chichester in May 1942, via Sweden, the aim was 'to re-establish the German nation on the basis of law and social justice'; and a friend of Helmuth Moltke's wrote in 1943 that the first essential was to break the fetters on human conscience and that 'the law which has been trampled under foot must be resurrected and placed in a position of full sovereignty over all aspects of human life'.

At the end of 1943 Goerdeler wrote in a draft government proclamation: 'The Government will begin its work by placing the sovereign power of the state on an ethical and legal basis. It will respect the individual, the family, religious confessions, professional organisations, local self-government and the free trade unions; but it demands of all citizens that they regard themselves in duty bound to work for the common good.'

234

Another draft for the government proclamation states that 'it is our wish to re-establish the fundamentals of morality in every sphere of private and public life'; freedom of the spirit, of conscience, of faith and of opinion must be restored, a divided people must regain mutual trust; the only schism should be between 'crime and unscrupulousness on the one hand and honesty and integrity on the other'.

The 'Appeal to the German People' which would have been read out in the name of General Beck immediately after the elimination of Hitler, says: 'Our aim is a true national community based on respect, charity and social justice. We want fear of God to replace fear of men who have tried to usurp His power; law and freedom to replace terror and force; truth and integrity, lies and self-interest.'

The most elaborate plans were made for the period immediately after the revolution and although there came together in the making young socialists and old conservatives, churchmen, soldiers and civil servants, men and women of the right and of the left and of the centre, there seems to have been genuine willingness to learn and to adapt, and genuine progress in finding common ground. The various plans and programmes were incomplete, many of them have been lost, and the situation for which they were devised never in fact existed, but the thoughts on the future organisation of the German state which crystallised at a time of such trouble and adversity, deserves respect.

The recognised leaders of the opposition movement, though their backgrounds varied from aristocratic tradition to socialist ideology, did not come together merely to oppose. They were united also in their will to act and in their espousal of the cause of reform. Importance has since been attached to the war-time meetings between aristocrats and socialist politicians, civil servants and trade unionists, Protestants and Catholics, who constituted the Kreisau Circle, named after Graf von Moltke's estate where they often met. Moltke himself was opposed to a *coup d'état*: the National Socialists were to be given no scapegoat, they were to be left to bear sole responsibility for the disaster they had brought on the German people, right up to the end. Many other members of the group were active participants in the attempt, others were sentenced although they had 'only thought'. The proposals of the Kreisau Circle represent in the main the ideas of the younger generation, as opposed to the older die-hards. They wanted a future based on freedom and humanity in general and on social progress and a European community in particular. Above all the nihilism of the Third Reich was to give way to Christianity: 'The Government of the German Reich sees in Christianity the foundation for the moral and religious revival of our people, for the dissolution of hate and falsehood, for the re-construction of the European community of nations.'

Many details were discussed. School and university reform, the right to work and property, the welfare of the family. Work should be organised, says the treatise of 1943, so that 'it promotes personal responsibility'. The memorandum to the Bishop of Chichester mentions that 'economic order should be re-established according to genuine socialist principles' and the problems of land reform, re-distribution of property and ownership of basic industries were also considered. But the main plan was for the transition period and the government proclamation lays stress on the belief that 'the economy must initially operate on a basis of rationing and controls.'

In the field of foreign policy the immediate aim was to make peace, and the highest duty, again according to the proclamation, was 'courageously and patiently to vindicate the oft dishonoured German name. We gave warning against this war which has brought so much suffering to all mankind, and we can therefore speak openly . . . What we demand for ourselves we must and wish to concede to others.'

The duty of restitution, especially to victims of racial persecution and of dealing with war criminals, was clearly accepted. The memorandum of May 1942 states that the German opposition envisaged a federation of European states, including Great Britain, which must work in close co-operation with other state federations; and in the new Europe, which should have a common executive, a free Poland and a free Czechoslovakia should have their rightful place. In August 1943 the programme stated that the free and peaceful development of civilisation and national culture could no longer be reconciled with absolute national sovereignty, and so it was necessary to strive for a supranational order. . . .

But the primary task was to end the war. As the 'Appeal to the German People' said:

'We want to rehabilitate our honour and thereby our reputation in the community of nations. We wish to contribute by every means at our disposal towards healing the wounds which this war has inflicted on all nations, and to revive confidence among them.

'Our aim is a just peace, in which self-destruction and the annihilation of other nations may turn to co-operation. Such peace can be founded only on freedom and equal rights for all nations.'

Those who fought for all this were themselves denied success. This implies no final judgment on the rebellion nor of the motives of the rebels. Their spiritual heritage remains.

CARLO MIERENDORFF

25 March 1897—4 December 1943

CARLO MIERENDORFF was born in Darmstadt, near
Frankfurt, the son of a minor official in the employ of the
Grand Duke of Hesse. In 1914 he volunteered for the army
and came back in 1918 as an officer, with high decorations.
From 1930 he was a Socialist member of the German *Reichstag*.
He was arrested in 1933 and held prisoner in concentration
camps until 1937. In the last few years before his death he
belonged to the close circle of men who were preparing
details of a new political order for the time after Hitler's fall.

*   *   *

Among the advertisements in the *Deutsche Allgemeine
Zeitung*, published in Berlin on Christmas Day 1943, there
appeared the following notice:

> On 4 December, the Lord over Life and Death took unto
> Himself our friend and companion Carlo Mierendorff. He was
> a victim of the air-raid on Leipzig.
> In the name of all his friends,

EMIL HENK	DR THEODOR HAUBACH
Heidelberg	Berlin-Grunewald

Kasimir Edschmid, a friend who spent much of his youth
with Theodor Haubach and Carlo Mierendorff, writes:

> 'The house where Theo Haubach lived was only a few yards
> away from ours, and we knew each other well as boys. My
> brother used to be Father Christmas for the Haubach family
> as well as for our own, and Theo, who later in life was afraid
> of nothing, was terrified of him in his disguise.
> 'At the outbreak of war in 1914 Theo introduced me to his
> school friend Carlo Mierendorff on the parade ground of an
> infantry regiment stationed at Darmstadt. He, like Theo, had
> just left school. He was a fair haired, well-built boy with bold,
> chiselled features, a defiant brow, a smile which was ironic at
> one moment and enthusiastic at the next; and for all his youth
> he had great dignity, which did not for a moment conceal the
> fact that he was a man who loved a fight. As the years went

Photo by Atelier Binder

by I noticed again and again that this fighting spirit was directed at everything unkind, anti-social, inhuman and bad, and was devoted to an unceasing struggle for freedom. About a year after Mierendorff had volunteered for the army he came under my care in a military hospital and, although himself a patient, helped me in a touching and unselfish manner to care for the wounded from the Balkans.

'About the same time a group of very young men had been formed in Darmstadt under the leadership of Josef Würth, the printer. By 1918 they had published 65 leaflets, Mierendorff sending contributions from the front. In the last number, published in November 1918, at the end of the war, he finished his message with the words: "We are waiting for you, my friends, for your enthusiastic support." This might well have been the passionate and guiding motto of his life.

'After the war he founded the periodical *Das Tribunal*, in Darmstadt, which was one of the most interesting magazines to appear in those troubled times. Among other things it published the famous appeal to French youth, which demanded a supra-national European community. Like many of the more responsible young socialists, Carlo Mierendorff was at that time a radical. For all his rashness, his eloquence and his literary passions, Mierendorff had a certain serenity bordering on wisdom, and indeed on real faith. This emerges also in his books, *Hätt' ich das Kino* ("If the cinema were mine"), is a *tour de force*.

'He studied at Heidelberg and took his degree there, joined the Social Democratic Party, became one of the youngest members of the *Reichstag* under the Weimar Republic, and when the barbarians stood on the threshold, challenged Dr Goebbels in a sensational manner. He made known to the public the contents of the Boxheim Documents, which outlined the first Nazi plan to seize power; and he chose an extract in which every paragraph ended with the words "to be shot".

'He later returned to Darmstadt to assist Wilhelm Leuschner, who was in charge of the Ministry of the Interior of Hesse. He knew the importance of impressive symbols in political warfare and introduced the "Three Arrows" as the badge of his sympathisers. This was in 1932, when they still hoped to defeat National Socialism, which was then showing signs of exhaustion. A few months later he was being dragged by the Nazis through the streets of Darmstadt like a captured beast.'

Mierendorff writes of these days in his notes from prison:

14 June, in the afternoon.

SS turned up at the L.K.P. (*Land* Criminal Police) Office. Departure under supervision of detectives Weiss and Augustin. Conflict over the SS car. Back to the L.K.P. Office. Negotiations with the SS. I must go along. Drive in the SS car to the Bismarckplatz. From there procession through the town: SS cars following me. Siren repeating—from the Main Post Office— 'Mierendorff the Press Chief of the Leuschner Government

14. 6. <u>nachmittags</u>.

S.S. scheint die L.K.P. aus. ...

...

...

...

Zelle 32.

(later: journalistic swine) . . . traitor to the workers'. Back once more from the prison—to fetch things from the car. Beatings, kicks. Body, face, neck. Human beings? . . . Cell 32.

The time he spent at camp Osthofen, just after this, was the worst, with terrible ill-treatment every night. In Papenburg-Börgermoor he had to dig trenches. In Torgau camp he was put into the so-called death cell with Wilhelm Leuschner. In Buchenwald he had to put up the first barbed wire and help to erect the new prisoners' barracks. In the fifth year of his imprisonment came the sudden dreaded summons from the place of employment, by two armed guards. Carlo Mierendorff expected to be executed. Instead, he was led into the administrative office and told that his release had been approved. He gave no answer but fell to the ground in a dead faint.

Once outside the barbed wire he found a means of earning his living, originally suggested by senior SS officials, in the social department of the Braunkohle- und Bensin A.G., Berlin. It was thought that in this National Socialist agency he would be under a certain control, but Mierendorff, active as before, made good use of his position, which also entailed business trips, at home and abroad, to revive his old political connections. As the possibility of revolt drew near, he was once more ready for action. It was he who declared: 'From now on, we can only go forward, to victory—or the gallows'. He prepared many of the plans designed to convert the public to new, democratic ideas; among other things he drafted, in 1943, the first speech intended for broadcasting, and devised a new symbol for the future. It showed the Cross of Christianity within the ring of social policy.

Carlo Mierendorff died in his forty-seventh year. He was a doomed man and the bomb only saved him from Freisler's death sentence. The news of his death filled his friends with horror and left among them a gap that could not be filled.

14.6. nachmittag.

S.S. scheint die L.K.P. Amt.
Abmarsch unter Aufsicht von Krim./Pol.
Dir. + Angestin. Konflikt am
Auto der S.-S. Zu ??? L.K.P. Amt.
??? verspricht mit S.S. Ich muss
mitgehen. Fahrt im S.-S Wagen
bis ???platz. Von dort ruhig
durch die Stadt;

hinter mir S.-S. Wagen. Sirene! Großsprech
– als Hauptpost – "M? (????chen) – das
??? der ??? (Hitler: ???heim)
??? – ????? – Arbeiter ????." ???
??? nochmal ????? – Jedes auch
den Wagen ???. Schläge, ??????. Leib-
??? – freie. Machthaber? – – –
– – – – – – – ,
Zelle 32.

(later: journalistic swine) . . . traitor to the workers'. Back once more from the prison—to fetch things from the car. Beatings, kicks. Body, face, neck. Human beings? . . . Cell 32.

The time he spent at camp Osthofen, just after this, was the worst, with terrible ill-treatment every night. In Papenburg-Börgermoor he had to dig trenches. In Torgau camp he was put into the so-called death cell with Wilhelm Leuschner. In Buchenwald he had to put up the first barbed wire and help to erect the new prisoners' barracks. In the fifth year of his imprisonment came the sudden dreaded summons from the place of employment, by two armed guards. Carlo Mierendorff expected to be executed. Instead, he was led into the administrative office and told that his release had been approved. He gave no answer but fell to the ground in a dead faint.

Once outside the barbed wire he found a means of earning his living, originally suggested by senior SS officials, in the social department of the Braunkohle- und Bensin A.G., Berlin. It was thought that in this National Socialist agency he would be under a certain control, but Mierendorff, active as before, made good use of his position, which also entailed business trips, at home and abroad, to revive his old political connections. As the possibility of revolt drew near, he was once more ready for action. It was he who declared: 'From now on, we can only go forward, to victory—or the gallows'. He prepared many of the plans designed to convert the public to new, democratic ideas; among other things he drafted, in 1943, the first speech intended for broadcasting, and devised a new symbol for the future. It showed the Cross of Christianity within the ring of social policy.

Carlo Mierendorff died in his forty-seventh year. He was a doomed man and the bomb only saved him from Freisler's death sentence. The news of his death filled his friends with horror and left among them a gap that could not be filled.

THEODOR HAUBACH

15 September 1896—23 January 1945

THEODOR HAUBACH matriculated in 1914, and so belonged
to the last generation of boys who were educated in the
'good old days' of the Kaiser and whose school-days were
undisturbed by war-time irregularities.

He grew up in his parents' home in Darmstadt, with
every prospect of security. With his keen intellect, his thirst
for knowledge and his aptitude for clear logic, it looked as
though he would go far in whatever field of study or research
he might choose. But when he was eighteen the question
of choosing a profession ceased to exist. He volunteered
for the army, was commissioned in the field, wounded eight
times and did not come back until the end of the war.

In 1919, with his usual initiative, he began to study
philosophy at Heidelberg. Like so many of his contemporaries, his experiences during the war had turned
him to socialism: 'Haubach and his friend Mierendorff soon
became leaders of the socialist students in Heidelberg,'
writes Emil Henk, a friend of them both. Haubach was
always quick to grasp fundamentals, and as a student he
bitterly opposed the Nationals—the future National Socialists
—in whom he recognised even at this early date an enemy
of the German people. In debates he was icily calm, and
appeared remote and unmoved in the midst of turmoil; but
he also in those days soon after the first war, fired his fellow
students with political energy and won many impressive
battles over his opponents. But practical politics were not
the end of the story, for he also mastered with rare thorough-
ness the ideology of socialism and the difficult, complicated
works of the 19th century philosophers.

It was perhaps in Hegel that Haubach found the closest
intellectual affinity, the precise definition, the passion for
ideas and the dialectic style which was most in sympathy
with his own; but unlike Hegel he never dreamed of explaining away the world as a creation of the mind. The logical
sceptic in him saw in philosophy the ultimate realm of human
knowledge, and as a young man he was interested only in

what could be proved, and denied the rest. But as he grew older and more mature he began with all care and humility to examine the problems of faith and to explore the unknown.

In 1923, the worst year of the inflation, Haubach took his degree as Doctor of Philosophy and went to the Institute for Foreign Affairs in Hamburg. A year later he became an assistant editor of the *Hamburg Echo* and also joined the executive of the Hamburg branch of the *Reichsbanner Schwarz-Rot-Gold,* as he wished to work actively for the protection of the Republic.

'The countless thousands of Germans who died in the war must surely have died for a new Germany,' he wrote in Hamburg, 'or else they died for nothing at all, there is no third possibility. This new Germany does not yet exist, but it is coming, we are struggling to help it, and when we fight for Germany, we are fighting for a new Europe.'

It was inevitable that the generation which faced the task of striving for this goal should pay attention to past German history. In his analysis of problems of military and political power, Haubach wrote: 'The influence of military ideology in the civilian sphere is at the root of the century-old failure of German national policy. All the contempt for things political, the rage against pen-pushers and gossip-mongers, is merely symptomatic of the lack of interest in political affairs which has persisted for centuries.'

Haubach wanted a republic 'which should assert itself and accept the full consequences of its will to survive, for that way and by definite limitations of power it will be possible to create a new political order, in which conflicts will be resolved not without power but at least without bloodshed, by negotiation'.

In 1930 he went to the Prussian Ministry of the Interior as press officer and then to the Berlin Police Headquarters as head of its press department. He became deputy chairman of the central executive of the *Reichsbanner* and suggested various dramatic measures to bolster up the Weimar Republic, but to his great disappointment they were not accepted by the responsible politicians.

In the first six years of the National Socialist régime Haubach was repeatedly arrested and imprisoned. He spent two years in the concentration camp at Esterwegen, and after his release earned his living as an insurance agent.

Photograph taken in the People's Court

After his third release, Victor Bausch, a friend of his who owned a paper factory, managed to get permission from the Gestapo for Haubach to work there in a job 'essential to the war economy'. In 1943 Haubach was approached by members of the Kreisau Circle and subsequently threw in his lot with them. He also worked in close co-operation with his old political friends, Mierendorff, Leuschner and Leber.

Haubach's various philosophical papers have been burnt

245

or destroyed and only his letters and reports of odd conversations remain to testify to his ardent struggle to solve the ultimate problems of mankind. As late as 6 July 1944, a fortnight before he and his friends were to string their bow at the might and power of the enemy, he wrote to a member of the clergy:

> 'The more I try to fathom the wisdom of the two testaments, the more I am bothered by the thought that past centuries have obscured one essential of the divine message: that man is not only a sinner, miserable, pitiful and small, but also a being who is capable of sharing the sublime to an extent which our declining age is no longer able to grasp. . . .'

On 9 August 1944, Theodor Haubach was arrested by the Gestapo. In January 1945 he was sentenced to death, and executed. He had often thought about the meaning of such sacrifice, and had written of it:

> 'Now the limits of violence are such that it may well destroy the person who resists, but not the force of resistance. Of course if it were actually possible to wipe out all the people who were inspired by the spirit of resistance against tyranny, the destruction would amount almost to the annihilation of the spirit itself; but what cannot be destroyed is the memory of the event, should such annihilation take place. . . .'

FRITZ-DIETLOF GRAF
von DER SCHULENBURG

5 September 1902—10 August 1944

On 10 August 1944, Fritz-Dietlof Graf von der Schulenburg, the heir of an old Mecklenburg family from which the Prussian kings had recruited many military leaders and civil servants, stood in the dock before Freisler. He faced a charge of high-treason, and he faced it with equanimity. But with the pride of a man who is making a profession of faith, he said to the President of the People's Court: 'We have taken this upon ourselves to save Germany from unspeakable misery. I am aware that I shall be hanged for it, but I do not regret my actions.' In this manner, a man who had believed ten years earlier that it might be possible to work with the National Socialists, threw caution to the winds and declared himself against the Hitler régime.

Fritz von der Schulenburg first became aware of the social misery which followed the first war while working as a lawyer in local administrative offices. His sympathy for the radical groups among the workers during riots at Reckling-hausen soon brought him into conflict with his superiors, so much so that he was transferred to East Prussia. In this way he came to Königsberg, where he was known as the 'Red Graf' and gathered about him a circle of friends who 'combined sound professional ability with minds open to new ideas'. Despite strong personal scruples against Hitler, Schulenburg joined the National Socialist Party, believing that it might combine patriotism with undogmatic socialism, and afterwards got to know Gregor Strasser and his friends. But he soon saw the legal abuse which was part and parcel of National Socialism. This uneasiness grew into political disillusionment and, after Gregor Strasser's 'liquidation' in 1943, into indignation.

While he was working in local administration in East Prussia, Schulenburg cleared off the public debt in the *Kreis* for which he was responsible and was able to put into practice some of his ideas for improving the civil service. He was

247

always on the look out for ways in which the cracks in the legal structure might be sealed, and for men who might help; but as usual opposition was hampered by Hitler's apparent success in foreign affairs, on the one hand, and by the methods of the Gestapo on the other.

In 1937 Schulenburg accepted the post of Deputy Chief of Police in Berlin. 'I had to decide whether I wished to leave the service or become the *Fouché* of Hitler; I chose the latter.'

He now had the opportunity to learn more of what was going on, and was all the more anxious to find kindred spirits. Goebbels soon began to distrust him. When Schulenburg became President of Lower and Upper Silesia in 1939, he was determined that his province should become a good example to others, but his energetic measures to this end soon got him into trouble with the Party and earned him the label 'politically unreliable'.

The war took him to the eastern front and, as in his civil job, 'Fritzi', now a platoon commander in an infantry company, was an example of composure, caution, conscientiousness and humour. His war experiences matured him and hardened his convictions, and later on when he was on the staff of General von Unruh, in Paris, he was willing and able to help and to spin the web.

He rarely—only in decisive moments—lifted the mask which hid his real intentions. He was particularly well informed on everything from Hitler's latest utterances to the position at the front, from blunders in the plans for industry and food economy to the content of the secret service files, and he had a sure instinct for discovering people who thought as he did. He spread his net over every group from Stauffenberg to the military administration in Paris, from the police to the reserve battalions, from Goerdeler to the trade unionists and Socialists, and again from the Kreisau Circle to the Army. He was to become Under-Secretary in the Ministry of the Interior after the fall of the Hitler régime.

His plan for the reform of the administration (he also worked with Beck, Popitz, Jessen and Planck on a new draft for a future constitution), was lost, though many of its characteristics have been preserved. Schulenburg saw as the main problem the foundation of a new German democracy and its further development in the conditions created by

248

Photograph taken in the People's Court

the industrial state; the question as to how the modern state is to be governed and administered so that each individual feels himself to be a responsible citizen. Schulenburg took as his starting point Baron von Stein's theories on national education and realised that, after dictatorship had been ousted, there would arise the unique opportunity for introducing basic democratic ideas which had never before been put into practice in Germany, and that a modern, social and lasting democracy could be set up. To this end he wished to

249

establish clear-cut spheres of responsibility in the various social and political fields. He was also convinced of the importance of practical planning for the reconstruction of destroyed towns.

On 20 July 1944, Fritz von der Schulenburg stood at Stauffenberg's side in the Bendlerstrasse. When it became evident that the attempt on Hitler's life had failed, he said: 'It looks as though the German people must drain this cup to the very dregs. We must sacrifice ourselves, but later on we shall be understood.' Then quite calmly, he destroyed the contents of his brief-case.

He preserved this calm to the end. At the trial, when asked by the judge what he had really in mind with the *coup d'état* he answered: 'Wait three months. The situation in which you will find yourself is exactly that from which we set out.' And after the trial he wrote to his wife: 'What we did was inadequate, but in the end history will judge and acquit us.'

A few hours later Fritz von der Schulenburg was executed at Plötzensee.

ADAM von TROTT ZU SOLZ

9 August 1909—26 August 1944

ADAM VON TROTT ZU SOLZ was born in Potsdam when his father was Minister of Education in the Prussian Administration. He studied law in Munich, Göttingen and Berlin, and philosophy, politics and economics as a Rhodes scholar at Oxford.

When he had passed his final law examinations in 1936, and after six months' preparation in the United States, he spent several years studying in East Asia, mostly in Peking (This was also made possible by the Rhodes Foundation). From the spring of 1940 onwards he worked in the Foreign Office in Berlin, in the Information Department, and was meanwhile in close touch with the Kreisau Group, with representatives of the working class and of the church and with friends among the aristocracy.

His thesis, *Hegel's Staatsphilosophie und das Internationale Recht* (Hegel's Political Philosophy and International Law), which appeared in 1932, and his publication in 1936 of the political and journalistic writings of Heinrich von Kleist, are enough proof of the extent of his intellectual study of the problems of the day and of National Socialism, which was the spur to his own determination to take an active part in politics. It also provided the motive for his journeys to other countries, which enabled him to gain a 'clearer picture of his own', an insight into the qualities of the peoples of the East and West and a new relationship to the Christian faith as the basis of conduct.

*   *   *

'War solves no problems'. With this thought in mind, Adam von Trott zu Solz, a man of extraordinary intellectual ability and moral courage, made, in 1939, a bold personal bid to prevent war. As late as July he was in London and was received by Chamberlain and Lord Halifax, and urged the Foreign Office to take up a strong attitude towards Hitler while there was still time before war broke out. After the outbreak of war he accepted an invitation to a conference in the United States, where he tried in a memorandum to win over President Roosevelt to a policy that might encourage

251

the anti-Hitler movement in Germany. Felix Morley, also a former Rhodes Scholar, wrote in his diary of von Trott's efforts in Washington at that time:

> 'But in fact he devoted most of his time to the attempt to arouse understanding here for the great change which, he believes, is to be expected in Germany. . . . The main problem is how to prevent a war of extermination against the Nazis from driving back into Hitler's arms all those forces which are now just beginning to concentrate to bring about Hitler's fall.'

In 1940 Adam von Trott returned to Germany via Japan, without success. Under cover of his official position as a counsellor in the Foreign Office, and always in danger, he fostered his connections in all parts of the world, his main object being to arouse enthusiasm and support abroad for the German resistance. He was in close touch with Leber and Stauffenberg.

At the beginning of 1944, on behalf of the forces that had resolved upon revolution, von Trott sent a message to the President of the United States, asking him in great urgency to let it be known to what extent foreign countries would be prepared to allow a new German government to safeguard democracy in Germany. About the same time his last treatise appeared under the title *Deutschland zwischen Ost und West* (Germany between East and West), of which his friends said that it was written with his life's blood.

Despite his frequent journeys and his endless opportunities, Adam von Trott was drawn as if by a magnet back to Germany, where he considered his duty to lie. In May 1944, for instance, he could easily have found some official reason to leave Verona for Rome, which was soon to be occupied by the Allies, and so have saved himself. But though he was reckoning with his own arrest at any moment, he wanted to get back to his friends in Berlin, and in June he left again for Sweden to find out how a successful uprising in Germany would be received in political circles there.

On 15 August, Adam von Trott zu Solz, who had been earmarked as the future Under-Secretary in the Foreign Office, stood with his friend, Hans-Bernd von Haeften, before the People's Court. On the evening of the same day he wrote to his wife:

Photograph taken in the People's Court

'You will know that what hurts me most is that I may never again be able to place my experience at the service of the country, the special abilities I have been able to develop by what was perhaps too single-minded concentration on foreign affairs and Germany's position among the powers. Here I could still have been useful. I should so much like to make some sort of summary of my ideas and proposals which might help other people, but I don't suppose I shall be able to. It was all an attempt, arising from love of my own country (for which I must thank my father) and knowledge of her strength, to protect her immutable rights among the changes and chances of

253

this modern world, and to preserve her profound and indispensable contribution to civilisation against the encroachment of powers and beliefs which are foreign to her. That is why I always hurried back in eager anxiety from foreign countries, with all their enticements and opportunities, to this one where I felt I was called upon to serve. What I have learnt and what I was able to do for Germany abroad would certainly have helped a great deal now, because there are so few people who have enjoyed such diverse opportunities in the last few years. So I must hope that even without me, understanding and assistance will be forthcoming from many of these connections, if it should ever again be wanted or necessary. But a sower is reluctant to leave germinating seed for others to look after, for between sowing and harvest there are many storms. . . .'

The death sentence against Adam von Trott zu Solz was carried out on 26 August 1944, in Berlin-Plötzensee.

JULIUS LEBER

16 November 1891—5 January 1945

JULIUS LEBER was born at Biesheim in Upper Alsace. When he left the village school the parson suggested that he should be sent to a secondary school at Breisach, but for financial reasons he had to break off his education and went into a wallpaper factory as an apprentice. In 1910 he won a scholarship to the *Oberrealschule* in Freiburg, and stayed there till 1912, earning his living by giving lessons and writing newspaper reports. He then studied political economy and history at the universities of Freiburg and Strasbourg, on a similar basis, until in 1914 he volunteered for the army. He served throughout the war as an officer and was decorated several times; in 1920 while an officer in the Frontier Defence Forces with strong republican convictions he took part in the defeat of the Kapp Putsch. After that he left the army and took his Dr rer. pol. degree.

At the age of thirty he was appointed editor of the *Lübecker Volksbote* and soon became a central figure among the workers in North Germany, and the unchallenged leader of the Lübeck Social Democrats. In this position, and while he was a member of the *Reichstag* from 1924 to 1933, he consistently fought the totalitarian parties of the right and of the left and dedicated himself by word and deed to the establishment of a living democracy in Germany.

On 16 January 1933, Julius Leber appealed to the working men: 'When it is a question of fighting for freedom, one does not ask what will happen tomorrow.' On the day the National Socialists came to power, he was arrested, and from 1 February 1933 onwards, with only a short break just before the March elections of that year, until the summer of 1937, he was dragged through prisons and concentration camps, always in danger of his life.

On 16 November 1933, he wrote from the Marstall Prison in Lübeck: 'There are all sorts of ways of frightening people, but love grows only from humanity and justice. And without love there can be no patriotism. Sometimes I wonder if I shall ever live to see a fatherland based on justice. On

1 August 1914, there descended on my generation a great curse, which it does not seem able to shake off.'

Julius Leber was a typical representative of the generation who, many of them influenced by their experiences in the first war, were ready to devote all their energies to the creation of a modern, democratic state in Germany, but who were frustrated by a series of tragic events and circumstances, and lost the chance ever to make something of their visions.

Leber was a severe critic of the weaknesses and half-measures of the Weimar Republic. He believed that a reliable fighting force and the determined administration of justice were essential to a live democracy; but that many of the responsible men 'relied on a colourless idealism and lived from hand to mouth'. In his opinion, a considerable share of the responsibility fell on his own party, which had too often failed to realise what was necessary and which hardly ever allowed creative and energetic personalities to come to the fore.

In prison, Leber wrote of his own experiences and said in conclusion: 'The high purpose has survived nerve-racking tensions and burdens, and political chaos: it is to build for the working man a better future, firmly based on justice and freedom.'

After his release from the concentration camp Leber made a living as a coal merchant in Berlin, and used the business as a cover for his political work. He quickly took up his old connections with friends all over the country and with many others who wanted to throw over the régime, for he regarded this as the most urgent and important task for which no plan was too dangerous and no stake too high. His mental energy and his unbounded will to action appealed particularly to the young, who strongly supported him for leadership in the new government, and according to the plans he was destined for the post of Minister of the Interior. What mattered to him was the building up of a workable democracy with a strong government, free from narrow party doctrines, and ready to work with all constructive and creative forces. He has been described as one of the outstanding figures of the German resistance movement, and Theodor Heuss said of him in a memorial address:

'Though he had no love for the barrack square Leber had,

Photograph taken in the People's Court

fundamentally, a soldierly nature and even laughed, without any attempt to deny it, when I told him that the Alsatian was made of the stuff out of which Napoleon moulded his marshals.' Gustav Dahrendorf, another friend, wrote: 'His whole life was action. Inspired by his great moral strength and his own strong will, he was at all stages of his life a soldier, a politician and a human being.'

Paul Sethe, who was present at the trial before the People's Court on 24 October 1944 (Leber had been arrested at the beginning of July), wrote afterwards:

'Deserving of death. . . . The man who stood there in front of that mighty and wicked judge, had done more than merely wonder if the war would be lost. He made no secret of the fact that he had tried to overthrow the government. One felt that Julius Leber had long known what his fate would be, but he was not at all overwrought, but calm and patient. He listened attentively to his enemy and then answered in a low voice, but distinctly and steadily. But Julius Leber was only human, and even though he had long known what would happen to him, there was perhaps deep in his heart a last vestige of hope, a thirst for life, a wish once more to taste freedom, to see the countryside and his family. His voice remained clear and he did not tremble. I could see from behind, from where the spectators sit, the heels of his shoes moving up and down (they were slightly worn down—oh, well, we are in the fifth year of the war and Leber is not a rich man), but he remained absolutely cool and controlled.

'It was clear from the beginning of the trial that the President in his red robe was hardly interested in convicting the prisoner. (After all what was there to do, in such a clear-cut case?) Freisler was not content with that: he wanted to drag down his victim into the dust, to humiliate him, to break his morale. His voice rang through the court, as he accused Leber of cowardice. Would Leber be stung to reply? Would he defend himself furiously? Only to be interrupted by that shrieking man, to be insulted anew, to be silenced? But the prisoner listened quietly to the raging of the judge, then answered quite calmly: "That is an error, in reality it was so..." One had the impression, as the duel went on, that the rôles had been reversed, that the man up there in the red robe began to recede, that he was losing his nerve, that the gramophone needed winding . . . Finally, he seemed disappointed, exhausted, cross. He ended the trial. He was still the man in power. He could deploy and command. But the other man, who now turned and went slowly back to the prisoner's dock, was the victor. Very much alone in that great hall, with only three or four friends, and they in the dock and as helpless as he was, faced with malicious opponents, judges, state lawyers, police and SS, with certain death before him; yet he had in the end outmanœuvred his adversary.

'Later, when the Counsel for the Defence, a State Counsel of course, rose to his feet, it was quite clear that Leber knew what was coming, that it was fatal and final. The counsel did not even plead extenuating circumstances. He simply stated that his client was fully aware of what he had done, and of what he must expect. When the sentence was read out, Julius Leber did not turn a hair, he denied his enemy that final pleasure. His face remained, as it had been all day, serene and calm. He looked into the distance surely far beyond the walls of the court . . . The world will never know what he was thinking, but when a little later the police took him away, back to his cell, he walked erect, as before. And in this manner too he will have gone when he started on his last walk, to a hard and bitter death.'

Just before Julius Leber was executed on 5 January 1945, he sent a message to his friends: 'One's own life is a proper stake for so good and just a cause. We have done what lay in our power. It is not our fault that all turned out like this, and not otherwise.'

CLAUS SCHENK GRAF von STAUFFENBERG

15 November 1907—20 July 1944

'WE have put ourselves to the test before God and before our conscience; it must be done, for this man is evil incarnate.' So said Claus Stauffenberg to Jakob Kaiser when he explained why he and his closest advisers now believed that no effort and no risk must be spared to remove Hitler. Jakob Kaiser said later that he would never forget that moment, for it gave him a sudden insight into Stauffenberg's struggle with his own conscience.

Claus Schenk Graf von Stauffenberg was thirty-six years old when, ten months before 20 July 1944, he took it upon himself to carry out the attempt on Hitler's life, the attempt which had so often been thought of, and on several occasions planned to the last detail. His decision sprang from the synthesis of ethics and energy which was the key to his character, and which came to the fore as he grew older and recognised the meaning of right and justice. In 1939, he was a young and unusually gifted regular officer and, whatever his secret misgivings, a conscious opponent neither of the National Socialists nor of their war. By the end of 1943 he saw through the system 'right down to the warped and morbid atmosphere of the eagle's nest'.

He found in Julius Leber a kindred spirit and a reliable friend, and when the latter was arrested on 5 July 1944, he sent a message to Frau Leber, on 17 July, saying : 'We know where our duty lies.'

*　　　*　　　*

Claus Stauffenberg came from the Swabian aristocracy; on his mother's side he was related to the Yorck family, and was a descendant of Gneisenau. At the time of his military training, he was regarded by many of his superior officers, and by his contemporaries, as the most gifted subaltern of his year, with a great future before him. In fun, he was called 'the new Schlieffen', and it was said of him that he had the strength 'to inspire the Army and the General Staff with a

260

new spirit and to compete with the narrow military point of view'. Later, a general of the old school described him as the 'only German General Staff Officer gifted with genius'.

At the outbreak of war Stauffenberg was a 1st Lieutenant in an armoured division, and fought in Poland and in the French campaign. He was not at all pleased when he was recalled to Headquarters, for he was still sure of victory and loth to leave the fighting troops. This was a new stage of a brilliant career, and he was called upon to deal with important tasks of organisation. But it was also the stage in which his resistance to the decisions of the *Führer* set in. At the beginning of 1943 he was transferred to North Africa, where he was wounded in the face, in both hands, and in the knee by fire from a low-flying plane. For days, as he lay in a military hospital in Carthage, he feared he might lose his eyesight completely; in fact he kept one eye and lost his right hand and half the left. During his convalescence his friends remarked that he seemed to have 'a new conviction and even greater energy than before'.

At that time, many senior officers criticised Hitler's war strategy among themselves, and some of them passionately condemned it, though fighting shy of decisive action against the régime. Claus Stauffenberg went much further than this, for he revised his whole attitude to life. He demanded the utmost of himself, and because he believed that the liquidation of the Hitler régime must be followed by genuine reform and by 'the building of a new, social state, which would win the confidence of the broad mass of the people', he sought to get in touch with the various resistance groups. As Chief of Staff to the Army Ordnance Department, and with the tacit consent of General Olbricht, he built up round Berlin a military net-work on which the resistance movement was to rely on the day of the revolution. The exponents of civil resistance came to regard Stauffenberg as the prototype of the young officers whose own future was in no danger, but who were inspired by the officer's sense of responsibility towards his troops on the one hand, and by an understanding of the obligations of one citizen towards the rest, on the other, to take decisive action. Even the Gestapo officials who took part in the investigation of the event of 20 July, were not quite unmoved by his spirit, and spoke of the vision and struggles of this man 'who wanted to combine ethical socialism with his aristocratic traditions'.

Stauffenberg also had a hand in the plan to reach an understanding with the western Allies before the crumbling eastern front broke down completely. Shortly before the Normandy landings he considered the possibility of helping the English through the German minefields, but the plan was discarded as it was clear that the idea of dividing the Allies was at that time quite unrealistic. After the Allied troops had actually landed, it remained only to curtail so far as possible the catastrophe of the drifting war, the immeasurable, senseless sacrifice, and to form a government from the resistance groups which even foreign countries would recognise. But all this pre-supposed the death of Hitler.

Twice, between 10 July and 20 July, he fixed the date for the attempt on Hitler's life, and twice his plans were defeated by circumstances. On 20 July he eventually succeeded in placing a time-bomb in a briefcase beside the conference table in Hitler's headquarters in East Prussia, almost at Hitler's feet. He left the room just before the explosion and hurried back to Berlin to expedite the military rising which had been so carefully planned. Back in the capital he learnt that by a piece of incredibly bad luck, although some of his staff had been killed, Hitler himself had escaped. Accidentally, an officer who was not informed of the plot had moved the briefcase with the bomb to the other side of the table.

Claus Schenk Graf von Stauffenberg was shot in the courtyard of the War Office in the Bendlerstrasse. One obituary said of him that with his wavy black hair and his tall, handsome figure, he was in every respect a true descendent of Gneisenau. His wife was arrested and kept in custody for a time, during which his fifth child was born. Stauffenberg knew that this last mission might lead to his death, and tried in the preceding days and weeks to write a simple political confession of faith embodied in an oath by which he and his friends should dedicate themselves to the protection and the future of all the forces of truth and right, forces 'long since tried and proven and just re-awakened'.

The essence of this dedication is: 'We wish for a new order which will make all Germans responsible for the state, and which will guarantee them right and justice.'

BIBLIOGRAPHY

(The numbers in brackets refer to the various publications listed on pp. 266-270)

THE information in this book has been compiled after extensive research and some indication of the sources and of the range of literature dealing with the various aspects of German resistance may be of interest. The origin of actual quotations is given in the text.

There are first of all statements and writings left behind by people who are now dead, accounts given by survivors and estimates of friends. The subject has been treated in documentary films, in broadcasts and of course in the press; and a number of books, written from many different points of view, have appeared since 1945. But in all probability the last word on German resistance has not yet been written; and the measures taken by the Nazis to obliterate every trace of opposition have made research all the more difficult.

Soon after the collapse of Germany in 1945 there appeared Rudolf Pechel's book (1) giving his own experiences, and about the same time a sensational summary of the resistance story (2) was published in the United States. A year or so later there appeared, also in the United States, a study by Hans Rothfels (3), of which a German edition was later published in Zürich; this is an able account of the development from 1933 to 1945 of the resistance which centred round the Kreisau group, although many new facts have come to light since its publication. Eberhard Zeller's book (4) deals very fully with Stauffenberg and his friends, with his part in the 20 July and, in less detail, with the previous history back to Beck's first attempts in 1938. It is of course mainly concerned with military resistance, and fundamental consideration of the problems involved in resistance of any kind and of the right and duty to resist, such as was later forthcoming in connection with the Remer proceedings (5), is essential to a balanced judgment. Günther Weisenborn's book (6) deals with many aspects of opposition to Hitler and in particular with the activities of the left-wing and radical groups.

There are a number of books dealing with the various personalities of the resistance movement (7) and in particular those who were involved in the trials before the People's Court which took place after 20 July (8). There are books

264

dealing with the persecution of the Jews (9) and many personal accounts, including a book by Fabian von Schlabrendorf (10), who worked closely with von Tresckow. Urich von Hassell's diary (11) throws some light on resistance work inside the German Foreign Office; and there are such various sources as the controversial memoirs of Hans Bernd Gisevius (12), a romantic biography of Canaris (13), Foerster's well-documented study of Beck (14) (which does not however go beyond the outbreak of war), and books by Kielmannsegg and Foertsch (15) on the Fritsch proceedings in 1938, the first visible crisis between Hitler and the *Wehrmacht*.

The struggle between the state and the churches has been discussed in many of the books on resistance, and it is perhaps remarkable, given the individual character of such resistance, that there should also be a number of publications devoted exclusively to it. There are for instance several books dealing with the activity of the Protestant Church (16), a collection of documents relating to Catholic resistance, particularly in the diocese of Berlin (17), the memoirs of the Protestant chaplain of Tegel prison (18); and many biographies, of which those of the parson Paul Schneider, of Bishop Graf von Galen (19), of Father Franz Reinisch and of Fritz Michael Gerlich (20), a journalist, are outstanding. There are also the accounts of individual prisoners (21), among which Dietrich Bonhoeffer's reflections, letters and poems (22) are of particular significance; and there is a study by Inge Scholl (23), dedicated to Hans and Sophie Scholl, Christoph Probst, Willi Graf, Kurt Huber, Alexander Schmorell and their friends; and another, compiled by friends of Kurt Huber (24) dealing with the same story. Finally, the memoirs of Thadden-Trieglaff and Lilje discuss other aspects of the struggle of the churches and deal fully with the terror and imprisonment which it involved (25).

The last letters of Helmuth von Moltke (26) are concerned with attitudes and activities which lay somewhere between the protests of the churches and direct political action against Hitler. They illustrate the ideas of the Kreisau group, whose plans for the social and Christian reform of Germany have been fully discussed in Theodor Steltzer's articles (27). Comparatively little has been written on socialist and trade-union resistance and the writings of Julius Leber (28), supported by notes from his friends, are an important contribution. A number of revealing personal sketches have also been published on Leber, Leuschner, Mierendorff (29), Haubach, Reichwein and von Moltke, Axel von Harnack's book (30) on his brother Ernst and Emil Henk's report (31) on the preparations for the 20 July also come under this category.

There is in fact a wide variety of literature on the subject of German resistance, much of it of serious historical and political interest. The books which have been mentioned here, to which many could be added (32), are not only documents of recent Germany history. They are also tributes to human integrity in an age of destruction.

1. PECHEL (Rudolf): *Deutscher Widerstand (German Resistance)*; Erlenbach-Zürich, 1947.
2. DULLES (Allen Welsh): *Germany's Underground*; published in the U.S., 1947; translated as *Verschwörung in Deutschland*, Zürich, 1948.
3. ROTHFELS (Hans): *German Opposition to Hitler*; published in the U.S., 1948; translated as *Die Deutsche Opposition gegen Hitler*, Krefeld, 1949.
4. ZELLER (Eberhard): *Geist der Freiheit, Der zwanzigste Juli (Spirit of Freedom, The Twentieth of July)*; Munich, 1952.
5. The articles appeared in *Geist und Tat*, No. 7, 1952, pp. 193-224; and *Frankfurter Hefte*, No. VI, pp. 475 ff.
6. WEISENBORN (Günther): *Der Lautlose Aufstand, Bericht über die Widerstandsbewegung des deutschen Volkes, 1933-1945. (The Silent Revolt, Report on the Resistance Movement of the German People)*; Hamburg, 1953.
7. *20 Juli 1944*; published by Hans Royce, Bonn, 1953.
8. *Die Wahrheit über den 20 Juli (The Truth about the 20 July)*; published by Eugen Budde and Peter Lütsches, Düsseldorf, 1952.
9. *Den Unvergessenen, Opfer des Wahns 1933 bis 1945 (To The Unforgotten, Victims of Madness, 1933-1945)*; Heidelberg, 1952.
10. SCHLABRENDORFF (Fabian von): *Offiziere gegen Hitler (Officers against Hitler)*; published by Gero von Schulze-Gävernitz, Zürich, 1947 (2nd edition, 1950).

11. HASSELL (Ulrich von): *Vom anderen Deutschland* (*The Other Germany*); extracts from his diaries, 1938-1944; Zürich, 1946.

12. GISEVIUS (Hans Bernd): *Bis zum bitteren Ende* (*To the Bitter End*); 2 vols.; Zürich, 1946 (2nd edition Hamburg, 1948).

13. ABSHAGEN (K. H.); *Canaris, Patriot und Weltbürger* (*Canaris, Patriot and Cosmopolitan*); Stuttgart, 9th-11th thousand 1950.

14. FOERSTER (Wolfgang): *Generaloberst Ludwig Beck, Sein Kampf gegen den Krieg* (*General Ludwig Beck, his Struggle against the War*); two editions, Munich, 1953.

15. KIELMANNSEGG (Johann A. Graf von): *Der Fritschprozess, 1938, Ablauf und Hintergründe* (*The Fritsch Trial, 1938, the Proceedings and the Background*); Hamburg, 1949; FOERTSCH (Hermann): *Schuld und Verhängnis, die Fritschkrise als Wendepunkt der nationalsozialistischen Zeit* (*The Fritsch Case as the Turning-point of the National Socialist Era*); Stuttgart, 1951.

16. *Kirchliches Jahrbuch für die Evangelische Kirche in Deutschland, 1933-1944* (*Ecclesiastical Yearbook of the Protestant Churches in Germany, 1933-1944*); Gütersloh, 1948; *Und folget ihrem Glauben nach, Gedenkbuch für die Blutzeugen Bekennenden Kirche* (*Follow Them in Their Faith: in Memory of the Martyrs of the Confessional Church*); published by Bernhard H. Forck, Stuttgart, 1949; HERMELINK (Heinrich): *Kirche im Kampf, Dokumente des Widerstands und des Aufbaus der Evangelischen Kirche in Deutschland von 1933 bis 1945* (*The Church Militant: Documents concerning the Resistance and Renaissance of the Protestant Church in Germany from 1933-1945*); Stuttgart, 1950; NIEMÖLLER (Wilhelm): *Kampf und Zeugnis der Bekennenden Kirche* (*Struggle and Testimony of the Confessional Church*); Bielefeld, 1948.

17. *Dokumente aus dem Kampf der Katholischen Kirche im Bistum Berlin gegen den Nationalsozialismus* (*Documents concerning the Struggle of the Catholic Church against National Socialism in the Diocese of*

Berlin); published by the Episcopal Secretariat of Berlin, 1946; *Blutzeugen des Bistums Berlin* (*Martyrs of the Diocese of Berlin*); published by Heinz Kühn, Berlin, 1952; ADOLPH (Walter): *Im Schatten des Galgens, zum Gedächtnis der Blut-Zeugen in der nationalsozialistischen Kirchenverfolgung* (*In the Shadow of the Gallows: in Memory of the Martyrs of the National Socialist Persecution of the Church*); Berlin, 2nd edition 1953; *Wo Seine Zeugen sterben, ist sein Reich* (*Where His Witnesses die, is His Kingdom*); letters of the executed parsons of Lübeck and reports of eye-witnesses, compiled by Josef Schäfer S.J., Hamburg, 1946.

18. POELCHAU (Harald): *Die letzten Stunden, Erinnerungen des Gefängnispfarrers Harald Poelchau* (*Their Last Hours: Memoirs of a Prison Chaplain*), Berlin, 1949.

19. *Der Prediger von Buchenwald, Das Martyrium Paul Schneiders* (*The Preacher of Buchenwald, the Martyrdom of Paul Schneider*), published by Heinrich Vogel, Berlin, 1953; PORTMANN (Heinrich): *Kardinal von Galen, ein Gottesmann seiner Zeit* (*Cardinal von Galen, a Churchman of his Time*); 2nd edition, Münster, 1950.

20. KREUTZBERG (Heinrich): *Franz Reinisch, ein Martyrer unserer Zeit* (*Franz Reinisch, a Martyr of our Time*); Limburg, 1952; ARETIN (Erwein Freiherr von): *Fritz Michael Gerlich, Ein Martyrer unserer Tage* (*Fritz Michael Gerlich, a Martyr of Our Days*); Munich, 1949.

21. Examples are: Poems by Hans Lehnert and Hilde Meisel, Hamburg, 1950; METZGER (Max Josef): *Gefangenschaftsberichte* (*Reports from Prison*); introduced and published by Hannes Bäcker, Meitingen bei Augsburg, 2nd edition 1948.

22. BONHOEFFER (Dietrich): *Widerstand und Ergebung: Briefe und Aufzeichnungen aus der Haft* (*Resistance and Humility: Letters and Notes from Prison*); Eberhard Bethge, Munich, 1951; *Auf dem Wege zur Freiheit, Dietrich und Klaus Bonhoeffer, Gedichte und Briefe aus der Haft*, Berlin, 1946.

23. Scholl (Inge): *Die Weisse Rose* (*The White Rose*); Frankfurt, 7th edition 1952.

24. *Kurt Huber zum Gedächtnis, Bildnis eines Menschen, Denkers und Forschers* (*In Memory of Kurt Huber: Portrait of a Man, a Thinker and a Scholar*); by his friends; published by Clara Huber, Regensburg, 1947.

25. Thadden-Trieglaff (Reinhold von): *Auf Verlorenem Posten?: Ein Laie erlebt den evangelischen Kirchenkampf in Hitlerdeutschland* (*A Lost Cause?: a layman witnesses the struggle of the Protestant Church in Hitler's Germany*); Tübingen, 1948; Lilje (Hanns): *Im Finsteren Tal* (*In the Valley of Shadows*); Nürnberg, 1947.

26. Moltke (Helmuth James Graf von): *Letzte Briefe aus dem Gefängnis Tegel* (*Last Letters from Tegel Prison*); Berlin, 4th edition 1953.

27. Steltzer (Theodor): *Von deutscher Politik, Dokumente Aufsätze und Vorträge* (*Documents, Articles and Lectures concerning German Politiks*); publ. Friedrich Minssen, Frankfurt-am-Main, 1949.

28. Leber (Julius): *Ein Mann geht seinen Weg* (*A Man goes on his Way*), writings, speeches and letters of Julius Leber; compiled and published by his friends, Berlin, 1952.

29. *Blick in die Welt*, Numbers 7, 9, 10, 11; publ. Kasimir Edschmid, Darmstadt, 1947; Zuckmayer (Carl): *Carlo Mierendorff, Porträt eines deutschen Sozialisten* (*Carlo Mierendorff, Portrait of a German Socialist*); Berlin, 1947.

30. Harnack (Axel von): *Ernst von Harnack, 1888-1945: ein Kämpfer für Deutschlands Zukunft* (*Ernst von Harnack, 1888-1945: a Fighter for the Future of Germany*); Schwenningen-am-Neckar, 1951.

31. Henk (Emil): *Die Tragödie des 20 Juli 1944, ein Beitrag zur politischen Vorgeschichte* (*The Tragedy of 20 Juli 1944: a Retrospective Contribution*); Heidelberg, 2nd edition 1946; Schlotterbeck (Friedrich): *Je dunkler die Nacht, desto heller die Sterne* (*The Darker the Night, the Brighter the Stars*), memoirs of a German working man; Zürich, 1945 and Berlin, 1948.

32. For example: Braubach (Max): *Der Weg zum 20 Juli*, a report of his research work, published in *Veröffent-*

269

lichungen der Arbeitsgemeinschaft für Forschung des Landes Nordrhein Westfalen, No. 13 (1953) and also a supplement to *Das Parlament,* 15 July 1953; CONZE (Werner): *Die deutsche Opposition gegen Hitler,* published in *Politische Literatur* 5/6 (1953), pp. 210-215; STADTMÜLLER (Georg): *Zur Geschichte der Deutschen Militäropposition 1938-1945 (On the History of German Military Resistance, 1938-1945);* published in *Saeculum* IV, No. 4 (1953), pp. 437-449.